Facebook

for dummies®
A Wiley Brand

6th edition

by Carolyn Abram

Facebook® For Dummies®, 6th Edition

Published by **John Wiley & Sons, Inc.**, 111 River Street, Hoboken, NJ 07030-5774, www.wiley.com

Copyright © 2016 by John Wiley & Sons, Inc., Hoboken, New Jersey

Published simultaneously in Canada

For general information on our other products and services, please contact our Customer Care Department within the U.S. at 877-762-2974, outside the U.S. at 317-572-3993, or fax 317-572-4002. For technical support, please visit www.wiley.com/techsupport.

Wiley publishes in a variety of print and electronic formats and by print-on-demand. Some material included with standard print versions of this book may not be included in e-books or in print-on-demand. If this book refers to media such as a CD or DVD that is not included in the version you purchased, you may download this material at http://booksupport.wiley.com. For more information about Wiley products, visit www.wiley.com.

Library of Congress Control Number: 2016934862

ISBN: 978-1-119-17903-0

ISBN 978-1-119-17905-4 (ePub); ISBN 978-1-119-17904-7 (ePDF)

Manufactured in the United States of America

10 9 8 7 6 5 4 3 2 1

Contents at a Glance

Introduction 1

Part 1: Getting Started with Facebook 5
CHAPTER 1: The Many Faces of Facebook 7
CHAPTER 2: Adding Your Own Face to Facebook 23
CHAPTER 3: Finding Your Way Around Facebook 37

Part 2: Day-to-Day Facebook 49
CHAPTER 4: The Daily Facebook: News Feed and Posting 51
CHAPTER 5: Timeline: The Story of You 77
CHAPTER 6: Privacy and Safety on Facebook 103
CHAPTER 7: Facebook on the Go 137

Part 3: Connecting with Friends on Facebook 171
CHAPTER 8: Finding Facebook Friends 173
CHAPTER 9: Just between You and Me: Facebook Messages 193
CHAPTER 10: Sharing with Facebook Groups 213

Part 4: What to Do on Facebook 237
CHAPTER 11: Filling Facebook with Photos and Videos 239
CHAPTER 12: Scheduling Your Life with Events 263
CHAPTER 13: Creating a Page for Promotion 273
CHAPTER 14: Using Facebook with Games, Websites, and Apps 305

Part 5: The Part of Tens 323
CHAPTER 15: Ten Ways to Make the Most of Your Facebook Content 325
CHAPTER 16: Ten Ways Facebook Uniquely Impacts Lives 331
CHAPTER 17: Ten Frequently Asked Questions 337
CHAPTER 18: Ten Tips for Parents of Teens on Facebook 345

Index 351

Table of Contents

INTRODUCTION 1

About Facebook For Dummies 1

Foolish Assumptions.. 2

Icons Used in This Book 3

Beyond the Book 3

PART 1: GETTING STARTED WITH FACEBOOK 5

CHAPTER 1: **The Many Faces of Facebook** 7

So . . . What Is Facebook, Exactly? 8

Discovering What You Can Do on Facebook 10

    Connect with friends..................................... 10

    Learn what's going on with your friends 10

    Establish a Timeline..................................... 11

    Communicate with Facebook friends....................... 12

    Share your thoughts 12

    Share your pictures...................................... 13

    Plan Events 14

    Join and create Groups................................... 14

    Facebook and the web 14

    Promote a cause or business 15

Keeping in Mind What You Can't Do on Facebook 15

    You can't lie.. 16

    You can't be twelve 16

    You can't troll, spam, or harass 16

    You can't upload illegal content. 17

Realizing How Facebook Is Different from Other Social Sites....... 17

How You Can Use Facebook 18

    Getting information...................................... 18

    Keeping up with long-distance friends..................... 18

    Moving to a new city 19

    Getting a job 19

    Reunions.. 20

    Organizing movements 20

CHAPTER 2: **Adding Your Own Face to Facebook** 23

Signing Up for Facebook..................................... 23

Getting Started... 25

    Step 1: Find Your Friends 25

    Step 2: Profile Picture 28

What to Expect in Your Inbox 30
    Confirmation 30
    E-mail outreach 31
Your New Home Page 31
Adding More Friends..33
Filling out Your Profile Information 34

CHAPTER 3: Finding Your Way Around Facebook 37
Checking Out the Blue Bar on Top 38
Search 41
The Left Sidebar...42
    The Favorites section 42
    Other sections 44
Viewing News Feed 45
Right On 46
The Littlest Links 47

PART 2: DAY-TO-DAY FACEBOOK.............................49

CHAPTER 4: The Daily Facebook: News Feed and Posting 51
Your Daily News . . . Feed..................................52
    Anatomy of a News Feed story 53
    Common story types.....................................54
Ticker..58
Interacting with News Feed 59
    Liking..59
    Reacting 60
    Liking Pages 60
    Commenting..61
    Sharing 63
    Liking and sharing across the Internet....................64
    Saving 65
Adjusting News Feed.......................................66
    Hiding posts and people.................................66
    News Feed preferences 67
Sharing Your Own News.....................................69
    Status updates...70
    What should I say?......................................70
    Status updates "plus" 70
    Controlling who sees your posts..........................73

CHAPTER 5: Timeline: The Story of You 77
Scrolling Through Time.....................................78
First Impressions 79

Add a profile picture that's already on Facebook 81
Add a profile picture from your hard drive 82
Take a photo of yourself using your webcam 83
Telling Your Story 84
Posts 85
Status. 85
Life events. 88
Editing posts. 90
The left column 91
All About Me. 92
Work and Education 93
Sections. 99
Your Friends and Your Timeline 101

CHAPTER 6: Privacy and Safety on Facebook 103
Know Your Audience. 104
Privacy on the Go. 106
Changing privacy 108
Privacy Shortcuts. 109
Who can see my stuff? 109
Who can contact me? 110
How do I stop someone from bothering me?. 111
Privacy Settings 111
Privacy. 111
Timeline and tagging. 113
Blocking. 117
Apps. 120
Ads. 124
Timeline Privacy. 126
All about privacy 126
Interested in privacy 127
Privacy Tools. 128
View As 128
Activity Log 129
Privacy Checkup. 130
Remembering That It Takes a Village to Raise a Facebook 131
Peeking Behind the Scenes 132
Protecting minors 132
Preventing spam and viruses 133
Preventing phishing 133
One Final Call to Use Your Common Sense. 134

CHAPTER 7: Facebook on the Go 137
The Facebook App. 138
Layout and navigation 139
News Feed 142

Posting from the app 143
Photo posts 144
Check-ins. 148
Checking out Timelines. 150
Using Groups 153
Events 155
Facebook Messenger 156
Navigating Messenger 157
Viewing and sending Messages. 158
The Facebook Family of Mobile Apps. 160
Groups. 161
Moments. 161
Paper 161
Hello 161
Rooms 162
Slingshot 162
Riff 162
Facebook on Your Mobile Browser. 162
Mobile Home 163
Mobile Timelines 164
Mobile Inbox 165
Facebook Texts 165
Mobile settings. 167
Mobile notifications. 168

PART 3: CONNECTING WITH FRIENDS ON FACEBOOK . . .171

CHAPTER 8: **Finding Facebook Friends** 173
What Is a Facebook Friend? 174
Adding Friends. 175
Sending Friend Requests 175
Accepting Friend Requests. 176
Choose your friends wisely 177
It's quality, not quantity 177
Finding Your Friends on Facebook 178
Import your friends. 178
People you may know. 181
Find classmates, co-workers, neighbors, and mutual friends. . . .181
Find what you're looking for: Search 183
Managing How You Interact with Friends 184
Friend Lists 185
Groups. 189
News Feed options 190
Following. 190
Unfriending. 191

CHAPTER 9: **Just between You and Me: Facebook Messages** . . . 193

Sending a Message 194
Sending links 195
Sending photos 196
Sending stickers 196
Sending GIFs 197
Sending payments 197
Sending attachments 198
Video chat 199
Message Options 199
Inbox 201
Conversations in the Inbox 202
Conversations with lots of people 205
The Chat Menu 207
Messaging on the Go 209

CHAPTER 10: **Sharing with Facebook Groups** 213

Evaluating a Group 214
Sharing with a Group 217
Using the Publisher 217
Reading and commenting on posts 220
Chat 221
Events 222
Files and docs 223
Creating Your Own Groups 225
Personalizing Groups 227
Group Dynamics 228
Controlling notifications 228
Searching a group 230
Adding friends to a group 230
Being a group administrator .231
Reporting offensive groups 234

PART 4: WHAT TO DO ON FACEBOOK 237

CHAPTER 11: **Filling Facebook with Photos and Videos** 239

Viewing Photos from Friends 240
Photos in News Feed 240
Photo viewer 241
The album view 242
Viewing photos on your mobile device 243
Viewing tagged photos and videos of yourself 244
Adding Photos to Facebook 244
Uploading photos 245
Creating an album 250

Editing and Tagging Photos 252
    Editing albums 253
    Editing a photo. 255
    Automatic albums 257
Working with Video 257
    Viewing videos 258
    Adding a video from your computer .258
    Adding a video from the Facebook app 259
Discovering Privacy 260
    Photo and video privacy. 260
    Privacy settings for photos and videos of yourself. 261

CHAPTER 12: Scheduling Your Life with Events 263
You're Invited! 263
Public Events 265
Viewing Events 266
Creating Your Own Events 267
    Inviting guests 268
    Adding an event photo 269
Managing Your Event 270
    Editing your event's info 270
    Canceling the event. 270
    Messaging your event's guests 271
    Removing guests 271

CHAPTER 13: Creating a Page for Promotion 273
Getting to Know Pages 274
    Anatomy of an Official Page. 274
    Community Pages 275
    Connecting and interacting with Pages 276
Creating a Facebook Page 277
    Do I need a Page? 277
    Creating your Page 278
    Getting started. 279
Sharing as a Page 282
    The Publisher 282
    Photos and videos. 285
    Events 287
    Milestones 287
    Notes. 288
Using Facebook as Your Page 289
    Liking, commenting on, and sharing posts 289
    Liking other Pages. 290

Managing a Page 290
    Messages 291
    Notifications 293
    Publishing Tools. 294
    Settings 295
Insights: Finding Out Who Is Using Your Page 301

**CHAPTER 14: Using Facebook with Games,
Websites, and Apps**. 305
What Apps Need 306
    The basics 306
    The slightly less basic 307
    Permission to act. 308
Games on Facebook 308
    Game Home pages on Facebook 309
    Sidebar links. 310
    Invitations and notifications. 310
    Posts 311
    The Game Center. 312
Using Facebook Outside of Facebook 313
    Log in with Facebook 313
Mobile Apps and Facebook 315
Managing Your Games, Websites, and Apps. 317
    App visibility 317
    Info you provide. 318
    This app can 318
    Learn more. 319
    Removing apps 319
    Apps others use. 319
    Opting out. 320
    Controlling what you see from friends. .320
    Reporting offensive apps 321

PART 5: THE PART OF TENS. 323

**CHAPTER 15: Ten Ways to Make the Most of
Your Facebook Content** 325
Remember the Past 325
Scrapbook Your Baby Photos 326
Say Thanks 327
Give Your Photos Some Flair 327
Review the Last Year (or Years) 327
Track Your Feelings 328
Add Tags 328

Riff with Friends 328
Use Stickers or GIFs in Your Messages. 329
Friend-a-versaries 329

CHAPTER 16: **Ten Ways Facebook Uniquely Impacts Lives** 331
Keeping in Touch with Summer Friends 331
Preparing to Head Off to School 332
Going on Not-So-Blind Dates. 332
Meeting People in Your New City or Town 333
Reconnecting with Old Friends 333
Keeping Up with the 'Rents . . . or the Kids 334
Facebook Networking. 334
Facebook for Good 335
Goin' to the Chapel 335
Hey, Facebook Me! 336

CHAPTER 17: **Ten Frequently Asked Questions** 337
Do People Know When I Look at Their Timelines? 338
I Friended Too Many People and Now I Don't Like Sharing
Stuff — What Can I Do?. 338
What's with the New Facebook — Can I Change It Back? 339
I Have a Problem with My Account — Can You Help Me? 340
What Do I Do with Friend Requests I Don't Want to Accept? 341
Why Can't I Find My Friend? 341
Will Facebook Start Charging Me to Use the Site? 342
How Do I Convince My Friends to Join Facebook? 342
What If I Don't Want Everyone Knowing My Business? 343
Does Facebook Have a Feature That Lets Me Lock
Myself Out for a Few Hours? 344

CHAPTER 18: **Ten Tips for Parents of Teens on Facebook** 345
Talk to Teens about General Internet Safety. 346
Beware of Strangers 346
Teach Teens How to Report Abuse. 346
Teach Teens How to Block People 347
Learn to Use Privacy Settings 348
Talk about Posts and Consequences 348
Remember the Golden Rule 348
Respect Teens' Boundaries 349
Don't Send Friend Requests to Teens' Friends 349
Make Space for Your Own Social Life, and Your Family Life,
on Facebook 350

INDEX 351

Introduction

Facebook connects you with the people you know and care about. It enables you to communicate, stay up-to-date, and keep in touch with friends and family anywhere. It facilitates your relationships online to help enhance them in person. Specifically, Facebook connects you with the *people* you know around *content* that is important to you. Whether you're the type to take photos or look at them, or write about your life, or read about your friends' lives, Facebook is designed to enable you to succeed. Maybe you like to share websites and news, play games, plan events, organize groups of people, or promote your business. Whatever you prefer, Facebook has you covered.

Facebook offers you control. Communication and information sharing are powerful only when you can do what you want within your comfort zone. Nearly every piece of information and means of connecting on Facebook come with full privacy controls, allowing you to share and communicate exactly how — and with whom — you desire.

Facebook welcomes everyone: students and professionals; grandchildren (as long as they're at least age 13), parents, and grandparents; busy people; socialites; celebrities; distant friends; and roommates. No matter who you are, using Facebook can add value to your life.

About Facebook For Dummies

Part 1 of this book teaches you all the basics to get you up and running on Facebook. This information is more than enough for you to discover Facebook's value. Part 2 teaches you about the basics of using Facebook — the sorts of things millions of people log in and do every day. Part 3 explains how to find friends and all the ways you can interact with them. Part 4 explores some of the special ways you might find yourself using Facebook once you're up and running. Finally, Part 5 explores the creative, diverse, touching, and even frustrating ways people have welcomed Facebook into their lives.

Here are some of the things you can do with this book:

>> **Find out how to represent yourself online.** Facebook lets you create a profile (called a Timeline) that you can share with friends, co-workers, and people-you-have-yet-to-meet.

>> **Connect and share with people you know.** Whether you're seeking close friends or long-lost ones, family members, business contacts, teammates, businesses, or celebrities, Facebook keeps you connected. Never say, "Goodbye" again . . . unless you want to.

>> **Discover how the online tools of Facebook can help enhance your relationships offline.** Photo sharing, group organization, event planning, and messaging tools all enable you to maintain an active social life in the real world.

>> **Take Facebook with you when you're not at your computer.** Facebook's mobile tools are designed to make it easy to use Facebook wherever you are.

>> **Bring your connections off Facebook and on to the rest of the web.** Many websites, games, apps, and services on the Internet can work with your Facebook information to deliver you a better experience.

>> **Promote a business, cause, or yourself to the people who can bring you success.** Engaging with people on Facebook can help ensure that your message is heard.

Foolish Assumptions

In this book, I make the following assumptions:

>> You're at least 13 years of age.

>> You have some access to the Internet, an email address, and a web browser that is not Internet Explorer 6 (Internet Explorer 7, Safari, Chrome, Firefox, and so on are all good).

>> There are people in your life with whom you communicate.

>> You can read the language in which this sentence is printed.

Facebook pages and features — such as the Facebook Groups or the Settings page — are called out with capital letters. Brackets like <this> denote generic text that will be different on your screen, such as looking at <Your Name>.

I often state my opinions throughout this book. Though I have worked for Facebook in the past, the opinions expressed here represent only my perspective, not that of Facebook. I am an avid Facebook user and became one long before I worked for Facebook.

Icons Used in This Book

What's a *For Dummies* book without icons pointing you in the direction of great information that's sure to help you along your way? In this section, I briefly describe each icon I use in this book.

The Tip icon points out helpful information that is likely to improve your experience.

The Remember icon marks an interesting and useful fact — something that you may want to use later.

The Warning icon highlights lurking danger. With this icon, I'm telling you to pay attention and proceed with caution.

Beyond the Book

In addition to what you're reading right now, this product also comes with a free access-anywhere Cheat Sheet that helps you build your Friends List; communicate with your friends in the many ways available on Facebook; and stay on top of important Facebook dates, such as friends' birthdays and events. To get this Cheat Sheet, simply go to www.dummies.com and search for "Facebook For Dummies Cheat Sheet" in the Search box.

1

Getting Started with Facebook

IN THIS PART . . .

What you can and can't do on Facebook

Signing up and getting confirmed

Looking around and navigating to different parts of Facebook

IN THIS CHAPTER

Discovering Facebook

Knowing what you can and can't do on Facebook

Finding out how Facebook is different from other social sites

Seeing how different people use Facebook . . . differently

Chapter 1

The Many Faces of Facebook

Think about the people you interacted with throughout the past day. In the morning, you may have gone to get the paper and chatted with a neighbor. You may have asked your kids what time they'd be home and negotiated with your partner about whose turn it is to cook dinner. Perhaps you spent the day at the office, chatting, joking, and (heaven forbid) getting things done with your co-workers. In the midst of it all, you may have sent an email to all the people in your book club, asking them what book should be next, and what date works for the most people. Maybe while you sat on the bus you read the newspaper, or called your mom to wish her a happy birthday, or searched on your phone for a good restaurant to go to for drinks with friends. This is your world, as it revolves around you.

Each of us has our own version of the world, and as we interact with each other, those worlds intertwine, interplay, and interlock. Maybe your best friend from college was the one to introduce you to the book club, and then someone from the book club recommended a good restaurant. This network of people you interact with — your friends, acquaintances, and loved ones — exists online. Facebook is the online representation of the web of connections between people in the real world. Facebook (and other Internet companies) likes to call this network the *social graph*.

Now, you may be asking, if this graph or network exists in the real world, why do I need it online, too? Good question (gold stars all around). The answer is that having it online facilitates and improves all your social relationships. In other words, Facebook makes your life easier and your friendships better. It can help with very practical things like remembering a friend's birthday or coordinating a party. It can also help with the more abstract aspects of relationships, things like staying close with family you aren't physically near or talking about your day with friends.

Getting set up and familiar with Facebook does take a little work (which you know, or else you wouldn't be starting out on this book-length journey). It may feel a little overwhelming at times, but the reward is worth it — I promise you.

So . . . What Is Facebook, Exactly?

"Yes, Carolyn," you're saying. "I know it's going to help me stay in touch with my friends and communicate with the people in my life, but what *is* it?"

Well, at its most basic, Facebook is a website. You'll find it through a web browser like Safari, Google Chrome, Firefox, or Internet Explorer, the same way you might navigate to a search engine like Google or to an airline's website to book tickets. (You can also access it using an app on your smartphone, but more on Facebook Mobile in Chapter 7.) Figure 1-1 shows what you will probably see when you navigate to www.facebook.com.

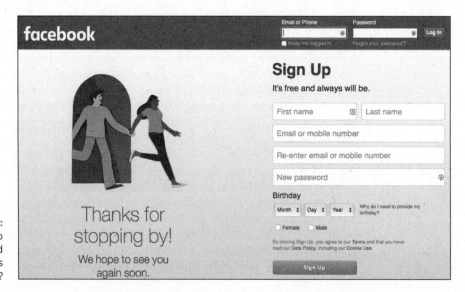

FIGURE 1-1:
Welcome to Facebook. Would you like fries with that?

If you're already a Facebook user and choose to stay logged in on your computer, www.facebook.com will likely look more like Figure 1-2, which shows an example of News Feed and your Home page.

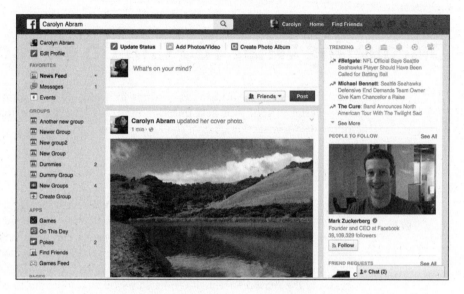

FIGURE 1-2:
Welcome back to
Facebook,
old friend.

Facebook is a website where you go to connect and share with friends. And just as there are a lot of different ways you interact with friends in the real world, there are a lot of ways to do so on Facebook. For example, you may go to Facebook to

>> Check out what your friends are up to today.

>> Tell your friends and family about your recent successes, show them your photos, or let them know you're thinking of them.

>> Share a tidbit from your day or something you've been thinking about.

>> Show off the pictures from your latest vacation.

>> Make a contact in a city you're moving to or at a company where you're applying for a job.

>> Plan an event.

>> Get in touch with an old friend.

>> Garner support for a cause.

>> Get recommendations from friends for movies, books, music, and restaurants.

>> Remember everyone's birthday.

So what Facebook *is*, exactly, is a website built to help you represent yourself online and share with your real-world friends online. The rest of it — how that's accomplished, what people typically share on Facebook, and how it all works — is what this book is all about.

Discovering What You Can Do on Facebook

Now that you know Facebook is a means by which you can connect with people who matter to you, your next question may be, "How?" More gold stars for you! In the next few sections, I give you an overview.

Connect with friends

As soon as you sign up for Facebook, you will start seeing prompts to "Add Friends." *Friendships* are the digital connections between you and your real world friends and acquaintances. On Facebook, it's pretty common to refer to *friending* people you know. This just means establishing the virtual connection. Friending people enables you to communicate and share with them more easily. Friends are basically the reason Facebook can be so powerful and useful to people. Facebook offers the following tools to help you find your friends:

>> **Facebook Friend Finder:** Enables you to scan the email addresses in your email address book to find whether those people are already on Facebook. Selectively choose among those with whom you'd like to connect.

>> **People You May Know:** Shows you the names and pictures of people you likely know. These people are selected for you based on commonalities like where you live or work or how many friends you have in common.

>> **Search:** Helps you find the people who are most likely already using Facebook.

After you establish a few connections, use those connections to find other people you know by searching through their connections for familiar names. I explain how to find people you know on Facebook in Chapter 8.

Learn what's going on with your friends

Whenever you log into Facebook, you'll see your *News Feed*. News Feed is the constantly updating list of stories by and about your friends. In less vague terms, every time one of your friends adds something to Facebook — a photo, a post about her day, a link to an article he liked — it creates a story that may appear when you log in. In this way, News Feed becomes an ongoing update about your friends. News Feed is how I know when my friends have gotten engaged, moved, or had a baby. It's how I know who had a funny thought while they were waiting for their coffee and who overheard an unintentionally hilarious conversation on the bus. It's how I know that there was an earthquake in California (don't worry, everyone's fine) and that people were really disappointed by the way the Seattle Seahawks played over the weekend. You can see a snippet of a News Feed in Figure 1-2. I spend a lot of time explaining News Feed in Chapter 4.

Establish a Timeline

When you sign up for Facebook, one of the first things you do is establish your *Timeline*, originally referred to as Profile. The reason Facebook calls this a Timeline and not a profile (other than to be a bit confusing) is because Timelines are much more than just an at-a-glance bio. Timelines become an ongoing history of your life on Facebook. When you (or your friends) are feeling nostalgic, you can explore your history the same way you might flip through an old photo album.

At first, the thought of putting a photo album of your entire life online may feel sort of scary or daunting. After all, that stuff is personal. But one of the things you'll discover about Facebook is that it's a place to be personal. The people who will see your Timeline are, for the most part, the people you'd show a photo album to in real life. They are your friends and family members.

REMEMBER

That "for the most part" is an important part of Facebook, too. You will encounter other people on Facebook, including potential employers or professional contacts, more distant friends, and casual acquaintances. This distinction — between your close friends and everyone else — is an important one to be aware of.

The Timeline, shown in Figure 1-3, is set up with all kinds of privacy controls to specify *whom* you want to see *which* information. Many people find great value in adding to their Timeline just about every piece of information and then unveiling each particular piece cautiously. The safest rule here is to share on your Timeline any piece of information you'd share with someone in real life. The corollary applies, too: Don't share on your Timeline any information that you wouldn't share with someone in real life.

Chapter 5 provides lots of detail about the Timeline and what you might choose to share there. For now, think of it as a personal web page that helps you share with your friends on Facebook.

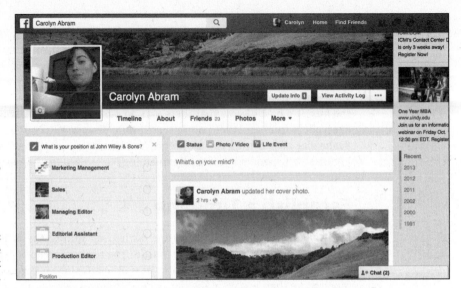

FIGURE 1-3:
An example of a Facebook Timeline.

Communicate with Facebook friends

As Facebook grows, it becomes more likely that anyone with whom you're trying to communicate can be reached. These days it's a fairly safe assumption that you'll be able to find that person you just met at a dinner party, an old professor from college, or the childhood friend you've been meaning to catch up with. Digging up a person's contact information could require calls to mutual friends, a trip to the white pages (provided you know enough about that person to identify the right contact information), or an email sent to a potentially outdated email address. Facebook streamlines finding and contacting people in one place. If the friend you're reaching out to is active on Facebook, no matter where she lives or how many times she's changed her email address, you can reach one another.

And Facebook isn't just about looking up old friends to say hi. Its messaging system is designed to make it easy to dash a quick note off to friends and get their reply just as fast. The comments people leave on each other's photos, status updates, and posts are real conversations that you will find yourself taking part in.

Share your thoughts

You have something to say. I can just tell by the look on your face. Maybe you're proud of the home team, maybe you're excited for Friday, or maybe you can't believe what you saw on the way to work this morning. All day long, things are happening to all of us that make us just want to turn to our friends and say, "You know what? . . . That's what." Facebook gives you the stage and an eager audience.

In Chapter 4, I explain how you can make short or long posts about the things happening around you and how they're distributed to your friends in an easy way.

Share your pictures

Since the invention of the modern–day camera, people have been all too eager to yell, "Cheese!" Photographs can make great tour guides on trips down memory lane, but only if you actually remember to develop, upload, or scrapbook them. Many memories fade away when the smiling faces are stuffed into an old shoe box, remain on undeveloped rolls of film, or are left to molder in obscurity on your phone's camera roll.

Facebook offers three great incentives for uploading, organizing, and editing your photos:

>> **Facebook provides one easy-to-access location for all your photos.** Directing any interested person to your Facebook Timeline is easier than e-mailing pictures individually, sending a complicated link to a photo site, or waiting until the family reunion to show off the my-how-the-kids-have-grown pics.

>> **Every photo you upload can be linked to the Timelines of the people in the photo.** For example, you upload pictures of you and your sister and link them to her Timeline. On Facebook, this is called *tagging* someone. Whenever someone visits your sister's Timeline, he sees those pictures; he doesn't even have to know you. This is great because it introduces longevity to photos. As long as people are visiting your sister's Timeline, they can see those pictures. Photo albums no longer have to be something people look at right after the event and maybe then again years later.

>> **Facebook gives you the power to control exactly who has access to your photos.** Every time you upload a photo or create a new photo album on Facebook, you can decide whether you want everyone on Facebook to see it, just your friends, or even just a subset of your friends based on your comfort level. You may choose to show your wedding photos to all your friends, but perhaps only some friends see the honeymoon. This control enables you to tailor your audience to those friends who might be most interested. All your friends might enjoy your baby photos, but maybe only your co-workers will care about photos from the recent company party.

I go over how to share your photos in Chapter 11.

Plan Events

Events are just what they sound like: a system for creating events, inviting people to them, sending out messages about them, and so on. Your friends and other guests RSVP to events, which allows the event organizers to plan accordingly and allows attendees to receive event reminders. Facebook Events can be used for something as small as a lunch date or something as big as a march on Washington, D.C. Sometimes events are abstract rather than physical. For example, someone could create an event for Ride Your Bike to Work Day and hope the invitation spreads far and wide (through friends and friends of friends) to promote awareness. I use Events to plan barbecues for my friends as well as to put together a larger reading series. I cover Events in detail in Chapter 12.

Join and create Groups

Groups are also what they sound like: groups of people organized around a common topic or real-world organization. One group may be intimate, such as five best friends who plan several activities together. Another group could be practical — for example, PTA Members of Denver Schools. Within a group, all members can share relevant information, photos, or discussions. My groups include one for my son's daycare classroom where parents can share information and coordinate playdates, one for my *For Dummies* editorial team so we can update each other on how the writing is going, and one for a group of friends who are all planning to take a trip together next year. Groups are covered in detail in Chapter 10.

Whenever you post something to Facebook, you can choose to share it only with members of a certain group. So if you just had a baby and know how much your family is jonesing for new photos, you can just share photos with your family group without inundating the world at large.

Facebook and the web

Facebook Photos, Groups, and Events are only a small sampling of how you can use Facebook to connect with the people you know. Throughout this book, you find information about how Facebook interacts with the greater Internet. You might see articles recommended by friends when you go to *The New York Times* website, or information about what music your friends like when you use Spotify, an Internet radio website. In Chapter 14, I explain in detail the games, apps, and websites that you can use with your Facebook information.

Many of these websites and applications have been built by outside developers who don't work for Facebook. They include tools to help you edit your photos;

create slideshows; play games with friends across the globe; divvy up bills among people who live or hang out together; and exchange information about good movies, music, books, and restaurants. After you become a little more comfortable with the Facebook basics, you can try some of the thousands of applications and websites whose services allow you to interact with your Facebook friends.

Promote a cause or business

Every day, you interact with your friends and family. You also interact with other beings: a newspaper or magazine, your favorite coffee shop, a celebrity whose marriage travails you can't help but be fascinated by, a television show that has you on the edge of your seat, or a cause that's near and dear to your heart. All these entities can be represented on Facebook through Pages (with a capital P). These Pages look almost exactly like Timelines, just for the not-quite-people among us. Instead of becoming friends with Pages, you can like them. So when you like a television show (say, *The Daily Show with Trevor Noah*), you'll start to see updates from that Page *(The Daily Show)* on your Home page. Liking Pages for businesses or causes helps you stay up-to-date with news from them.

If you're the one managing something like a small business, a cause, or a newsletter, you can also create a Page. After you've created that Page, your users/customers/fans can like it, and then you can update them with news about whatever's going on in the world of your store/cause/thing. I talk about all the ins and outs of Pages in Chapter 13.

Keeping in Mind What You Can't Do on Facebook

Facebook is meant to represent real people and real associations; it's also meant to be safe. Many of the rules of participation on Facebook exist to uphold those two goals.

TECHNICAL STUFF

There are things you can't do on Facebook other than what's listed here. For example, you can't send multiple unsolicited messages to people you're not friends with; you can't look at the photos of someone who has really tight privacy settings; you can't spin straw into gold. These rules may change how you use Facebook, but probably won't change *whether* you use it. The following four rules are highlighted in this section because if any are a problem for you, you probably won't get to the rest of the book.

You can't lie

Okay, you can, but you shouldn't, especially not about your basic information. Facebook's community standards include a commitment to use an "Authentic Identity." What this means is that Facebook wants you to create only one Timeline for yourself, and use your real name there. If you create fake accounts or Timelines, there is a good chance these will be flagged, disabled, and removed from Facebook.

You can't be twelve

Or younger. Seriously. Facebook takes very seriously the U.S. law that prohibits minors under the age of 13 from creating an online Timeline for themselves. This rule is in place for the safety of minors, and it's a particular safety rule that Facebook does enforce. If you or someone you know on Facebook is under 13, deactivate (or make him deactivate) the account now. If you're reported to the Facebook User Operations team and they confirm that you're underage, your account will be disabled.

You can't troll, spam, or harass

On the Internet, *trolling* refers to posting deliberately offensive material to websites in order to get people upset. *Spamming* refers to sending out bulk promotional messages. When I talk about *harassment,* I mean deliberately tormenting or bothering another person or group of people. If you do any of these things on Facebook, there's a good chance your account will be shut down.

The logic for this is that Facebook is about real people and real connections. It's one thing to message a mutual friend or the occasional stranger whose Timeline implies being open to meeting new people if the two of you have matching interests. However, between Facebook's automatic detection systems and user-generated reports, sending too many unsolicited messages is likely to get your account flagged and disabled.

Similarly, Facebook aims to be a "trusted" environment for people to exchange ideas and information. If people deliberately disturb the peace with pornographic, hateful, or bullying content, that trust is pretty much broken.

Chances are that you have no intention of breaking this trust, so keep in mind that if you see trolling, spam, or harassment taking place, you can report the content or person to Facebook (you can find out how to report a photo, for example, in Chapter 11), and its User Operations team investigates the report. If you're getting warnings about things like spamming, chances are you just need to tweak *how* you're using Facebook. For example, you may need to create a Page instead of using your personal account for mass messaging. You can find out how to promote your business (or yourself) in Chapter 13.

You can't upload illegal content

Facebook users live in virtually every country in the world, so Facebook is often obligated to respect the local laws for its users. Respecting these laws is something Facebook has to do regardless of its own position on pornography (where minors can see it), copyrighted material, hate speech, depictions of crimes, and other offensive content. However, doing so is also in line with Facebook's value of being a safe, happy place for people 13 and older. Don't confuse this with censorship; Facebook is all about freedom of speech and self-expression, but the moment that compromises anyone's safety or breaks any law, disciplinary action is taken.

Realizing How Facebook Is Different from Other Social Sites

Lots of social sites besides Facebook try to help people connect. Some popular sites are Twitter, LinkedIn, Instagram, Tumblr, and many others.

I'll start with the biggest reason Facebook is different. Literally, the biggest: Facebook has over one *billion* users across the world (yes, billion with a *b*). Other social sites might be popular in one country or another, but Facebook is popular pretty much everywhere.

REMEMBER

If you're going to use only one social networking site, choose Facebook — everyone you want to interact with is already there.

You'll see a lot of similar functionality across different sites: establishing connections, creating Timelines, liking content, and so on. However, each site brings a slightly different emphasis in terms of what is important. LinkedIn, for example, helps people with career networking, so it puts emphasis on professional information and connections. Match.com, on the other hand, is about matchmaking, so it's not exactly meant for those of us who aren't looking to get a date. Twitter encourages its members to share short *tweets*, 140-character posts with their connections; and Instagram (which is actually owned by Facebook) encourages its members to share cool photos taken with mobile phones.

You might find some or all of these sites useful at different points in time, but Facebook wants to be the one that is always useful in one way or another — so it tries to offer all the functionality I just mentioned . . . *and more.*

How You Can Use Facebook

Now that you know what you can do, generally, on Facebook, it's time to consider some of the specific ways you may find yourself using Facebook in the future. The following list is by no means comprehensive, and I've left out some of the things already mentioned in this chapter (things like sharing photos and events and groups). These are more specific-use cases than an advertisement for Facebook's features.

REMEMBER

One billion people use Facebook, but not all of them can see your whole Timeline. You can share as much or as little with as many or as few people as you so desire. Put under lock and key the posts or parts of your Timeline you *don't* want to share with everyone. Chapter 6 goes into much greater detail on how to protect yourself and your information.

Getting information

At any age, you may need to find someone's phone number or connect with a friend of a friend to organize something. Facebook can make these very practical tasks a little bit easier. As long as you can search for someone's name, you should be able to find her on Facebook and find the information you're looking for.

Keeping up with long-distance friends

These days, families and friends are often spread far and wide across state or country lines. Children go to college; grandparents move to Florida; people move for their job or because they want a change of scenery. These distances make it hard for people to interact in any more significant way than gathering together once per year to share some turkey and pie (pecan, preferably). Facebook offers a place where you can virtually meet and interact. Upload photos of the kids for everyone to see; write posts about what everyone is up to. Even the more mundane information about your life ("I'm at jury duty") can make someone across the world feel like, just for a second, she's sitting next to you and commiserating with you about your jury summons.

AM I SIGNING UP FOR A DATING SITE?

Throughout this book, you read about ways to communicate: messages, chatting, poking, liking, and commenting. These fairly neutral activities can take on a whole new meaning and spark when they happen between two people interested in each other.

Although Facebook is not technically a dating site, plenty of people do take advantage of its social nature to boost their dating lives in different ways:

- You can inform people through your Timeline whom you're looking to meet (women, men, or both).

- You can certainly use Facebook's systems to flirt, get to know, and yes, do a little background research on dating prospects.

- If you're happily ensconced in couple-dom, listing your relationship status and linking to your partner's Timeline is an easy way to broadcast, "Move along; I'm taken."

Moving to a new city

Landing in a new city with all your worldly belongings and an upside-down map can be hugely intimidating. Having some open arms or at least numbers to call when you arrive can greatly ease the transition. Although you may already know some people who live in your new city, Facebook can help connect with all the old friends and acquaintances you either forgot live there or have moved there since you last heard from them. These people can help you find doctors, apartments, hair stylists, Frisbee leagues, and restaurants.

As you meet more and more new friends, you can connect with them on Facebook. Sooner than you thought possible, when someone posts about construction slowing down his commute, you know exactly the street he means, and you may realize, *I'm home.*

Getting a job

Plenty of people use Facebook as a tool for managing their careers as well as their social lives. If you're looking at a particular company, find people who already work there to get the inside scoop or to land an interview. If you're thinking about moving into a particular industry, browse your friends by past jobs and interests to find someone to connect with. If you go to a conference for professional development, you can keep track of the other people you meet there as your Facebook friends.

Reunions

Thanks to life's curveballs, your friends at any given time may not be the people in your life at another. The memories of people you consider to be most important in your life fade over the years so that even trying to recall a last name may give you pause. The primary reason for this lapse is a legitimate one: There are only so many hours in a day. While we make new, close friends, others drift away because it's impossible to maintain many intense relationships. Facebook is an extremely powerful tool; however, it hasn't yet found a way to extend the number of hours in a day, so it can't exactly fix the problem of growing apart. Facebook can, however, lessen the finality and inevitability of the distance.

Because Facebook is less than ten years old (and because you're reading this book), you probably don't have your entire social history mapped out. Some may find it a daunting task to create connections with everyone they've ever known, which I don't recommend. Instead, build your graph as you need to or as opportunity presents. Perhaps you want to upload a photo taken from your high school graduation. Search for the people in the photo on Facebook; form the friend connection; and then *tag*, or mark, them as being in the photo. Maybe you're thinking about opening a restaurant, and you'd like to contact a friend from college who was headed into the restaurant business after graduation. Perhaps you never told your true feelings to the one who got away. For all these reasons, you may find yourself using the Facebook Search box.

TIP

Frequently, I receive reports from adopted children who connect with their biological parents or estranged siblings who find each other on Facebook. I once heard from my sixth-grade bully, who found me on Facebook and apologized for his behavior as a kid. I, in turn, used it to apologize to someone I treated terribly around the same time.

Organizing movements

In the summer of 2014, you couldn't look at a News Feed without encountering a video of someone dumping a bucket of ice water over their head. It wasn't some sort of bizarre hazing ritual; it was the ALS ice bucket challenge, designed to raise awareness of amyotrophic lateral sclerosis (also known as Lou Gehrig's disease). This awareness campaign hinged entirely on social sites like Facebook to spread. People would "challenge" their friends to either donate to an ALS-related charity or dump ice water over their heads and post the video of it to Facebook (or, ideally, do both). One person would post her ice-bucket video, challenge five friends, and then those five friends would post their ice-bucket videos, and so on and so on. The campaign spread through Facebook and the ALS association reported that it had more than doubled the amount of money raised over the previous summer.

The term *movement*, here, can apply to anything. People have used Facebook to agitate against terrorist groups, to raise money for victims of natural disasters, to spark conversation about suicide clusters at elite schools. Whatever the cause or movement may be, Facebook can be used to bring support and spread the word.

THE BIRTH OF THE 'BOOK

In ye olden days, say, the early 2000s, most college freshmen would receive a thinly bound book containing the names and faces of everyone in their matriculating class. These *face books* were useful for matching names to the students seen around campus or for pointing out particular people to friends. There were several problems with these face books. If someone didn't send his picture in, the books were incomplete. They were outdated by junior year because many people looked drastically different, and the books didn't reflect the students who had transferred in or who were from any other class. Finally, they had little information about each person.

In February 2004, Mark Zuckerberg, a sophomore at Harvard, launched an online "book" to which people could upload their photos and personal information, a service that solved many of these problems. Within a month, more than one-half the Harvard undergraduates had signed up.

Zuckerberg was then joined by others to help expand the site into other schools. I was the first Stanford student to receive an account. During the summer of the same year, Facebook moved to Palo Alto, California, where the site and the company kept growing. By December 2004, the site had grown to one million college students. Every time Facebook opened to a new demographic — high school, then work users, then everyone — the rate at which people joined the site continued to increase.

At the end of 2006, the site had more than 10 million users; 2007 closed out with more than 50 million active users. At the time of this book's publication in 2016, that final count has grown to in excess of one billion people across the globe using Facebook to stay in touch.

IN THIS CHAPTER

Signing up and getting started

Adding information about yourself

Finding friends

Getting confirmed and managing emails

Chapter 2

Adding Your Own Face to Facebook

I n Chapter 1, I cover why you might want to join Facebook. In this chapter, I actually get you signed up and ready to go on Facebook. Keep a couple of things in mind when you sign up. First, Facebook becomes exponentially more useful and more fun when you start adding friends. Without friends, it can feel kind of dull. Second, your friends may take a few days to respond to your Friend Requests, so be patient. Even if your first time on Facebook isn't as exciting as you hope, be sure to come back and try again over the following weeks. Third, you can have only one account on Facebook. Facebook links accounts to email addresses or phone numbers, and your email address (or number) can be linked to only one account. This system enforces a world where people are who they say they are on Facebook.

Signing Up for Facebook

Officially, all you need in order to join Facebook is a valid email address or phone number. When I say *valid email,* I just mean that you need to be able to easily access the messages in that account because Facebook emails you a registration confirmation. A *valid phone number* means a mobile phone number that can send and receive text messages, since Facebook will text you your registration confirmation. Figure 2-1 shows the crucial part of the sign-up page, which you can find by navigating to www.facebook.com.

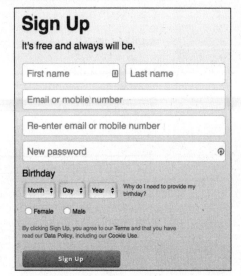

Sign Up

It's free and always will be.

First name | Last name

Email or mobile number

Re-enter email or mobile number

New password

Birthday

Month ⬍ | Day ⬍ | Year ⬍ Why do I need to provide my birthday?

○ Female   ○ Male

By clicking Sign Up, you agree to our Terms and that you have read our Data Policy, including our Cookie Use.

Sign Up

FIGURE 2-1:
Enter information
here to create a
Facebook
account.

As you can see, you need to fill out a few things:

>> **First and Last Name:** Facebook is a place based on real identity. Sign up with the name people know you by. I don't recommend signing up with a fake name or alias because that will make it hard for you to be found by friends. After you've signed up, you can add nicknames or maiden names to your Timeline to make it even easier for friends to find you. But for now, just use your real first and last names.

>> **Email or Mobile Number:** You need to enter your valid email address or phone number here. Facebook asks you to enter this information twice to make sure that there are no typos and your emails or texts will actually get to you.

If you're signing up for Facebook with a phone number, it needs to be a mobile phone number. Your home phone number can't get texts so it won't help you sign up for Facebook.

REMEMBER

>> **Password:** As with all passwords, using a combination of letters and numbers is a good idea for your Facebook password. It's probably not a good idea to use the same password for every site you join, so I recommend using something unique for Facebook.

>> **Birthday:** Enter your date of birth. If you're shy about sharing your birthday, don't worry: You'll be able to hide this information on your Timeline later.

>> **Sex (Female or Male):** Facebook uses your gender information to construct sentences about you on the site. For example, you might see a News Feed story that reads "Carolyn updated her profile picture." If you are transgender or use a nonstandard gender pronoun, you'll have the ability to change this in your settings.

After you fill out this information, click Sign Up (that's the big green button). Congratulations: You officially joined Facebook!

REMEMBER

When you click Sign Up, you're agreeing to Facebook's Terms of Service and Data Policy. Most websites have fairly similar terms and policies, but if you're curious about just what Facebook's are, you can always follow the Terms and Data Policy links just above the big green Sign Up button.

Getting Started

Although you have this book to help guide you through the ins and outs of Facebook, lots of Facebook users do not. (How sad for them!) That's why Facebook puts all its users through a two-step Getting Started Wizard to help start them out on the right foot. This is one of those places where what I think you should do and what Facebook thinks you should do line up exactly, so I'll go through the steps together, covering what to enter as well as why these steps are important to using Facebook.

WARNING

In certain cases, depending on whether you were invited to join Facebook by a friend or you joined with an email address from your workplace or school, you may get slightly different steps than those detailed as follows. You may not even see a Getting Started Wizard as it appears in the screenshots. Don't worry; the same principles apply — you want to find your friends and set up your profile.

Step 1: Find Your Friends

The Find Your Friends step, shown in Figure 2-2, is first because it's that important to enjoying Facebook. Without friends, Facebook can feel a little bit like going to an amusement park alone. Sure, the rides were fun, and the food was greasy, but no one was there to appreciate it with you.

REMEMBER

You have many ways to find friends on Facebook. I go over all of them in Chapter 8, as well as talking more about what friendship really means on Facebook. The method Facebook is highlighting in this step is the *Friend Finder*.

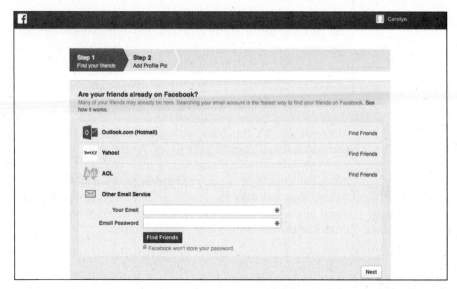

FIGURE 2-2:
Find your friends
early and often.

The Friend Finder works by allowing Facebook access to your email account. Facebook then combs through your email contacts and matches the emails it finds with emails attached to the Facebook accounts of the people you email. So if Joe Smith, your friend, emailed you from `jsmith@email.com` and also had a Facebook account he created with that email address, the Friend Finder presents you with Joe's name and profile picture and asks if you want to be friends on Facebook.

To use the Friend Finder, follow these steps:

1. **Select the email provider you're using.**

This may be Outlook.com (or Hotmail), Yahoo!, AOL, or another email client. Facebook automatically selects a provider based on the email you used to register.

I used a nonstandard domain, so Figure 2-2 shows nothing prefilled.

TIP

Depending on what email service you use, importing your contacts and looking for friends may entail a few extra steps. You may even be brought to the website of your email provider to log in to your email account. Log in and follow any necessary prompts to allow Facebook to access your contacts list.

2. **Enter your email address and email password.**

Remember to enter your email password, not the password you just created for Facebook.

3. **Click Find Friends.**

Behind the scenes, Facebook searches your contact list and presents you with the people in your email Contacts list who are already on Facebook. By default, all these people are selected to be your friends.

4. **Look through the list and choose the people you want to be friends with on Facebook.**

I talk more about *who,* exactly, should be your Facebook friends in Chapter 8, but for now, a good rule is to look for people you're friends with or related to in real life. You can deselect the people you don't want to add by clicking their faces or the check boxes.

This isn't your only opportunity to use the Friend Finder. If you aren't sure about adding a lot of people right away, that's okay. Chapter 8 shows you how to get back to these steps at any point in time.

REMEMBER

5. **Click Add as Friends.**

This sends *Friend Requests* to all the people you selected in Step 4. On Facebook, all friendships have to be agreed to by both people. A request to your friend needs to be approved by her before you are officially Facebook friends.

After you add friends, Facebook looks at the email addresses it didn't find matches for and asks you whether you want to invite those people to join Facebook.

6. **Select people you want to invite to join Facebook.**

Much like selecting friends to add, you can select and deselect friends' email addresses by selecting the check box next to their emails.

If you don't want to invite anyone to join Facebook just yet, look on the bottom right of the screen for a Skip link. It's right next to the Send Invites button.

TIP

7. **Click Send Invites to send out invitations to your friends via email.**

They'll receive emails from Facebook letting them know you invited them to join.

The Friend Finder is very useful when you're just getting started on Facebook because it allows you to find a whole bunch of friends all at once. If you had to look for each of your friends by name, it could take a while. Friend Finder allows you to speed up that process.

Step 2: Profile Picture

Your *Facebook Profile*, or *Timeline*, is the online representation of who you are. Most likely, you have online profiles for various websites. Facebook Timelines tend to be a little more comprehensive and dynamic, for reasons that I detail in Chapter 5.

Your Profile Picture is one of the most important parts of your Timeline. It's a good first step towards starting to tell your friends all about you. And, significantly, it helps your friends identify you. Remember all those friend requests you sent while you were using the Friend Finder? When those friends see your request, it will be much easier for them to verify that you're *you* if they can see a photo of you. Step 2, adding a profile picture, is shown in Figure 2-3.

TIP

If you've already been through the Getting Started Wizard or aren't seeing the wizard as it appears in Figure 2-3, click the Edit Profile link on the right side of the screen and then click Add Profile Picture when you arrive on the Edit Profile page. The instructions below assume you are looking at the Getting Started Wizard, so may not match the steps you take from the Edit Profile page exactly, though they are very similar.

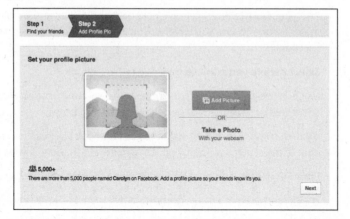

FIGURE 2-3: Add a profile picture to get your own face on Facebook.

You can add a profile picture in one of two ways. You can either upload a photo from your computer's hard drive or, if you have a computer with a built-in webcam, you can take a photo you want to use.

To add a profile picture from your hard drive, make sure you have a photo you want to use saved somewhere you can find it, and follow these steps:

1. **Click Add Picture.**

   This opens a window for browsing your computer's hard drive. Use it to navigate to wherever you saved the photo you wanted to use as a profile picture.

2. **Select your desired photo and click Choose or OK.**

   This brings you back to the Getting Started Wizard, except now there's a preview of your new profile picture.

3. **Click Next.**

If you want to use your computer's webcam to take a profile picture, follow these steps:

1. **Click the Take a Photo link.**

   This opens a dialog box for accessing your computer's webcam. You may have to click Allow before Facebook is able to work with your computer to show an image of you.

2. **Strike a pose and click the Take Photo button.**

   Once the photo has been taken, it displays in the dialog box. You can choose to retake the photo if you don't like the way your smile looks.

3. **Click Save.**

TIP

I talk a lot about your profile picture and the many ways it's used on Facebook in Chapter 5, but here are a few quick tips on selecting a profile picture:

» **Make a good first impression.** Your profile picture is one of the first ways people interact with your Timeline and how you choose to represent yourself. Most people pick pictures that are flattering or that represent what's important to them. Sometimes, profile pictures include other people — friends or significant others. Other times, the location matters. If the first photo you see of someone is at the beach versus at a party or sitting at his desk, you may draw different conclusions about that person. What picture represents you?

» **Consider who will see your profile picture.** By default, your profile picture appears in search results that are visible to all of Facebook and can even be made available to the larger Internet population. So, generally, people who search for your name can see that picture. Make sure it's something you're comfortable with everyone seeing.

» **Pick a photo *you* like.** As you use Facebook, you actually wind up seeing your own photo quite often. Small versions appear wherever you make a comment, post something, or are part of a group. So pick a photo you like looking at.

» **You're not stuck with it.** After I put all this pressure on you to pick the perfect photo, keep in mind that you can easily change your profile picture at any time. Is it the dead of winter, and that photo of you on the beach last summer is just too depressing to look at? No problem; simply edit your profile picture, which you can find out how to do in Chapter 5.

What to Expect in Your Inbox

Having made it through the Getting Started Wizard, you may think you are all done. You *have* made great progress (back pats all around), but there's still more to do. The first thing Facebook will prompt you to do is to confirm your email address or phone number. And, once you have confirmed your email, Facebook will contact you fairly frequently to try and get you fully integrated into the Facebook world.

Confirmation

Confirmation is Facebook's way of trying to make sure that you are really you and that the email address you used to sign up is really yours. After you finish the earlier two Getting Started steps, you may see a yellow banner across the top of your Home page, asking you to check your email to finish signing up for Facebook.

When you click the Sign Up button (as I describe earlier), Facebook sends you an email asking you to confirm your account. In other words, Facebook is double-checking that you are the person who owns your email address.

To confirm that you are, in fact, you, and that the email address is, in fact, yours, go to your email, look for that message, and open it. (It will usually have a subject like *Just One More Step to Get Started on Facebook* or *Facebook Confirmation.*) That email contains a link or button. Click the link or button in that email, and you will be confirmed.

You may have already confirmed your email address by using the Friend Finder or other normal activities. If Facebook isn't bugging you about it with banners or follow-up emails, you can pretty much assume you're good to go.

Email outreach

Once you've confirmed your email address and added a few friends, Facebook considers you a full-fledged member of the site. However, it doesn't want you to just show up once and leave, as a result, after you sign up, it may email you to remind you that you are now a Facebook user. These outreach emails have various subject lines, ranging from a notice that one of your new Facebook friends has updated his status, to a general notice that "You have more friends on Facebook than you think." Clicking the links in these emails will open up Facebook in your browser.

If you don't like receiving these emails, you can unsubscribe by clicking the "Unsubscribe" link in the bottom of any individual email. This will also open up Facebook in your browser, asking if you are sure you want to unsubscribe from that type of email. Click Confirm to make it official.

WARNING

When Facebook asks if you want to unsubscribe from "this type" of email, it is being very specific. Email updates about your friends (Carolyn added new photos on Facebook) are a different type than general prompts to find more friends. You may have to click unsubscribe from more than one email before you stop receiving emails altogether.

Your New Home Page

After you complete your Getting Started Wizard, you arrive at your Home page. This is where Facebook starts to look like the Facebook you would see if you'd been using the site for a while already. The Home page is what you see when you log in to Facebook.

What's interesting about the Facebook Home page is that while some parts remain the same (such as the big blue bar on top, and the menu on the left-hand side), the bulk of what you see is constantly changing. This is because the Home page (also known as the News Feed) updates to show you what your friends are posting, sharing, and talking about on Facebook.

At the beginning of this chapter, I point out that Facebook gets exponentially better once you have friends. This is absolutely true on the Home page. Until your friends respond to your requests, you may not see much here except prompts to learn more about Facebook, find more friends, or fill out more profile information beyond your profile picture. After you add the people you know as friends, take a break. Stretch. Take a walk. Drink some water. Come back over the next few days to see the interesting photos, status updates, and links your friends are sharing.

AM I TOO OLD FOR FACEBOOK?

No. Most emphatically, no. This is a common misconception, mainly because Facebook was originally exclusive to college students. Facebook's origins, even its name, are rooted in college campuses, but its utility and nature aren't limited to being useful to only college students.

Everyone has networks of friends and people with whom they interact on a day-to-day basis. Young or old, in college or working, this is true. Facebook tries to map these real-world connections to make it easier for people to share information with their friends.

If you're reading this section and thinking maybe you're just too old for Facebook, you're wrong. More and more people in older age demographics are signing up for Facebook every day to keep in touch with old friends, share photos, create events, and connect with local organizations. Almost everything I discuss in the book is non-age-specific.

Obviously, how people use the site can be very different at different ages, but you will discover these nuances when you use Facebook more and more. Generally, you should feel confident that you and your friends can connect and use Facebook in a meaningful way.

More than one billion people are using Facebook, and that number isn't made up of "a bunch of kids." Rather, it's a bunch of people from every age group, every country, and every walk of life.

TIP

As you navigate around Facebook for the first time, you may notice small boxes popping up in different parts of the screen (there's an example of one such box in Figure 2-4). Don't ignore these guys! They are trying to teach you tips and tricks to get you comfortable using Facebook.

FIGURE 2-4:
These little boxes point out how and why to use different Facebook features.

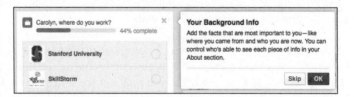

Adding More Friends

As a new user logging into Facebook, there seems to be one overwhelming thing that Facebook wants you to do — add more friends. You may be seeing the updates of friends in your News Feed, but you are almost certainly seeing previews of people you may know with big buttons prompting you to Add Friend. You may see these previews on the right side of your Home page, in your News Feed, even on your Timeline or on your friends' Timelines.

Facebook finds people to recommend you add as friends based largely on the people you are already friends with (this is a vastly oversimplified explanation of the find friends algorithm, but the longer explanation involves more math). Each time you see a "Person You May Know" you can choose to ignore the suggestion by clicking the tiny X button in the upper right corner or click the Add Friend button.

I always hesitate to give too much advice in terms of whether or not you should add someone as a friend. In general, especially when you are just starting out, I lean towards adding everyone you know and care about. Family, friends, coworkers, teammates, classmates — add 'em all. Adding more friends will make your News Feed more interesting, and Facebook will learn over time whom, exactly, you find most interesting.

REMEMBER

On Facebook, friendships are *reciprocal*. You don't officially become Facebook friends with others until they have approved your friend request.

On the flip side, I would not recommend adding people you don't actually like as friends. Yes, I mean that one person from your last job who was always super nice to you but secretly drove you insane. Or that second cousin twice removed who always asks you inappropriate questions about your love life. Don't feel obligated to click Add Friends simply because you *know* someone.

WARNING

Categories of people you may not want to add as friends are teachers, doctors, students, or other people you know and like but who you would like to maintain a more professional distance from. Facebook is often a place where people are casual, let their (virtual) hair down, and don't censor. It can be weird or even inappropriate to see your therapist venting about her patients or for your boss to see photos of you relaxing at the beach when you claimed you were home sick.

There is a lot more information about the nuances of friendship and how to know who to add in Chapter 8.

Filling out Your Profile Information

Getting your Timeline set up is not a requirement for starting to use Facebook. In fact, your Timeline is something that gets built up over time (and doing so is covered in Chapter 5) so I wouldn't give you such a Herculean task right away.

However, there are a few basic pieces of information that will help you find your friends on Facebook, as well as helping your friends identify you when you send them a friend request. These are your current workplace, current city, any schools you've attended, and your hometown. Especially if you have a common name, this information can really help someone who is regarding a friend request figure out if you are in fact Jane Smith from Portland (who they definitely want to be friends with) or Jane Smith from Seattle (who, maybe not so much).

To add this basic profile information, follow these steps:

1. From your Home page, click the Edit Profile link in the upper left corner of the screen.

This link can be found beneath the Facebook logo in the blue bar on top of the page, directly underneath your name and profile picture preview. Clicking it takes you to the About section of your Timeline, shown in Figure 2-5. By default, you are looking at the Work and Education subsection.

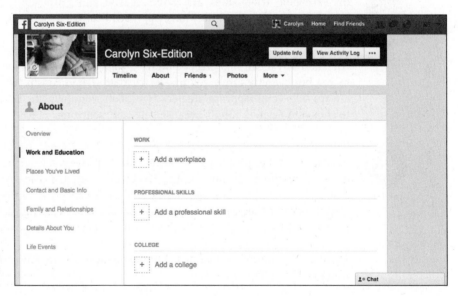

FIGURE 2-5:
Add Profile
Information here.

2. **Click Add a workplace, Add a college, or Add a high school.**

   Clicking any of these links opens up an interface for typing in the name of your workplace, college, or high school, respectively.

3. **Start typing the name of your workplace or school.**

   Facebook *autocompletes*, or attempts to guess at what you're typing as you type. So, for example, if you start typing "m-i-c" Facebook will display a menu of possible company matches — Microsoft, Mic Media, Michael Kors, and so on.

4. **Select your workplace or school when you see it appear in the autocomplete menu.**

   If your workplace doesn't appear in the autocomplete menu, simply finish typing its name and press Enter.

5. **(Optional) Add more details about your work or school.**

   You can add information like your specific job title, major, year of graduation, and more.

6. **Click Save Changes.**

   The blue Save Changes button is at the bottom of the section you are editing.

TIP

To the left of the Save Changes button, a small globe icon and the word "Public" lets you know that once you save it, this information is publicly available. Anyone can see it. I talk more about what this means in Chapter 6.

To add your hometown and current city from the About section of your profile, click the Places You've Lived link on the left side of the page (underneath Work and Education). You can then click to add your current city and hometown the same way you added your work and education information. You can also edit this information from the Overview section.

IN THIS CHAPTER

Navigating Facebook

Looking around the Home page

Using Search

Finding those less frequently used links

Chapter 3

Finding Your Way Around Facebook

ere's the thing about using Facebook: It has a lot of options. Now, this is actually one of the best things about Facebook. You can upload photos, look at photos, chat with a friend, message a friend, read updates from friends . . . the list goes on and on. What does get a little confusing is that there's no one way to do anything on Facebook. Depending on what page you're on, you'll see slightly different things. Depending on who your friends are, you'll see slightly different things. Using Facebook can't exactly be broken down into ten easy steps.

However, you can learn to recognize a few more constant places. Starting from when you log in, you will always start on your *Home page.* The Home page, though continually evolving, has a few constants that I detail in this chapter. If you ever find yourself lost on Facebook (it happens; trust me), click the Home link or the Facebook logo to go to the Home page, where you'll be able to reorient yourself.

Figure 3-1 shows a sample Home page. This chapter details the elements of the Home page that you're likely to see, too: menus and links to other parts of the site. Some of these links can be found no matter where you are on Facebook, some appear only when you're on your Home page, and some will be there, well, sometimes. Learning about these links helps you understand how to find your way around Facebook and enables you to work with some of Facebook's features and options.

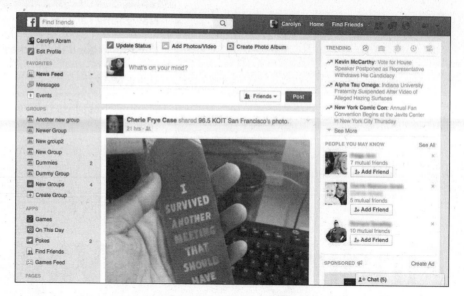

Checking Out the Blue Bar on Top

I happen to spend a lot of time in coffee shops working alongside writers, students, businesspeople, and hobbyists — all drinking steamy beverages and manning laptops. I can always tell at a glance when someone is browsing Facebook by the big blue bar across the top of the page. The blue bar is home to many of the important navigational links on Facebook. And anytime you're looking at a Facebook page, you'll have the blue bar accompanying you, like a really loyal puppy. Figure 3-2 shows the blue bar.

Here's what you need to know about the different parts of the blue bar:

>> **Facebook logo:** The "f" Facebook logo on the left of the blue bar serves two purposes. First, it reminds you what website you're using. Second, no matter where you are on Facebook, if you click this icon, you're back at the Facebook Home page.

>> **Search:** The big white box next to the Facebook logo is the search box. This text area is where you can type any sort of search query. Simply click that text

and start typing what you're looking for. After you click, Facebook opens up a menu with suggested searches. I talk more about how to find people and other Facebook content later on in the "Search" section of this chapter.

TIP

The text within the search box will actually change depending on where you are on Facebook. For example, when you're on a friend's Timeline, it will show your friend's name. When you're exploring a group, it will show the group's name. This is one way to keep from getting lost.

» **<Your Name> and Profile Picture:** If you share a computer with other people, glancing at this link whenever you use Facebook is an easy way to make sure you're using your Facebook account and not your spouse's or kid's account. Clicking this link brings you to your Timeline.

» **Home:** This link is always there to bring you back to the Home page. When in doubt, just go Home and start over.

» **(New Users) Find Friends:** If you're a new user of Facebook or don't have very many friends, Facebook adds this link to your blue bar to make it as easy as possible for you to go get more friends. Clicking it brings you to the Find Friends page, where you can use Facebook's various tools for finding and adding your friends. I cover all the ways to find friends in Chapter 8.

» **Friend Requests:** Next to the Home link is an icon of two people, intended to depict friends. Clicking this icon reveals a menu that shows you any pending Friend Requests you may have. Whenever you receive brand-new Friend Requests, a little red number totaling the number of new requests shows up on top of this icon. When you view the new requests, regardless of whether you respond to them, the red flag goes away. I cover sending and receiving Friend Requests in more detail in Chapter 8.

» **Messages:** An icon depicting two speech bubbles lets you access a preview of your Messages Inbox. Clicking it shows you snippets from your most recent messages, as well as links to use if you want to send a new message or go to your Inbox. As with the Friend Requests, a little red flag appears to show you how many new messages you have. When you click that flag and view the preview of the new messages, the flag disappears. I cover Facebook Messages in Chapter 9.

» **Notifications:** When someone on Facebook has taken an action that involves you, you're notified by a red flag on top of the next icon — the globe. Maybe the person has tagged you in a photo, posted to your Timeline, liked a comment you made, or posted something to a group you belong to. Click the globe to scroll through your most recent notifications, as well as a link to change your notification settings or see all your notifications on another page.

>> **Privacy Shortcuts:** The little padlock icon represents the Privacy Shortcuts menu. Knowing who can see what on Facebook is one of the keys to feeling comfortable sharing on Facebook, and this shortcut menu makes it easy to check up on yourself. This menu provides an easy way to find out the answers to three basic privacy and safety questions: Who can see my stuff? Who can contact me? and How do I stop someone from bothering me? I go over why these questions are important and how to understand the answers to them in Chapter 6.

>> **Account menu (down arrow):** In this book, I reference the *Account menu.* That's the menu that appears when you click this arrow. Here's a rundown of some of the categories you can find on the Account menu:

- *Your Pages:* In Chapter 13, I go over creating a *Page,* or special profile for businesses or organizations. If you create or manage Pages, you'll be able to find links to use Facebook on behalf of your Pages from the Account menu. You can also find links to create new Pages or manage your existing Pages.

- *Groups:* Chapter 10 explains how to create and use Groups to communicate and share with smaller groups of people within Facebook. The account menu contains links to create groups, check out your new groups, and manage and groups you have created.

- *Ads:* I also briefly cover ads in Chapter 13. If you create an ad to be shown on Facebook, you'll find links to manage and create more ads in this menu.

- *Activity Log:* I talk about Activity Log when I talk about privacy in Chapter 6. It's a way to keep track of all the actions you have taken recently on Facebook and who may be able to see those actions. You can get to your Activity Log from this menu.

- *News Feed Preferences:* Your News Feed is a constantly updated list of stories by and about your friends. It's what you see front and center on your Home page every time you log in to Facebook. In Chapter 4, I talk about how you can influence what you see in News Feed using the News Feed Preferences.

- *Settings:* Choosing this brings you to the Settings page, where you can change your name, your email address or password, your mobile information (which allows you to access the site from a mobile phone), or the language you want to use on the site. This is also where you go to find privacy settings (detailed in Chapter 6), notification settings, and to deactivate your account.

- *Log Out:* Clicking this ends your Facebook session. If you share your computer with others, always be sure to log out to ensure that another person can't access your Facebook account.

WARNING

If you have the Remember Me option selected when you log in, you won't ever be logged out until you click Log Out. Remember Me keeps you logged in despite closing the browser; therefore, I recommend using the Remember Me option only on a computer you don't share with others.

- *Help:* There are a few different ways to access help from the Account menu. Clicking Help switches over to a Help menu with links to frequently asked questions and a search box. If you ever have a problem and you can't find the answer in this book, the Help menu and the Help Center are good places to start. The Support Inbox is where you'll go if you ever have a problem that requires you contacting Facebook's Help team. Any correspondence with that team will take place in your Support Inbox. If you ever see something on Facebook you think you shouldn't (such as harassment or porn), you can go to the account menu and choose to Report a Problem.

Search

Search has become an integral part of using the Internet. It's the way we find the info we need — whether that's a businesses address, a person's contact info, or the year of the great San Francisco earthquake. Facebook's search is also important, though it works a bit differently from the way a search engine like Google or Bing does.

Most of the time, you will use Search to hop quickly to a friend's Timeline or to check out a Page you follow. Simply start typing your friend's name into the search box in the big blue bar on top of the page. Facebook displays an *autocomplete menu* as you type, showing possible matches as you add more and more letters. When you see the name of the person you are looking for, click on her name or picture to go to her Timeline.

Even though the most simple use of Search is what you'll use most of the time, it's worth noting that Facebook has an incredible database of information that you can search through at any time. You can search through friends' posts, photos, videos simply by entering a search term into the search box. Given the amount of information you might see in your News Feed on any given day, it can be incredibly helpful to search to find that one piece of information you are looking for (I *know* someone posted a link to the best place to pick apples in the fall, but I can't remember when . . .). The search results page allows you to filter for the latest results, or to look only at people, photos, videos, Pages, or places.

The Left Sidebar

The left side of the Facebook Home page is taken up by what Facebook calls the *sidebar.* The sidebar is the menu on the left side of the page that provides links to frequently used areas of the site.

The sidebar is divided into a few sections. The top section provides links to go to and edit your Timeline. The Favorites section provides links to the parts of Facebook you use most. The other sections are based on different parts of Facebook — Groups, Apps, Pages, and so on. Depending on how you use Facebook (for example, you may belong to many groups or no groups), the sidebar will appear slightly different to you. Figure 3-3 shows a sample sidebar.

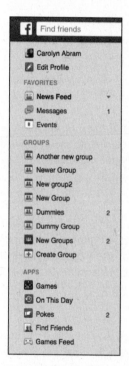

FIGURE 3-3:
A sample sidebar.

The Favorites section

By default, the Favorites section shows you links to News Feed, Messages, and Events. You cannot remove News Feed from this section; Facebook has simply decreed that News Feed will be one of your favorite parts of Facebook (and, in this case, I'm not inclined to disagree). Facebook will also add items to this section as you use Facebook. For example, if you start to spend a lot of time posting and commenting on a particular group, Facebook will automatically add it to your Favorites section. Because you might not always agree with Facebook, it's always possible to change which links appear here and the order in which they appear.

To remove a link from the Favorites section, follow these steps:

1. **Hover your mouse over the link you want to remove.**

A small gear icon appears to the left of the link.

2. **Click the gear icon.**

A menu opens over the gear icon with two options: Remove from Favorites or Rearrange (see Figure 3-4).

FIGURE 3-4:
Use this menu
to Remove or
Rearrange.

3. **Click Remove from Favorites.**

The menu closes and the link disappears from the Favorites section.

You may also want to rearrange the links that appear in your Favorites section so that your most favorite of favorite links are at the top and your least favorite of favorite links are at the bottom of the list. To do so, follow these steps:

1. **Hover your mouse over any of the links in the Favorites list.**

A small gear icon appears to the left of the link.

2. **Click the gear icon.**

A menu opens over the gear icon.

3. **Select Rearrange.**

When you do so, your cursor changes from an arrow or hand to a four-way arrow or compass icon. Also, an icon with three horizontal bars appears to the right of each item in the Favorites section (except for News Feed). This indicates that you can move these items around.

4. **Click and drag the items into your preferred order.**

Each link needs to be moved individually, so you may need to repeat this step a number of times.

5. **Click Done.**

The Done link appears below the last item in your Favorites section.

Other sections

The rest of the sections you may find in your left sidebar represent parts of Facebook that you may or may not use. A few of the sections (such as Interests and Developer) are used so infrequently, I've even left them off the following list.

>> **Groups:** Groups are a way for (you guessed it) groups of people to communicate and share with each other. Groups can be small or large, and can represent real world groups or not. Each group you join appears in the Groups section of the sidebar. You can click on the group name to navigate to that group's page. You can also hover over a group's name and click the gear icon that appears in order to add that group to the Favorites section, edit your settings, or leave the group. Groups are covered in detail in Chapter 10.

>> **Events:** Facebook's Events feature allows people to easily organize and invite people to an event. Any upcoming events you've RSVP'd to appear in the Events section of your sidebar, as well as a link to create an event. You can learn more about creating and managing events in Chapter 12.

>> **Pages:** *Pages* are Timelines for everything that's not a regular person. Public Figures like Barack Obama or Lady Gaga have Pages, as do small businesses, fictional characters, television shows and movies, pets of all hues and stripes, and pretty much everything else you can think of. If you are a Page owner (meaning you use Facebook to represent something other than yourself), your Pages appear in a list in this section, as well as links to create a Page, or create Ads to promote your Page. Chapter 13 covers creating and managing Pages.

>> **Friends:** Friend Lists are a feature that allows you to create clusters (or lists) of friends and then easily share directly with those friends. Think of sharing with a list as more like sending out an email blast and sharing with a group as more of a post to a message board. Facebook automatically creates certain lists (such as Close Friends) and you can create your own lists that you find useful to using Facebook. All your lists appear in the Friends section of your sidebar.

>> **Apps:** Much like apps that you may use on your smartphone, apps on Facebook are features and functionality you may use to enhance your Facebook experience. Technically things like Groups and Events are apps, though they are considered important enough to merit their own sidebar sections. Apps can be built by Facebook or by other companies. Any apps you use appear in this section of the sidebar. You can learn more about apps and how they integrate with Facebook in Chapter 14.

TIP

You can add a group, Page, app, or friend list to your Favorites menu by hovering over the item you want to add, clicking the gear icon, and selecting Add to Favorites.

Viewing News Feed

This chapter is about navigating Facebook, which is why the blue bar and the sidebar are so important. At the same time, these menus aren't really the focus of the Home page. Instead, these menus serve as a bit of a background to the main event in the center of the page: News Feed. As I mention earlier, News Feed is what you see as the main focus of your Home page.

So what is News Feed? Imagine that your morning paper, news show, or radio program included an additional section that featured articles solely about the specific people you know. That's what News Feed is. As long as the people you know are active on Facebook, you can stay up-to-date with their lives via your News Feed. A friend may post photos from his recent birthday party, another may write a post about her new job, and another may publish a public event for her upcoming art show. These may all show up as stories in your Facebook News Feed. A News Feed bonus: You can often use it to stay up-to-date on current events just by seeing what your friends are talking about or by liking the Pages of real-world news organizations and getting their updates in your News Feed. When there's unusual weather, I find out about it on Facebook first because I see a flurry of posts asking if that was really hail.

News Feed is possibly one of the best and most interesting things about Facebook, but also one of the hardest to explain. This is because no matter how I describe seeing a photo of my friend and her new baby pop up in my News Feed, it won't be as exciting as when *your* friend posts those photos. I do my best to capture at least a bit of this excitement in Chapter 4.

At the very top of News Feed is what's called the *Publisher* or *share box*, shown in Figure 3-5. This box is what you use to add your own content to Facebook: status posts, photos, links to articles you find interesting, and so on. These posts also go into News Feed and may appear in your friends' News Feeds. Your friends can then comment, like, and generally interact with you about your post. I go into more detail about how to use the Publisher in Chapter 4.

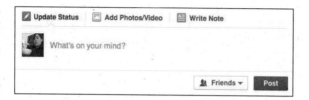

FIGURE 3-5: Share what's on your mind from the Publisher.

Right On

Much like the left sidebar, the items you see on the right side of the page change depending on how you use Facebook. If you're a newer user you may see different things than if you have been using Facebook for a long time. People with many friends may see something different than people with fewer friends. Here are some of the items you may see on the right side of your Home page:

>> **Reminders:** You may see reminders for things like upcoming events, friends' birthdays, or requests you need to respond to.

>> **Trending:** Trending topics shows a taste of what *everyone* is talking about on Facebook. For example, if everyone is talking about a particular presidential candidate or a particularly hilarious video of a rat stealing a pizza slice, those topics will appear under the heading of Trending Topics. You can click on any of the trending topics to learn more about them. You can also click to see more, or use the filters next to the word Trending to see trending topics in politics (state building icon), science and technology (atomic icon), sports (soccer ball icon), or entertainment (movie reel player icon).

>> **Ticker:** Earlier in this chapter, I mention News Feed and how it is a constantly updated list of posts from your friends and Pages you like. Well, one of the things to know about Facebook is that it actually isn't *all* of your friends' posts. For most people, it would be overwhelming to get an update every time every friend did something on Facebook. News Feed tries to show you the best of the best. Ticker, on the other hand, shows you everything. Ticker itself shows an abbreviated summary of what happened (for example, Juliana likes Martha's link). You can then hover your mouse over that item to see details about the link Martha shared and who else likes or commented on it.

>> **Facebook Suggestions:** Facebook's suggestions are generally ways for you to continue to find and interact with people and things you may find interesting. Facebook may suggest people it thinks you would want to add as friends, Pages you might like, groups you might want to join, and so on. These suggestions are based on people, Pages, and groups you already have interacted with.

>> **Sponsored Ads:** Ads on the right side of the page appear in a section labeled "Sponsored." Facebook is 100% free for you to use, and one of the ways it pays the bills is by selling ads like these.

The Littlest Links

At the very bottom of the rightmost column are a handful of important, but infrequently needed links. These links all appear in grey text.

>> **English (US):** If you signed up for Facebook on a computer in the United States, Facebook defaults to English. If for any reason you want to change the language in which you use Facebook, click this link to select your desired language.

>> **Privacy:** Details the Facebook Data Use Policy, if you're looking for a little light bedtime reading.

>> **Terms:** This link takes you to a page where you can view all of Facebook's Terms and Policies, including the Statement of Rights and Responsibilities (which you agreed to when you signed up), the Data Policy, and its Community Standards.

>> **Cookies:** Sadly, clicking this link doesn't make chocolate chip cookies suddenly appear in your hand. Instead, it brings you to a page that explains how Facebook uses *web cookies,* or stored data on your web browser. Cookies are used on many websites to keep your experience more convenient (for example, automatically displaying Facebook in the language of whatever country your computer is in) and also to deliver ads to you.

>> **Advertising:** Click this link to create or manage ads that you've posted to Facebook.

>> **Ad Choices:** Clicking this link brings you to the Facebook Help pages where you can learn more about how Facebook targets ads to you, and what you can do to adjust what ads you see.

>> More: Clicking this link opens a menu of still more links. Click any of these options to navigate to different parts of Facebook:

- **About:** Facebook's About page is where you can learn more about Facebook, the company, and what it's been doing in the news lately.

- **Careers:** If you're considering applying for a job at Facebook, check out its careers page first.

- **Create Page:** If you want to create a Page for a band, brand, celebrity, or other non-person entity, you can use this link.

- **Developers:** If you are a software engineer looking for ways to build apps that use Facebook, click this link to learn more about the Facebook Platform.

- **Help:** A duplicate of the link in your Account menu, this takes you to the Facebook Help Center.

2

Day-to-Day Facebook

IN THIS PART. . .

Logging in and reading News Feed

Sharing your status, photos, and links

Checking out what's going on with friends

Interacting via comments, likes, and sharing

Using Facebook on your mobile phone

Managing your privacy

IN THIS CHAPTER

Finding out what your friends are up to by reading News Feed

Interacting with friends via comments, likes, and sharing

Sharing your own thoughts using the Publisher

Chapter 4

The Daily Facebook: News Feed and Posting

Sometimes after I've explained the basics of Facebook to someone — it's a website that lets you connect and share with your friends — they follow up with a fairly obvious question: But what do you *do* with it?

The answer to that question is both very simple — you keep up with your friends — and somewhat complicated. There are so many tiny actions and interactions on Facebook that add up to a sense of being surrounded by your friends. It's that sense of friendship that keeps people coming back to Facebook day after day (and, with smartphones, minute after minute).

This book tells you how to do virtually everything you could ever want to do on Facebook, but chances are you won't create a photo album or plan an event every single day. Chances are that as you go about your day online — reading articles, watching videos, shopping, and more — you'll check in on Facebook, find out news big and small from your friends and the Pages you follow, share a few of your own thoughts or observations, and go on your way. This chapter covers those very basic activities in depth.

The main way people find our news and generally keep in touch on Facebook is through News Feed, the constantly updating list of stories about content people are posting to their Timelines. I talk about News Feed at length in this chapter, and also about the ways you interact with what you see there. News Feed isn't just about reading the posts you see there; it's also about comments and likes.

You can also keep up with friends by sharing your own content — things like status updates, photos, and links to articles you read. You can post your own content from the top of News Feed and your friends will, in turn, be able to see it, like it, and comment on it.

Your Daily News . . . Feed

News Feed is the centerpiece of your Home page. When you log in to Facebook, you see the familiar blue bar on top and the left sidebar, but mostly you see News Feed.

So what is News Feed? It's a constantly updating list of stories by and about your friends. *Stories* here refers to actions that your friends have taken on Facebook — things like writing a status update, sharing a photo or link, or becoming friends (in fact, there are a lot of different types of stories which are all detailed below in the "Common story types" section). You may also see stories from Pages that you follow. Facebook sometimes refers to stories as posts, and I use the terms interchangeably here as well.

Back in the day, a common refrain around the Facebook office was, "News Feed is a robot." More accurately, News Feed is an algorithm. It doesn't show you *everything* from your friends; instead, it tries to show you things it thinks you will find interesting. News Feed makes its selections based on a complicated calculus of who is posting what and when. News Feed will likely show you more stories from people you interact with more often on Facebook. It also has a tendency to show you "big events" like engagements or new babies even from more distant acquaintances. News Feed also learns the sorts of stories you are likely to click on, like, or comment on, and will try to show you more of those. Simply browsing News Feed and interacting with the things you see helps News Feed to improve. There are ways for you to manually fine-tune News Feed as well, which I cover in the "Adjusting News Feed" section.

Because News Feed tries to show you what it thinks you'll find most interesting, stories might not always appear from newest to oldest. There is some bias toward new stories (especially if you log into Facebook frequently), but you might see a popular photo that a friend posted several days ago appear at the top of your News Feed instead of one from this morning if it got a lot of likes or comments.

Additional likes or comments can also cause a post to reappear in your News Feed even if you've already seen it.

Anatomy of a News Feed story

Figure 4-1 shows a sample News Feed story. In this case, it's a status update from a friend. In Facebook world a *status update* refers to any text people post that answers the question "What's on your mind?"

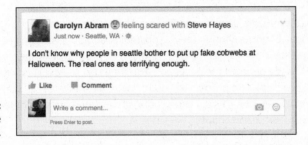

FIGURE 4-1:
Just your average
status update.

Even in this tiny example, there are six significant parts of the story:

TIP

>> **Name and profile picture:** The first part of any story is who it's about or who wrote it. Both the name and picture are links to that person's Timeline. In addition, if you hover the mouse cursor over a person's name, you'll see a miniaturized preview of the person's Timeline with information about your relationship (that you are friends and following him, in most cases) as well as a button you can click to message him.

Hovering the mouse cursor over any bolded text in a News Feed story generates a preview for a Timeline, Page, or interest with specific buttons for adding friends, liking, or following.

>> **Feeling/Activity info:** Not every status includes this, but Facebook provides a list of emotions and activities that can be appended to any status update or post. In this case, the emoticon (and words) depict my fear of spiders.

>> **Tags:** Tags are a way of marking who or what is with you when you post something to Facebook. You might tag a person who is with you when you write a post, or you might tag a TV show you are watching. Tags in posts are displayed as links in blue text. You can hover the mouse cursor over these tags to view more info about that person, Page, place, or thing.

>> **Timestamp:** The little gray text near the profile photo in the post tells you how long ago this post was added.

>> **Privacy Info:** The gray icon next to the timestamp represents the privacy of that post. Hover the mouse cursor over the icon to see who else can see the post. Usually posts are visible either to everyone (Public) or just to that person's friends.

>> **Content:** The content section of a News Feed story is the most variable. It might be a preview of an article, or a video, or a photo album. It could also be a location where someone has *checked in,* or marked her location via GPS, using her phone. The content is the part of the story that is the most important; it's the whole reason for the story existing. In Figure 4-1, the content is a status update about spiders in Seattle.

>> **Like, Comment, and Share:** These links allow you to interact with your friends about the content they've posted. In addition, you can see how many people have already liked a post, and you can see any comments that have been made beneath the post itself. You may also see a text box next to your own profile picture prompting you to "Write a comment . . . ." I talk more about commenting, liking, and sharing in the "Interacting with News Feed" section later in this chapter.

Common story types

News Feed is made up of all sorts of stories. Although the basic anatomy is the same, here are some of the common story types you might encounter:

>> **Status updates:** The status update post appears in Figure 4-1. Status updates are the short little posts that your friends make about what's going on in their lives.

>> **Links:** Figure 4-2 shows a post sharing a link. This is one of the chief ways I get my news: Friends share links to articles, and the previews are so interesting to me I have to read the whole article. Click the links (or the article's title) to go to the articles.

>> **Photos:** Figure 4-3 shows a story about photos. When people add photos or are tagged in photos, it creates this type of story, with information about who was tagged and a sample of the photos that were added. Click the photos to see bigger versions and browse the entire album.

>> **Videos:** Figure 4-4 shows a video story. As you scroll through News Feed, videos will begin playing; however, the sound will be muted. Hover the mouse cursor over the video to display the video's progress bar and other controls. Click the volume icon to turn on the sound. When the video stops, you can click the Play button to start it again. You may see videos that have been added directly to Facebook, or videos from other sites like YouTube or Vimeo.

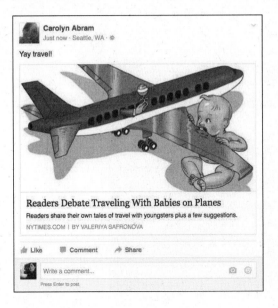

FIGURE 4-2:
Use your status
to share links to
articles.

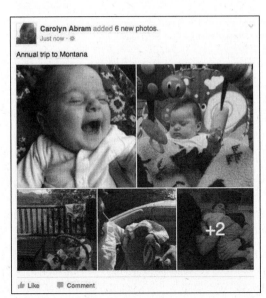

FIGURE 4-3:
A photo story.

>> **Timeline Posts:** Figure 4-5 shows a Timeline post story between two friends. The first person wrote the message on the second person's Timeline.

Usually, you only see Timeline post stories when you're friends with both of the people involved.

REMEMBER

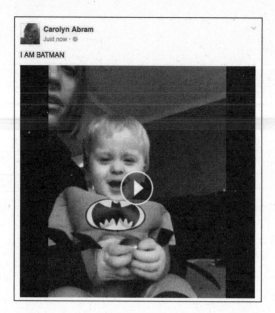

FIGURE 4-4:
A video story.

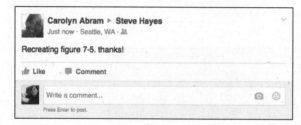

FIGURE 4-5:
A Timeline post
between friends.

>> **Group and event posts:** When people post to a group or event you're a member of, it may show up in your News Feed. These stories look very similar to the Timeline posts; the second friend's name is simply replaced with the group or event name.

>> **Life Events:** People can create Life Events from their Timelines. These events can be for an event as small as buying a new pair of sunglasses, but in my experience people use them to mark big moments: weddings, babies, moving, getting a pet, buying a house, and other things that tend to be truly major developments in one's life. Figure 4-6 shows a Life Event post.

>> **Check-ins:** A check-in is a way of marking where you are. Stories about check-ins show a preview of information about the location where that person checked in, as well as a list of other friends who have checked in there in the past.

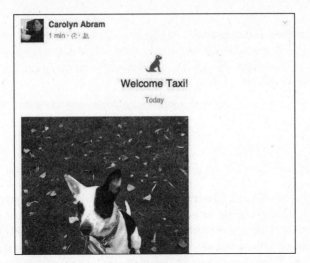

>> **Tags:** Stories about tags let you know what photos or posts your friends have recently been tagged in and include a preview of the photos with your friend in them. Because of the way tags work, you may be seeing photos that were added by someone who is not your friend.

>> **Likes and comments:** Stories about likes and comments let you know what Pages, posts, or articles your friends have liked or commented on recently. Usually whatever your friend has interacted with is shown and linked so that you can check it out for yourself.

>> **Read/Watch/Listen:** Certain services and websites, such as the book-reading site Goodreads, may be allowed to automatically post specific actions people take on their site to Facebook. See Chapter 14 for more information about how these applications work.

>> **Friendships:** Friendship stories might be about just two people becoming friends or about one person becoming friends with lots of different people.

>> **Changed cover and profile pictures:** These stories often look very similar to a regular photo story. Click through to look at the new photos on your friends' Timelines in their full-sized glory.

>> **Events:** Stories about events (usually letting you know which friends have RSVP'd *yes* to an event) include a link to the event, so if you're looking for someplace to go, you can say *yes,* too. Only public events show up here, so if you've added a private event, don't worry about people who weren't invited seeing it in News Feed.

>> **Sponsored and suggested:** Suggested and sponsored stories are ads. Ads are what keep Facebook free to use, so there's no way to remove them. These ads are hopefully relevant to you and your life and may even help you find Pages or services you find interesting.

Ticker

Remember, News Feed doesn't show you *everything.* It shows you the stories and posts you are most likely to want to see. It favors certain friends over others and certain types of stories over others. If you want to see absolutely everything look over in the rightmost column for your *ticker.* Ticker is continuously updating a list of story headlines that appear as they happen. Instead of a full post (like the one talked about way back in Figure 4-1) you see only the headline: Alexander commented on Elizabeth's photo. Anjelica likes Aaron's post. You can hover the mouse cursor over any item in Ticker to expand the story and see all of the details. There's an example of an expanded Ticker story in Figure 4-7. Ticker itself is on the right side of the image, and the expanded story covers up News Feed. You can click, comment on, and like the content in the story just as you would a regular News Feed story.

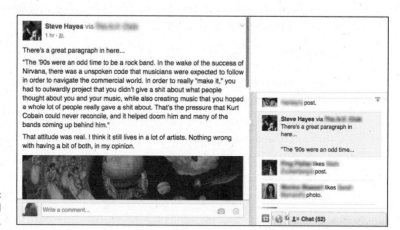

FIGURE 4-7:
An expanded
ticker story.

TIP

If you don't have very many friends or your friends aren't very active on Facebook, you might not see ticker at all.

To stop the ticker from appearing on the right side of the page, hide it by clicking the icon in the upper right corner of the Ticker section (it looks like an arrow pointing up into a bar). Click the icon again to show Ticker again.

If you find yourself spending more time looking at Ticker than at News Feed, you can change News Feed to show the most recent stories first, as opposed to the "top stories" that News Feed culls from the wealth of stories available to it.

1. **Click the small down arrow next to the words *News Feed* in the Favorites section of the left sidebar.**

   A menu opens.

2. **Select Most Recent.**

   News Feed shifts to show stories in the order they happened on Facebook, as opposed to promoting older stories that you might find more interesting to the top of News Feed.

Interacting with News Feed

Unlike the newspaper on your doorstep in the morning, News Feed is not just a method of delivering news. It's actually more of a starting place, meant to facilitate more interactions between you and your friends. Each story has three options at the bottom of it: Like, Comment, and Share. Each of these options allows you to interact with your friend and their content. You can also save content you see on Facebook to go back to at a later time.

Liking

Liking is one of the simplest actions on Facebook. Here's how you like something:

1. **Click Like.**

It really is that easy. Anytime you see something that is just good, you can click Like to let the person who shared it know that you liked seeing it. Like buttons make appear as text or as a thumbs up icon (or both). When you like something, the person who shared it will be notified (and trust me, being notified that someone liked something you shared is a great feeling). Additionally, other people seeing that story may see that you have liked it. If you ever like something by accident, simply click Unlike to undo it.

I don't want to overcomplicate liking by over-explaining when you might like something, when you might like something instead of commenting on it, when you might like something *and* comment on it. Suffice it to say that if you enjoyed something you saw, or that you agree with something your friend said, or that, well, you liked that content, then clicking Like communicates the sentiment loud and clear.

Reacting

Liking is the simplest way to let someone know you saw and appreciated something they posted. Sometimes, however, Like just doesn't seem appropriate. People often post stressful or sad things on Facebook; it would be insensitive to respond to "My dog had to be put down today" with *Like*. On the other side of things, sometimes Like isn't a strong enough term. Do you like that baby smiling, or do you *love it so much you want to eat its face?* Historically, you might see people commenting on these sorts of posts with one-word responses: Love. Dislike. LOL. Sad. Reactions is Facebook's way of providing more than just one button to express your sentiment. To leave a Reaction other than a Like, simply hover the mouse cursor over the Like button or link and wait for the Reactions menu to open. You can then choose your Reaction from the following options:

>> **Like:** The old standby. Click on the thumbs up icon to let your friend know you liked their post.

>> **Love:** The heart icon lets your friend know you loved their post.

>> **Haha:** The laughing smiley face lets your friend know you thought what they posted was funny.

>> **Wow:** The smiley face gaping in awe lets your friend know that you were impressed if not flabbergasted by their post.

>> **Sad:** Express a little empathy by clicking the crying smiley face. It is the virtual equivalent of a gentle pat on the back.

>> **Angry:** The virtual equivalent of a little "grrrrr," clicking the glowering smiley face lets your friend know that you are angry.

When you click any of these reactions, your friend receives a notification that you reacted to their post.

Liking Pages

You can like almost anything on Facebook. You can like a photo or a status; you can even like a comment on a photo or status. But there's a slight difference between liking this sort of content and liking Pages.

Pages are sort of official profiles that companies, bands, and public figures make to represent themselves on Facebook. They mostly work like Timelines (the key differences are covered in Chapter 13), except instead of friending Pages, you like them.

This sort of liking has one big implication you should be aware of. It means you may start seeing posts and updates from the Page in your News Feed, alongside stories from your friends. These sorts of updates can be really interesting and cool if you're into the particular company or brand (for example, Old Spice Guy or *The New York Times*). If they start to bother you, you can always hide that Page from your News Feed.

Commenting

Liking something is the quickest and easiest way to let your friend know that you saw what they had to say and enjoyed it. Commenting is also pretty simple, and it takes you from a reaction — I liked this! — to a conversation. The only requirement for a comment is that you to have something to say.

Adding a comment

To comment on anything on Facebook, follow these steps:

1. **Click Comment.**

   The comment box expands. Frequently, this box is already expanded, in which case you can simply go on to Step 2.

2. **Click in the text box that appears.**

3. **Type what you want to say.**

4. **(Optional) Click the camera icon to add a photo to your reply.**

   This opens an interface for navigating your computer's hard drive, so make sure you know where the photo is that you want to add.

5. **(Optional) Click the smiley face icon to add a sticker.**

   This opens a menu for selecting from Facebook's sticker collection. Stickers are a collection of cartoons that depict various emotions. (You can see a sticker in one of the comments in Figure 4-8.) Simply choose the sticker that best represents your sentiment.

6. **When you're finished, press Enter.**

After you comment on something, you'll be notified about subsequent comments so that you can keep up on the conversation. If you decide, on second thought, that maybe you didn't really want to say that thing, you can always delete your comment by hovering the mouse cursor over it and clicking the X that appears. You can do the same when someone comments on something you've posted and you don't like what she says.

You can tag a friend in a comment by typing the @ symbol (that's Shift+2) and then typing your friend's name. Facebook will auto-complete as you type and you will be able to select the person's name from a menu that appears. People use this to bring their comments (or the original post) to the attention of other friends, as tagging someone sends them a notification.

Replying to and liking comments

As I mention earlier, commenting on something is a way of starting a conversation, and the way to continue that conversation is by liking or replying to comments. At the bottom of any comment, you can see two small links to Like or Reply.

Liking a comment is generally a way of saying "I agree" or "Right on!" or "That's funny." Click Like next to any comment to let the commenter know how much you enjoyed what he had to say.

Replying to a comment is as easy as clicking the Reply link beneath the comment you want to respond to. This opens a text box that says `Write a reply....` You can then follow the same commenting steps detailed earlier.

Replies show up indented from the original comment, as shown in Figure 4-8.

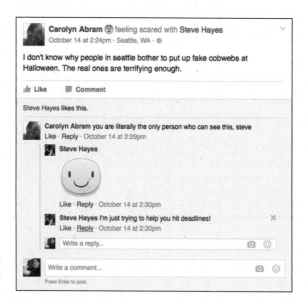

FIGURE 4-8:
A comment leads
to a conversation.

Sharing

You've probably noticed the word *Share* being used a lot on Facebook. In addition to the Share box (also called the *Publisher*) at the top of your News Feed and Timeline, Facebook has a specific Share feature, designed to make it easy to post and send content that you find both on Facebook and on the web.

TIP

Sharing is a variation of using the Publisher, or Share box. I go over using the Publisher in the "Sharing Your Own News" section of this chapter.

Perhaps you've already noticed the little Share links all over Facebook. They show up on albums, individual photos, events, groups, News Feed stories, and more. They help you share content quickly without having to copy and paste.

If you're looking at content on Facebook that you want to show someone, simply click the Share link near it. This opens a small menu with several options:

» **Share Now (<Privacy>):** This is the quickest way to share something. Choosing this option simply posts the content to your own Timeline (and, by extension, your friends' News Feeds). The <Privacy> notice reminds you who normally sees content that you share on Facebook. It might say "Public" or "Friends" or "Custom" depending on your privacy settings.

» **Share:** This option opens a full Share box that allows you to add your own commentary on the content you are sharing before you share it. Use the drop-down menu at the top (pictured in Figure 4-9) to choose how you'd like to share the content.

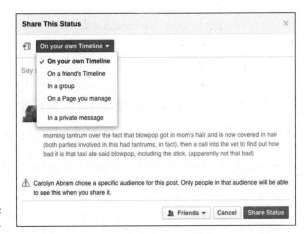

FIGURE 4-9:
Share here.

>> **On Your Own Timeline:** This option posts the content to your Timeline the same way you post a link or a photo from your Share box. This means it will go into your friends' News Feeds as well. This is redundant with the Share Now option, except you also get to add any comments to your post about your friend's post before you share it.

>> **On a Friend's Timeline:** This option is the same as copying and pasting a link into a post you leave on your friend's Timeline (but it's much easier than all that copy/paste nonsense).

>> **In a Group:** This option allows you to post the content to a specific group you're a member of. You can find more about sharing with groups in Chapter 10.

>> **On a Page You Manage (for Page owners only):** If you're the admin of a Page — a Timeline for non-people — you can share things as a post from your Page.

>> **In a Private Message:** This accomplishes the same thing as copying and pasting a link into a message to a friend. In other words, only the friend you send it to will see the link, whereas sharing via the Timeline means anyone viewing your friend's Timeline can also see the content. I talk about messages in Chapter 9.

If you're choosing to share on your own Timeline, you can click the privacy drop-down menu next to the Share button to change who can see the post.

>> **Send as Message:** This option opens a message box where you can type in names you would like to message with your friend's post. You can also add a comment to the "Say something about this" section to let your friend(s) know why you are sharing it with them.

If you click Share on a friend's post, the friend who originally shared it is given a credit. So if you reshare an article, the post that your friends see will say Via *<Friend's Name>* so that everyone knows where you found it.

Liking and sharing across the Internet

If you're a reader of blogs, you may notice that the Share and Like links and icons appear in lots of places. For example, at the bottom of blog posts on Jezebel, a Gawker Media blog, a little Like button counts the number of people who have liked any particular post.

You can like posts on any website you're viewing, and those likes will be recorded on your Timeline and may appear in your friends' News Feeds. Through *Social Plugins,* Facebook allows other website developers to enable certain Facebook features like the Like button on their own websites. If you're currently logged in to

Facebook, you may start noticing these buttons all over the Internet. This is a really quick way to let your Facebook friends know about the most interesting content you've come across online.

TIP

Other websites have Share links that generate the same Facebook Share box that you find on Facebook itself. So from an entirely separate website, you can choose to post to a friend's Timeline, your own Timeline, to a group, or to a message thread.

Saving

For me, News Feed is one of the best sources I have for articles, videos, and legitimate old-fashioned news that I might find interesting. I follow a number of Pages for newspapers and magazines, and my friends are the nerdy type who read and share articles that they find interesting as well. The only problem with this is that sometimes I see articles that look really interesting when I don't actually have time to click through and read them. That's why the Save feature is one of my favorite hidden Facebook features. Saving articles, videos, and other posts is an effective way to make a reading list for later, when you have more time. This is also a good way to bookmark helpful websites you might need later (like a list of the best pumpkin patches to visit in the fall).

To save a post, click the small down arrow in the upper right corner of the post you want to save. This opens the News Feed menu (see Figure 4-10). Click the Save post option (usually in the middle of the menu). This automatically adds the post to your Saved section (which appears by default in the Favorites section of your left sidebar). You can get to your saved posts at any time by clicking Saved in your Favorites section. Facebook may also occasionally show you a selection of your saved items in your News Feed in case you forgot about them.

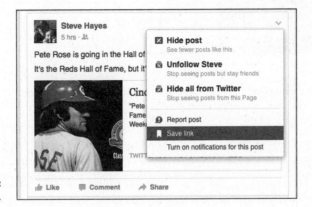

FIGURE 4-10:
Saving a link.

Adjusting News Feed

News Feed is designed to learn about what you like and whom you care about and to show you stories accordingly. As you use News Feed, it learns what you like based on your clicks, comments, and likes. You can give News Feed more information to work with in order to make News Feed even better for you.

Hiding posts and people

There are ways to tell News Feed explicitly who you do and don't want to see (and I go over these in the "News Feed Preferences" section). But chances are you might not know what you like, or more often, what you don't like until you see it. Sometimes you'll realize that you will simply explode if you have to see another baby photo from a particular coworker. Sometimes someone you know just won't stop posting political screeds. And sometimes one particular post will just bug you and you won't want to see it anymore.

As soon as you realize you don't like what you are seeing, you can easily give this feedback to News Feed using the menu of options found as part of any News Feed story. To open this menu, click on the small down arrow in the upper right corner of any News Feed story. This menu is shown in Figure 4-11.

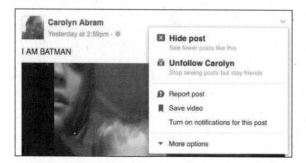

FIGURE 4-11:
Use this menu to hide posts and people.

This menu gives you at least two options with regard to the story you are looking at

>> **Hide post:** Selecting this option will immediately hide that post from your News Feed. Additionally, Facebook will try to show you fewer posts "like this." In other words, depending on the type of story you are hiding (such as a photo story or life event) Facebook will try not to show you as many of that story type.

>> **Unfollow <Friend or Page Name>:** Selecting this option will semi-permanently prevent stories from this friend from appearing in your News

Feed at all. I say semi-permanently because you will be able to undo this option at a later time if you wish.

Selecting either option will hide the story you are looking at and display a small confirmation message to let you know that you have successfully hidden that post or unfollowed your friend. You can click undo here if you regret your actions.

If you are looking at a post that involves multiple people, such as a story about Lina (your friend) tagged in a photo by Connor (not your friend), you may see additional options to Hide All from Connor. If someone is sharing a post from a Page or an App, you may also see options to hide posts from that Page or App.

REMEMBER

Unfollowing friends is different from unfriending them. Unfriending them severs the link between your Timelines and may mean you are no longer able to see certain parts of their Timeline. Unfollowing simply removes their posts from your News Feed.

News Feed preferences

Hiding posts and people is a good way to incrementally adjust your News Feed over time. But if you're looking to make a bigger impact right away, you may want to adjust your News Feed preferences instead. Your News Feed preferences allow you to choose friends you want to see first, unfollow friends you already know you don't want in your News Feed, and reconnect with people you may have unfollowed in the past.

To get to the News Feed Preferences menu, hover the mouse cursor over the News Feed link in the Favorites section of your left sidebar. Click the gear icon that appears to the left of the words News Feed and then click Edit Preferences in the menu that appears. This opens the Preferences menu shown in Figure 4-12.

There are three sections of preferences you can use to influence News Feed.

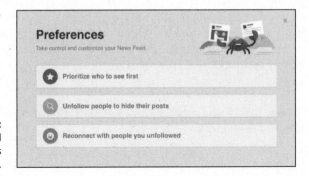

FIGURE 4-12:
The News Feed
Preferences
menu.

Prioritize

Prioritizing friends is a way of designating people you *always* want to see in News Feed. I prioritize people like my best friends and my husband. I also have prioritized a more distant friend who I think posts really hilarious stuff, so I want to make sure I don't miss what she has to say.

Posts from prioritized friends will always be at the top of your News Feed when you log in. Unfortunately, if your friends don't post very often, there still won't be anything to show you. News Feed needs something to work with. You can see a prioritized post in Figure 4-13. The only thing that differentiates such a post (other than the fact that it's at the top of News Feed when you log in) is a tiny blue star in the upper right corner of the post.

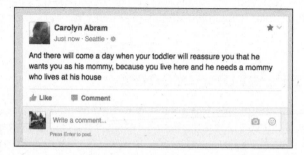

FIGURE 4-13:
A prioritized post in News Feed.

Click Prioritize Who to See First to open a menu for choosing people from your friend list. Facebook displays the people it thinks you'll likely want to see first at the top, you may have to scroll down a bit to find whom you're looking for. Click on any friend's face to select him (and click again to deselect him). When you're finished, click the blue Done button to save your choices.

Unfollow

By default, when you become friends with them you also start following them. This means that their posts may appear in your News Feed. However, as not all friendships are created equal, unfollowing is a simple way to stop seeing stories while still maintaining the friendship. You don't need any particular reason to unfollow people (or unfollow a Page). You can do it because they post too frequently, or you don't like what they post, or because they just broke your best friend's heart.

To select people (and Pages) you'd like to unfollow, follow these steps from the News Feed Preferences menu:

1. **Click the Unfollow People to Hide Their Posts section.**

   This opens an interface for selecting people and Pages.

2. **Click on the people or Pages you want to unfollow.**

   When you have selected someone to unfollow, that person's profile picture will be outlined in blue and the word "Unfollowed" will appear below her name.

3. **Click Done to save your selections.**

Reconnect

If your News Feed is ever feeling a little stale or bland, you might want to consider refollowing people you had previously unfollowed. Clicking this section of the Preferences menu opens a menu for choosing from people whom you have previously unfollowed. Click on any face to add them back into the News Feed mix and then click Done.

Sharing Your Own News

While there are millions of things to do on Facebook (and this book tries to cover every single one of them), the most basic action on Facebook is sharing. The previous parts of this chapter cover how you see and interact with the things your friends have shared. Now it's time to put yourself out there and start sharing things for yourself.

First thing's first: Take a look at the *Publisher* (also called the Share box) at the top of your News Feed. It's shown in Figure 4-14. The Publisher is what you use to create and share posts with your friends. Any posts you make from the Publisher will go on your Timeline and may appear in your friends' News Feeds.

FIGURE 4-14: Start sharing here.

Like much of Facebook, there's a lot packed into this little box. Before going into all the details of what you can share and how, I start with the most basic type of post: a status update.

Status updates

A status update is a way of reporting what's going on with you right now. Facebook uses the phrase "What's on your mind?" to prompt a status update. So you can share what you're thinking about, what you're doing, or really anything. To update your status, follow these steps:

1. **Click into the Publisher, where it says "What's on your mind?"**
2. **Type your status.**
3. **Click Post.**

Like I said, sharing on Facebook is meant to be easy.

Once you've shared your status, your friends will likely see it in their News Feeds and they will be able to like and comment on your status.

What should I say?

There isn't a simple answer to the question of what you should or shouldn't post as a status update. The question "What's on your mind?" is meant to provoke whatever it is you'd like to share.

In general, sharing where you are or what you're doing are basic status reports that make sense as status updates. When I see updates from my friends they often are sharing a random thought that passed through their heads as they were out and about during the day. If there's a football game on I can often figure out what's happening based on my friends' status updates. Check out your own friends' posts to see what they are talking about.

You might share something notable you saw recently; you might tell a quick and funny story (or a longer one, as there isn't a word limit on status updates) about your day. Originally, status updates all started with the words "<Carolyn> is. . ." and for the most part status updates tend to be about what you're doing or thinking about right now. If you're feeling uninspired, feel free to post that you are reading *Facebook For Dummies*.

Status updates "plus"

Now that you know the basics of posting a status update, you can learn more about all the extra information you can add to a status. Adding links to your updates allows you share interesting things you've found all over the Internet. You can also click any of the buttons at the bottom of the Publisher to add photos, tags, and details about what you're doing and where you are. You can combine almost all of these additions to your posts, but you can't add both links and photos from your hard drive at the same time.

Adding links

To add content from another website to your post, simply copy and paste the link into the Publisher. Facebook will automatically generate a preview for the content based on the link. Previews usually include an image, a headline, and a description. You can edit any of these sections by hovering the mouse cursor over them. You can choose to remove an image and edit any text associated with the preview of the link.

Once you get your preview looking the way you want, you can delete the original link (the preview will remain) and use the space above to share your thoughts about your link.

Adding a photo

Click the Camera icon at the bottom of the Publisher to add a photo to your post. When you click this, it opens an interface for navigating your computer's hard drive to find the photo you want to add.

TIP

Often some of the best photos you want to share on Facebook are on your phone. You can learn how to share photos directly from your smartphone in Chapter 7.

Once you've selected the photo (or photos) you want to add, click choose. This brings you back to the Publisher. The photos you've added will appear as small square thumbnails within your post. Hovering the mouse cursor over this thumbnail causes two new icons to appear. Select the left icon (a person with a tag) to *tag* the people who are in that photo. Tagging is a way of linking a photo to one of your friends' Timelines. That way people will know who is in your photo, and your friend's friends will be able to see the photo as well.

Select the Paintbrush icon (on the right side of the photo thumbnail) to edit your photo. Clicking this opens up a larger preview of your photo with editing options along the bottom of the screen. The options for editing are: filters, tag, add text, and add stickers. For more information on these options, see Chapter 11.

Adding a tag

A *tag* is a way of linking someone or something else to your own content on Facebook. Most often tags are used to let people know who is in a photo, but tags can also be used in status updates to let people know who is with you. People also use tags to bring certain friends' attention to something they are posting. For example, you might see a status update that says something like "Who's up for a 5k at

Thanksgiving? **Brian, Mike, Janet, Gail?**" Each bolded name links to a friend's Timeline. Additionally, those friends get notified when the post is published, which means they definitely see the invitation to go running.

There are two ways to tag someone in your post. The first is to type the @ symbol (that's shift + 2) and begin typing the name of the person you want to tag. Facebook auto-completes as you type. When you see your friend's name highlighted, hit enter or select it with your mouse. When you tag someone this way, the tag appears as part of the post: "Kicking **Jeremy**'s butt at foosball."

The second way that you can add a tag is by clicking the Tag People icon at the bottom of the Publisher (it looks like a person with a plus sign). Clicking this opens a small text field at the bottom of the Publisher that asks "Who are you with?" Again, start typing your friend's name and press Enter when you see it highlighted in the auto-complete menu. When you tag people this way, their name gets appended to the top of the post: "Kicking butt at foosball — with **Jeremy**." You can see both of these types of tags in Figure 4-15.

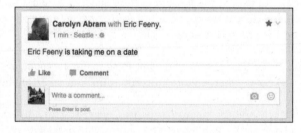

FIGURE 4-15:
Tag your friends when they are with you.

TIP

In addition to people, you can tag Pages. For example, you might want people to know that you are very excited about the new *Star Wars* trailer. Type the @ sign and start typing **Star Wars**, and you'll find that it also appears in the auto-complete menu.

Adding what you're doing or feeling

Clicking the smiley face icon opens a menu of choices to explain what you are doing, thinking, or feeling while writing your status update. You may be feeling blessed, or baking cookies, or traveling to the Grand Canyon. The options here are virtually endless. The information you enter here gets appended to your post, often with an *emoji*, or icon, that further illustrates what you are doing or feeling. Additionally, if something you are doing has a page or information about it on Facebook, Facebook may add a preview of that information to your post. Figure 4-16 shows an example of a post with information about what I am listening to. There is the emoji of headphones to denote that I am listening to something, and a preview of the Hamilton the Musical Page added to the post.

You can only add one thing you are doing or feeling to a post, so unfortunately you cannot be both feeling confused and watching *True Detective* at the same time, as far as your posts go.

Checking in with your location information

Facebook uses information it gets from your browser to automatically append at least a small amount of location information (usually your city) to your posts. You can click the location pin to add more specific location information, also known as a *check-in.* Clicking the location pin icon opens a small text field that asks "Where was this?" Start typing where you are — that might be a place like a coffee shop or an airport, or a city or a landmark. Facebook auto-completes as you type; when you see your desired location highlighted, press Enter to check in there.

Controlling who sees your posts

The big question people often have before they share something on Facebook is "Who is going to see this?" Facebook makes it easy to know who will see a post as you are creating it. Right next to the big blue Post button is the Privacy menu, shown in Figure 4-17.

There is a very simple way to control your privacy, and then more advanced options beyond that. The simplest privacy distinction is shown in Figure 4-17: the choice between "Public" and "Friends."

Public posts

By default, when you sign up for Facebook, your posts are public. When something is public, it means that anyone can see it. It doesn't mean, however, that everyone *does* see it. Due to the volume of content on Facebook (one billion people adding even one post a day is a *lot* of posts) the chances of a true stranger seeing your post is actually pretty low. Rather, the people in the "public" who will likely see your post are friends of your friends or other people whom you in some way interact with on Facebook — through a shared group, for example. If someone were to search you out and visit your Timeline, that person would be able to see any public posts you've made there.

Friends only posts

The second main option presented to you in the privacy menu is "Friends." Posts that are visible to friends are only visible to people you have added as friends. You already know that when you post something, it may appear in your friends' News Feeds; the same holds true when you set your privacy to Friends. Friends of friends will not be able to see your post, even if your friend comments on it. Someone searching you out and viewing your Timeline would not be able to see your post. This privacy option is why I recommend that you never accept friend requests from strangers. When you know everyone whom you are friends with, it is easy to know who can see your posts.

Privacy is a way of controlling who can see what, but the easiest way to measure it is not in counting the number of people who can see something. If you have a huge Friend List (and many people do) does the difference between something being available to 500 people or to 1,000 people or to 1,000,000,000 people matter? Well, maybe. The way I usually measure privacy is not numerical but emotional. Do you feel comfortable? Do you feel safe? These are the questions I think you should answer when you are choosing between making something public or visible only to friends.

Whichever option you choose, the next time you go to post something, that same option will be selected. Facebook assumes that most of the time you are interested in sharing with the same people — either friends or everyone — so it doesn't force you to change your privacy each time you post.

Advanced sharing options

Often, people ask me about sharing content with a subset of their friends. This might be because they are only comfortable sharing with a small group of people, or because their Friend List includes people like their bosses or family members whom they don't want to share everything with. People also sometimes worry about being annoying to their friends. Parents on Facebook often get teased about adding too many photos of their babies, so a new mom or dad might want to share all those baby photos with a smaller group of people who *definitely* want to see them. There are three main ways to accomplish this: Friend Lists, groups, or custom privacy.

FRIEND LISTS

Friend Lists are a way of sorting friends into categories. These categories remain private to you; friends aren't notified when you add them to a friend list. Facebook also creates some lists for you automatically (you can edit those lists later, if you want). If you click on "More Options" in the privacy menu, you will see some of these lists appear: Close Friends, Family, <Current City>, and any other lists you have created. Selecting the list you want to share with means that only those friends will be able to see whatever it is you are posting. So if you want to post your thoughts about a ballot measure in your local elections, you could choose only to share that with friends in your city. Friend Lists are covered in Chapter 8.

GROUPS

Groups are a lot like lists when you use them to categorize your friends, except that groups provide a destination for all members to share content together. When you add friends to a group, Facebook notifies them of it and they must decide whether or not to join the group. Groups can be a really easy way to share content with a smaller circle — the aforementioned dilemma of new parents with lots of photos of their babies can be relieved by creating a "Photos of Junior" group and inviting friends to join. Friends who would rather not see your baby photos all the time can decline to join, and people who do join knows what they are signing up for.

To share something with a group, navigate to that group's Home page from your left sidebar. Then use the Publisher there (it works the same as the Publisher at the top of your News Feed) to share your post. By default, friends in a given group are notified when you post something and also may see that post in their News Feed. Groups are covered in greater detail in Chapter 10.

CUSTOM PRIVACY

Another option when you select More Options from the privacy menu is custom privacy. Custom privacy allows you to be incredibly specific in terms of choosing who can and cannot see your post. You can use it to specify that people in Seattle can see your post, but not Josh or David. Or that your friends can see it, but not people you went to high school with. I've seen people plan surprise parties this way: by posting a reminder about Phil's birthday and then reminding people that Phil can't see that post. I go over exactly how to use the Custom Privacy menu in Chapter 6.

REMEMBER

When you choose a new privacy option, that same choice will remain the next time you post something.

IN THIS CHAPTER

Navigating the Timeline

Filling out and editing your Timeline information

Sharing with your friends through your Timeline

Chapter 5

Timeline: The Story of You

One of the fun things about writing *Facebook For Dummies* has been noting what's important in my life based on the examples I use to explain certain concepts. When I wrote the first edition, I was just out of college and every example usually related to Ultimate Frisbee, whether it was posting photos (of a Frisbee game) or planning an event (like a Frisbee match). By the second edition, I'd been working a little bit longer and used examples related to some really fun travels I'd taken. The third edition was all about my wedding, the fourth about my time in grad school, the fifth about my new baby, and for this edition, my second baby makes more than a few cameos. As it turns out, your life can change a lot over the course of several years.

That moment of looking backward and seeing how far you've come is the idea behind the Facebook Timeline. Like many websites, Facebook wants you to establish a profile with the basic biographical information — where you're from, what you do, where you went to school. But in addition to that, Facebook also wants you to keep updating and posting and sharing and marking events that define you. Then it turns all that information into a virtual scrapbook that you and your friends can explore. That virtual scrapbook is your Timeline.

Although Facebook does a lot of the work, this is *your* Timeline, so all aspects of it can be edited, modified, and changed based on how you want to represent yourself and your history. This chapter covers all the ways you edit the information and appearance of your Timeline, as well as who can see what on your Timeline.

Scrolling Through Time

Figure 5-1 shows the top of a Timeline. The Timeline has a few different portions: the big cover photo and the smaller profile picture, the navigation tabs beneath the cover photo, the About box, the Share box, and the Timeline itself, extending from the present back and back and back to the day you were born.

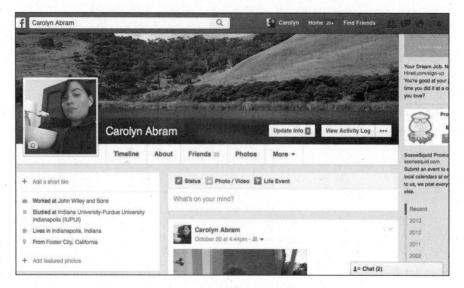

FIGURE 5-1
The top of a Timeline.

In terms of navigating the Timeline, the most important thing to know is that *you scroll down the page to go back in time.* As you scroll down, posts you and your friends have made and life events you have added keep on showing up. When you start scrolling down, a new menu appears at the top of the page (below the blue bar at the top). I call this the *Timeline navigator* (see Figure 5-2).

FIGURE 5-2:
Use the navigator to activate your nostalgia.

The Timeline navigator uses a series of drop-down menus to help you jump around in time. Click any of the buttons to view a drop-down menu of options:

>> **Timeline:** This drop-down menu lets you switch from the Timeline itself to the About section of your Timeline. I cover the About section in the "All About Me" section later in this chapter.

>> **Year:** This drop-down menu lets you hop from year to year on your Timeline. As you go further back by year, an additional drop-down menu appears that lets you jump from month to month within a year.

First Impressions

If you're brand new to Facebook, your Timeline may seem a little empty compared to those of your friends. That's okay; your Timeline will fill up as you start to update your status, post links, and so on (see the upcoming "Telling Your Story" section). But before you do all that, you want to get the basics filled out so that people can find you, recognize you, and learn a little bit about you. This section covers the very first thing people see when they arrive on your Timeline: your cover photo and your profile picture.

These two photos at the top of your Timeline present the first impression to all visitors to your Timeline. The cover photo is the larger photo that serves as a background to your Timeline. People often choose visually striking photos or images that speak to who they are and what they love. To change your cover photo, follow these steps:

1. **Hover over your existing cover photo.**

   A camera icon appears in the upper left corner of the existing cover.

2. **Click the camera icon.**

   The Update Cover Photo menu appears with four options: Choose from My Photos, Upload Photo, Reposition, and Remove.

   If you're using a Facebook Mobile app that syncs with your phone, you may also see an option to Add Synced Photo.

   TECHNICAL STUFF

3. **Click Choose from My Photos to select a cover photo from photos you've already added to Facebook.**

   The Choose from My Photos window appears, as shown in Figure 5-3. By default, it shows Recent Photos. You can get to a full list of your photos by clicking Photo Albums in the upper right corner.

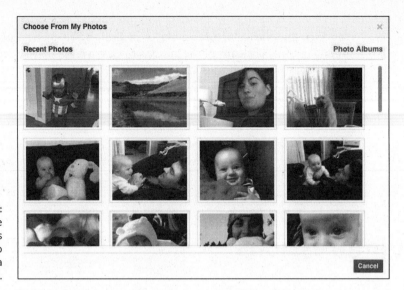

Choose From My Photos   ✕

Recent Photos   **Photo Albums**

Cancel

FIGURE 5-3:
Use the Choose from My Photos window to choose a cover photo.

4. **Choose Upload Photo to select a cover photo from your computer.**

    A window for navigating your computer's files appears.

5. **Select your cover photo from the options either on Facebook or on your hard drive.**

    This brings you back to your Timeline, where you should see the new cover photo in place with the overlaid message, Drag to Reposition Cover.

TIP

Because the cover photo spans the width of your Timeline, you may occasionally find that when you try to add some photos as your cover, you get an error telling you that it isn't wide enough. Make sure your cover photo is at least 720 pixels wide to ensure that it will fit.

6. **Click and drag your cover photo to position it correctly within the frame of the screen.**

7. **Click Save Changes.**

    Your new cover photo is now in place.

TIP

If you don't like the way your cover photo is positioned, you can use the same Change Cover menu to either reposition or remove your cover photo. You can change your cover as often as you want.

Your profile picture is the smaller photo. This photo is what sticks with you all around Facebook, appearing wherever you comment or post something. For example, your friends may see your status post in their News Feeds, accompanied by your name and profile picture. Most people use some variation on a headshot for their profile picture. There are several ways to add a profile picture.

Add a profile picture that's already on Facebook

If you skip to Chapter 11, you'll see that Facebook is the number-one photo-sharing site on the web, which means there's a good chance someone has already added a photo of you to Facebook that you might like to use as a profile picture.

Use these steps to change your profile picture to one that is already on Facebook:

1. **Hover your mouse over your existing profile picture.**

The Update Profile Picture button appears.

2. **Click the Update Profile Picture button.**

The Update Profile Picture window (shown in Figure 5-4) appears. Across the top are three options: Upload Photo, Take Photo (assuming you have a computer with a built-in webcam), and Edit Thumbnail (denoted by a pencil icon). The bottom part of this menu displays photos that are already on Facebook that you may want to choose as your profile picture.

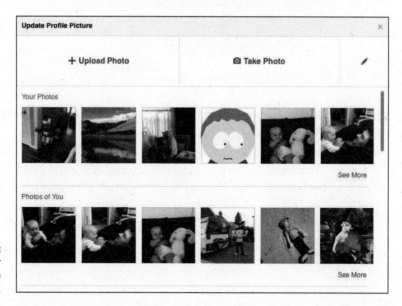

FIGURE 5-4:
Choose your profile picture here.

3. **To choose from the photos of you on Facebook, browse the displayed photos.**

This window displays several rows of photos. Each row shows a certain category of photos such as Your Photos (photos you've previously added to Facebook) and Photos of You (photos in which you've been tagged). You can see more photos in any category by clicking the See More link on the right side of any row of photos.

4. **Select the photo you want as your profile picture by clicking it.**

This brings you to the photo cropping interface, as shown in Figure 5-5.

FIGURE 5-5:
Crop profile picture to focus on just you.

5. **Using the cropping functions, choose the portion of the photo you want as your profile picture.**

Move the transparent box around the photo by clicking and dragging it. Zoom in and out using the plus and minus buttons. Zooming out will include more of the photo in the profile picture, zooming in will allow you to zero in on your own face.

6. **Click Crop and Save when you've finished.**

This step takes you back to your Timeline. The new profile picture should be visible.

Add a profile picture from your hard drive

If there aren't any photos of you on Facebook that would make suitable profile pictures, you can choose a photo from your computer's hard drive:

1. **Hover the mouse over your existing profile picture.**

   The Update Profile Picture button appears.

2. **Click the Update Profile Picture button.**

   The Update Profile Picture window appears (refer to Figure 5-4). Across the top are three options: Upload Photo, Take Photo (assuming you have a computer with a built in webcam), and Edit Thumbnail (denoted by a pencil icon). The bottom part of this menu displays photos that are already on Facebook that you may want to choose as your profile picture.

3. **Select Upload Photo.**

   An interface for navigating your computer's hard drive appears.

4. **Locate and click the desired photo.**

5. **Click Open or Choose.**

   This brings you to the photo cropping interface, shown in Figure 5-5.

6. **Using the cropping functions, choose the portion of the photo you want as your profile picture.**

   Move the transparent box around the photo by clicking and dragging it. Zoom in and out using the plus and minus buttons. Zooming out will include more of the photo in the profile picture, zooming in will allow you to zero in on your own face.

7. **Click Crop and Save when you've finished.**

   This step takes you back to your Timeline. The new profile picture should be visible.

Take a photo of yourself using your webcam

If you have a camera built into your computer or an external webcam, you can also take a photo to be your profile picture by following these steps:

1. **Hover the mouse over your existing profile picture.**

   The Update Profile Picture button appears.

2. **Click the Update Profile Picture button.**

   The Update Profile Picture window (shown in Figure 5-4) appears. Across the top are three options: Upload Photo, Take Photo (assuming you have a computer with a built-in webcam), and Edit Thumbnail (denoted by a pencil icon). The bottom part of this menu displays photos that are already on Facebook that you may want to choose as your profile picture.

3. **Select Take Photo.**

An interface for shooting a photo using your computer's webcam appears. You may need to click to allow Facebook access to your webcam.

4. **Click the button at the bottom of the screen to take your photo.**

Remember to smile!

5. **If you're happy with the photo, click Save.**

The photo is added and appears in place of your old profile picture.

Much like your cover photo, you can change your profile picture as often as you choose. Every photo you select as your profile picture is automatically added to the Profile Pictures album.

REMEMBER

Your cover photo and profile picture are visible to anyone who searches for you and clicks on your name. Make sure you're comfortable with everyone seeing these images.

Telling Your Story

Getting back to the main focus of your Timeline, take a look at the stuff below the cover photo. Two columns run down the page:

>> The skinny column on the left side is full of interests, recent activity, and application activity (I cover these parts of your Timeline in the upcoming "Sections" section).

>> The wider right column is where posts and life events live. These posts might be something you've added to Facebook, like a status or a photo or something someone has added to Facebook about you, like a photo tag. These posts constitute your Timeline. As you scroll down your past, you can see what you were posting last week, last month, last year.

Whether you joined Facebook yesterday or five years ago, you can use Facebook to highlight important events in your life that are happening now or in years past. This section goes over the basics of sharing your story, from the ongoing process of status updates and photo posts to the posting of life events to the capability to curate your Timeline to highlight your favorite posts and events.

Posts

Posts are the type of sharing you'll be doing most often on Facebook. These are the bread and butter of sharing. People post multiple times a day about an array of topics. And they post things from the Share box, also known as the Publisher. The Publisher is the text field at the top of your Timeline's right column, as shown in Figure 5-6.

FIGURE 5-6:
The Publisher on
the Timeline.

The Publisher is what you use to post content — statuses, photos, places, links, and so on — to your Timeline. When you post content, you can also choose who can see it. Friends and subscribers then may see these posts in their News Feeds when they log in.

The Publisher on your Timeline is very similar to the Publisher at the top of your News Feed. Both are used to create posts. You can use either one to add a status, photo, or link. You can add tags, emotions, and location information to posts made in either Publisher. The main difference is that the Publisher on your Timeline also lets you create life events, and lets you change the date of your post to add content (like photo albums) to the proper point in your history.

Status

The most common type of post that you see people make from the Share box is a basic text update that answers the question, "What's on your mind?" On Facebook, people refer to this type of post as a *status update* or just as their *status.* Status updates are quick, short, and completely open to interpretation. People may update them with what they may be doing at that moment ("Eating a snack"), offer a random observation ("A cat in my backyard just caught a snake!"), or request info ("Planning a trip to India this summer. Anyone know where I should stay?"). It's very easy for friends to comment on statuses, so a provocative update can really get the conversation going. I comment on commenting in Chapter 4.

Status updates sound small and inconsequential, but when they're added together, they can tell a really big story for one person or for many people. For close friends, these statuses let you keep up-to-date on their daily lives and share a casual laugh over something that you might never hear about otherwise. As a collective, statuses are how news spreads quickly through Facebook. Because your posts go into your friends' News Feeds, a single update can have a big impact and is somewhat likely to be repeated in some way or another. For example, news of a minor earthquake in my area spread faster on Facebook than it did on news sites.

To update your status, follow these steps:

1. **Click in the What's on Your Mind field of the Share box.**

This step expands the Share box.

2. **Type your comment/thought/status.**

3. **(Optional) Click the person icon in the bottom gray bar of the Share box to add tags to your post.**

Tags are ways of marking people you're with when you're writing a status update. The tags link back to your friends' Timelines and notify them of your update. When you tag someone, an additional bit of text is added to the status, so it looks like this:

Off to play board games — with *<Eric>*.

Eric then receives a notification that you tagged him.

TIP

If you want to tag someone as part of a sentence as opposed to just noting that he's with you, add an @ symbol and begin typing the person's name. Facebook auto-completes as you type, and the tag appears as part of your status update: for example,

<Eric> kicked my butt at Settlers of Catan.

4. **(Optional) Click the location pin icon to add a location.**

You can click this pin and begin typing a city or place name, and Facebook tries to auto-completes the place where you are. Letting friends know where you are (also called *checking in*) is a great way to increase the chances of serendipitous encounters. I've often had a friend text me when she sees a status to ask if I'm still at the coffee shop, wanting to know if she can swing by to say hi.

5. **(Optional) Click the smiley face icon to add info about what you're doing, interacting with, or feeling.**

Much like tagging a person, or checking in to a location, you can add details to your status about what you're reading, watching, listening to, feeling, doing, and so on. Facebook looks to auto-completes things as you type, so if you add that you're at the movies, you can start typing in a movie's title, and Facebook will automatically add it to the list of movies that you've watched.

6. **(Optional) Click the audience menu in the lower right corner to change who can see this particular post.**

You can choose from two basic privacy options: Public or Friends. Whatever you select will be saved for your next status post. In other words, if I post a link to Friends, the next time I go to update my status, Facebook assumes I also want to share that with Friends. I go over post privacy, including more advanced privacy options, in Chapter 6.

7. **Click Post.**

If that made you feel like updating your status requires wayyyy too much work, I want to remind you how many of those steps are optional. You can follow the abridged version of the preceding if you prefer:

1. **Click in the Share box.**

2. **Type your status.**

3. **Click Post.**

POSTS WITH LINKS

Frequently, people use their status updates to bring attention to something else on the Internet. It may be an article they found interesting, or an event, a photo album, or anything else they want to publicize. Usually, people add a comment to explain the link; other times, they use the link itself as their status, almost as though they're saying, "What I'm thinking about right now is this link."

Posts with links mean you can share something you like with a lot of friends without having to create an email list, call up someone to talk about it, or stand behind someone and say, "Read this." At the same time, you're almost more likely to get someone to strike up a conversation about your content because it's going out to more people, and you're reaching a greater number of people who may be interested in it.

To post a link, simply follow the instructions for updating a status and copy and paste the link you want into the field where you normally type a status. This automatically expands a preview of what your post will look like, including a preview of the content (as shown in Figure 5-7).

A preview usually contains a headline, a thumbnail photo, and teaser text. Hover over either the headline or teaser text and click to edit what appears in the preview. You can also edit your own comment.

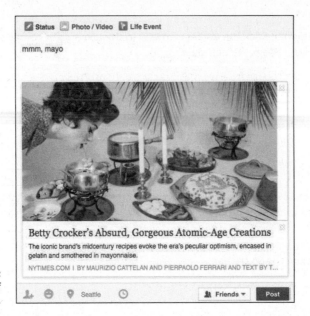

mmm, mayo

Betty Crocker's Absurd, Gorgeous Atomic-Age Creations

The iconic brand's midcentury recipes evoke the era's peculiar optimism, encased in gelatin and smothered in mayonnaise.

NYTIMES.COM | BY MAURIZIO CATTELAN AND PIERPAOLO FERRARI AND TEXT BY T...

Seattle · Friends ▾ · Post

FIGURE 5-7:
A preview of your post.

TIP

If you delete the URL text from the Share box, it doesn't actually remove the link from your post. In fact, deleting the link can make your post look cleaner and leave more room for your own thoughts about the link.

PHOTOS AND VIDEOS

Facebook is actually the Internet's number-one photo-sharing website. In other words, people love to share photos, and they post a lot of them on Facebook. In Figure 5-6, you can see that Photo/Video is one of the options at the top of the Publisher. You can also click the camera icon to add photos to a status update. Consider these facts a teaser trailer for Chapter 11, where I go over the entire Photo application, including adding photos and videos from the Publisher.

Life events

Part of what's nice about Facebook is the way it lets you connect with friends over the small stuff: a nice sunset on your walk home, a funny observation in the park (cats in strollers! Hilarious!). But Facebook is also awesome for letting you connect over the big stuff. Babies being born, houses being purchased, pets being adopted. The milestones, if you will. The Life Events section lets you make a note of that event on your Timeline.

Although it's not required, you may also feel an urge to fill out your history on your Timeline. If you're new to Facebook, you may want to expand your Timeline back past the day you joined. Life Events is a good way to think about what you want to add in your history.

To add a life event, follow these steps:

1. **Click the Life Event section in the Publisher.**

A menu of various types of life events appears. The categories are listed here although when you click each one, you'll find many subcategories as well:

- *Work & Education*
- *Family & Relationships*
- *Home & Living*
- *Health & Wellness*
- *Travel & Experiences*

TIP

Milestones can be big or small; if you check out the subcategories, you'll see things that range from getting your braces removed to learning a new hobby to having a baby. And you should feel free to make up your own. Lots of people use Life Events to represent small accomplishments in a humorous way. For example, one of my friends posted a life event to commemorate the day he successfully canceled his cable service.

2. **Select the event you want to create from the menu.**

This opens a pop-up window with specific text fields to fill out and space for photos to go along with the event. You can see an example in Figure 5-8.

3. **Fill out the details you want to share.**

TIP

You don't have to fill out all the fields, but it's pretty important to fill in the date of the event so that it goes to the right place on your Timeline.

FIGURE 5-8:
Add a life event from the recent or distant past.

4. **Add a photo to illustrate the event.**

   Click Choose from Photos if there is already a photo on Facebook you want to use, or choose Upload Photos to add photos from your computer.

5. **Use the Privacy menu to choose who can see this event in your Timeline.**

   You have the same basic options as you have all over Facebook: Public, Friends, or Custom.

6. **Click Save.**

   The event is then added to your Timeline, with any photos you've added featured prominently.

As you scroll down through your history, you may realize that you want to add an event or milestone. Don't worry about scrolling back up to the top of the page. The Timeline navigator should be following you as you scroll down, showing your name and the year you're looking at. Click the Life Event icon on the right side of this bar to add a milestone to your past.

Editing posts

If you've been on Facebook for a while and start scrolling backward through time, you may notice that you're not actually seeing everything. You see everything that you've done in the last week, sure. And most things from the last month. If you scroll back a year, you might not see every photo you added, but maybe one photo from a big event that a lot of people commented on.

Facebook knows that not all posts are created equal, so it attempts to create a selection of the best posts to represent your history, and it calls these posts *Highlights.* When you look at your Timeline highlights, you see what Facebook thinks are the most important posts and bits of information. Facebook does this based on algorithms that look at things like how many likes or comments a certain post got. It favors things like photos. But Facebook doesn't always get it right, so you can always go back and choose your own highlights.

Click the tiny grey down arrow in the upper right corner of any post to reveal the Edit Post menu, shown in Figure 5-9. This menu allows you edit the content or details of any post, as well as to Highlight, Hide, or Delete that post. Editing the content includes changing things like the date or what you wrote, and adding things like tags or locations to that post. Click Highlight to make sure that a given post appears in the highlights of your Timeline. After you select Highlight, a blue bookmark style banner gets added to the upper right corner of your post.

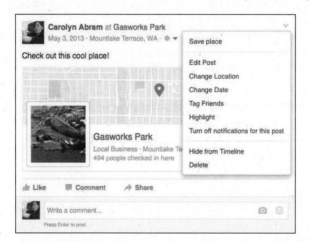

Hiding a post is different from deleting it. When you hide a post, you keep that post from appearing on your Timeline, but the post still exists. So if, for example, you hide a particularly bad photo from your Timeline, the photo album still exists. Anyone with permission to see it could navigate to your Photos section and check it out. But it's not going to get called out on your Timeline. If you delete a post, it's gone forever; even you won't be able to find it on Facebook.

TIP

If you're looking to remove things like photos or videos that exist only on Facebook, keep in mind that once they're gone from Facebook they're gone forever. It might be more practical to change the audience that can see the photo album than to delete it entirely. Trust me; one hard-drive crash, and your photos are Facebook-only.

The left column

The right column of your Timeline features your posts and life events and updates every time you add something new. The left column of your Timeline is bit more static and provides snapshots of three parts of your profile that people tend to look for when they visit a Timeline:

TIP

>> **Intro:** The Intro box shows a portion of the information you may have added to your About section (which I cover soon in the "All About Me" section). The part it does show includes the things that help identify you as you.

I think of it as "dinner party introduction." These pieces of info — where you work, where you live, where you went to school, who your spouse is — are the sorts of things you might talk about the first time you meet someone.

>> **Photos:** The Photos box shows thumbnails of photos you've added or been tagged in, starting with the most recent one. Clicking on any photo thumbnail will open an album view of all your photos.

>> **Friends:** The Friends box shows thumbnail photos of, you guessed it, your friends. Friends with new posts will appear at the top, followed by friends you have added most recently.

All About Me

The About box gives you (and your friends) the dinner party basics: where you live, what you do, where you're from, whom you're with. But there's a lot more information about you that Facebook gives you the opportunity to share. Clicking the About link beneath your cover photo opens the expanded About section of your Timeline (see Figure 5-10). By default, you see an overview of all your information — from here you can choose different sections to edit.

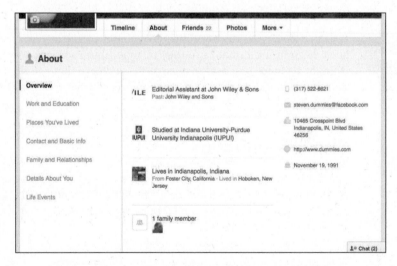

FIGURE 5-10:
The About section of your Timeline.

This page houses lots of information about you: Work and Education, Contact and Basic Information, Places You've Lived, Relationships and Family, Details About You, and Life Events. Much of this information won't change very much over time, so it needs to be edited only once or when something big happens, like you move to a new city. Click on any of the sections to edit or add to the information there. You can also edit who can see it. Unlike the cover photo and profile picture, you choose who gets to see this information. By default, your information is public, meaning everyone can see it. I go over changing your privacy in more detail in Chapter 6.

Work and Education

Your work and education information is actually very important information to add to Facebook. This is the information that helps old friends find you for reunions, recommendations, or reminiscing. It is also what helps people identify you as you, as opposed to someone else with a similar name.

To add an employer, follow these steps:

1. From the Work and Education section, click the Add a Workplace link.

2. Start typing the name of the company where you worked or currently work.

Facebook tries to find a match while you type. When that match is highlighted, or when you finish typing, press Enter.

3. Enter details about your job in the fields that appear.

These include

- *Position:* Enter your job title.

- *City/Town:* Enter where you physically went (or go) to work.

- *Description:* Provide a more detailed description of what it is you do.

- *Time Period:* Enter the amount of time you worked at this job. If you select I Currently Work Here, it appears at the top of your Timeline.

4. Select who you want to see this information using the privacy drop-down menu.

By default, this information is public. You can choose to only make it available to Friends, Friends except Acquaintances, Only Me, or a custom set of people or friend list. These more advanced privacy options are covered in Chapter 6.

5. Click the Save Changes button.

You can change any of the information about this job (or others) in the future by clicking the Options link next to the workplace you want to change and selecting Edit from the menu that opens.

TIP

If you're interested in using Facebook for professional networking, you can also add specific projects to your work history. For example, underneath my job at *Facebook For Dummies,* I could click Add a Project and fill out information about the most recent edition: who my editors are, how long the project took, and a description of what I'm doing.

To add a college, follow these steps:

1. **From the Work and Education section, click the Add a College link.**

2. **Start typing the name of the college you attended (or attend).**

   Facebook tries to find a match while you type. When that match is highlighted, or when you finish typing, press Enter.

3. **Enter details of your school in the fields that appear.**

   These include

   - *Time Period:* Click the blue text Add Year to show when you started and finished your degree.

   - *Graduated:* You can check the graduated box to note that you actually received a degree (or uncheck it to denote you did not).

   - *Description:* Add details about your time at school that you think may be relevant.

   - *Concentrations:* List any majors or minors you had.

   - *Attended For:* Choose whether you attended as an undergraduate or a graduate student. If you select Graduate Student, you will have additional space to enter the type of degree you received.

4. **Select who you want to see this information using the privacy drop-down menu.**

   By default, this information is public. You can choose to make it available only to Friends, Friends except Acquaintances, Only Me, or a custom set of people or friend list. These more advanced privacy options are covered in Chapter 6.

5. **Click the Save Changes button.**

To add a high school, follow these steps:

1. **From the Work and Education Section, click the Add a High School link.**

2. **Start typing the name of the high school you attended (or attend).**

   Facebook tries to find a match while you type. When that match is highlighted, or when you finish typing, press Enter.

3. **Enter details of your school in the fields that appear.**

   These include

   - *Time Period:* Click the blue text Add Year to show when you started and finished your degree.

- *Graduated:* Check this box if you graduated from this school.

- *Description:* Add details about your time at school that you think may be relevant.

4. **Select who you want to see this information using the privacy drop-down menu.**

   By default, this information is public. You can choose to only make it available to Friends, Friends except Acquaintances, Only Me, or a custom set of people or friend list. These more advanced privacy options are covered in Chapter 6.

5. **Click Save Changes.**

   You can change any of the information you just entered in the future by clicking the Options link next to the school you entered and selecting Edit from the menu that opens.

Places You've Lived

This section allows you add your hometown, current city, and any other place you've lived. If you haven't previously added your current city or hometown, click the Add Your Current City or Add Your Hometown links to do so. If you need to edit your current city, hover your mouse over the current city displayed, and click the Edit link that appears on the right side of the screen. As you type in your city, Facebook will auto-complete as you type. Simply select your city when you see it appear. Remember to click Save Changes when you've successfully entered your current city and hometown.

From this section of your About section, you can also create a life event to represent other places you have lived. To do this, click the Add a Place link under the Other Places Lived section. This automatically creates a life event about moving. You can then fill out all the fields related to moving (including when it happened) and even add photos from your move.

Contact and Basic Information

Your Contact and Basic Information is just what it sounds like: the very basics about you and how to get in touch with you. Contact information includes:

>> **Phone numbers:** You can add as many phone numbers as you have — home, mobile, and work.

>> **Address and Neighborhood:** You can choose to add this information in case anyone ever needs to mail you a present.

>> **Email address(es):** You can add as many email addresses as you want, and choose who can see those addresses.

>> **Website and Other Accounts:** You can add information about your account handle for other websites or services like Skype, Instagram, Twitter, and so on. You can also add a link to any personal websites you have.

>> **Facebook Username:** Facebook automatically creates a custom URL for your profile page when you join to make it easy to direct people to your Timeline. Usually usernames try to make use of your name, so a typical username might look something like: www.facebook.com/carolyn.abram.

You can add contact info you've never added by clicking the links to Add <Contact Info>. You can edit any existing contact information by hovering your mouse over the line of info you'd like to change and clicking the Edit button that appears. When you edit something, you can also edit *who* can see it by using the privacy drop-down menu. When you are done editing your information or privacy, remember to click the Save Changes button.

I know, it may seem a little scary to add your contact information to the Internet, and if you're not comfortable with it, that's okay. Facebook itself is a great way for people to reach you, so you shouldn't feel that it's required that you add other ways for people to contact you, as well.

That being said, it can be very useful for your friends to be able to find your number or address if needed, and there are privacy options (which are discussed in Chapter 6) that can help you feel more comfortable sharing some of this information.

Your Basic Information includes the following categories:

>> **Birth Date and Birth Year:** You entered your birthday when you registered for Facebook. Here, you can tweak the date (in case you messed up) as well as decide what people can see about your birthday. Some people don't like sharing their age, their birthday, or both. If you're one of these people, use this drop-down menu to select what you want to share.

WARNING

Although you can change your birthday and year at will most of the time, Facebook's systems prevent you from shifting to under 18 after you've been listed as over 18. If, through a legitimate mistake, this happened to you, contact Facebook's User Operations team from the Help Center.

>> **Gender:** You entered your gender when you signed up for Facebook, and Facebook mirrors your selection here. If you're transgender or have a preference in how people refer to your gender, you can choose to edit your gender and enter in whatever word best describes you. You can also choose what pronoun should be used in News Feed stories and around Facebook.

- >> **Interested In:** This field is primarily used by people to signal their sexual orientation. Some people feel that this section makes Facebook seem like a dating site, so if that doesn't sound like you, you don't have to fill it out.

- >> **Languages:** Languages might seem a little less basic than, say, your city, but you can enter any languages you speak here.

- >> **Religion:** You can choose to list your religion and describe it.

- >> **Political Views:** You can also choose to list your political views and further explain them with a description.

REMEMBER

By default, your basic information (with the exception of your birthday) is public. Click Edit and then use the Privacy menu to change who can see any item of information.

Family and Relationships

The Relationship section and the Family section provide space for you to list your romantic and family relationships. These relationships provide a way of linking your Timeline to someone else's Timeline, and therefore require confirmation. In other words, if you list yourself as married, your spouse needs to confirm that fact before it appears on both Timelines.

You can add a relationship by following these steps:

1. **From the Family and Relationships section of the About section, click Add your relationship status.**

   An area for adding this information appears.

2. **Click the Relationship Status menu to reveal the different types of romantic relationships you can add.**

   These include Single, In a Relationship, Engaged, Married, It's Complicated (a Facebook classic), Widowed, Separated, Divorced, In a Civil Union, In an Open Relationship, and In a Domestic Partnership.

3. **You can either stop here or choose to link to the person you're in this relationship with. Type the person's name into the box that appears.**

   Facebook auto-completes as you type. Press Enter when you see your beloved's name highlighted. This sends a notification to that person.

4. **(Optional) Add your anniversary using the drop-down menus that appear.**

   If you add your anniversary, your friends will see a small reminder on their Home pages on that date.

5. Click Save.

If you ever need to change this information, hover over it and click the Edit link to reopen this interface.

TIP

For many couples, the act of changing from Single to In a Relationship on Facebook is a major relationship milestone. There's even a term for it: Facebook official. You may overhear someone saying, "It's official, but is it Facebook official?" Feel free to impress your friends with this knowledge of Facebook customs.

You can add a family relationship by following these steps:

1. From the Family and Relationships section of the About section, click Add a Family Member.

A menu for editing this information appears.

2. Click in the text box for Family Member and start typing your family member's name into that box.

Facebook tries to auto-complete as you type. When you see your sister's or mother's or whomever's name appear, click to select it.

3. Select the type of relationship from the drop-down menu.

Facebook offers a variety of family relationships ranging from the nuclear to the extended.

4. Click Save Changes.

Details About You

The Details About You section is a bit of a catch-all section for details that don't really fit anywhere else:

» **About You:** This section is a free form place for you to describe yourself, if you so choose.

» **Name Pronunciation:** If people are always mispronouncing your name, you can choose to add a phonetic spelling of it. This pronunciation will be displayed on your profile with an audio component that people can choose to play to learn the proper way to say your name. This information is always public.

» **Other Names:** You can add nicknames, maiden names, or any other names people might use to search for you. This information is always public.

» **Favorite Quotes:** If you have any quotations you live by, you can add them to this free form field.

Life Events

You can see a summary of all the life events that exist on your Timeline in this space. If you see big gaps in your history that you'd like to fill, you can click Add a Life Event. You then can select from the same categories and fill out the same forms that I talk about in the Telling Your Story section.

Sections

Sections are parts of your Timeline you and your friends can jump to in order to see compilations of, for example, places you've checked in or what books you've read. To view your sections, click on the More tab underneath your cover photo. Some common Sections you see listed here are listed below:

>> **Likes:** The Likes section shows pages that you have liked, starting with the most recent one. As you scroll back in time, this box shows pages you liked at particular times. You can also click to view likes by category (such as Restaurants or Books).

>> **Places or Check-ins:** The Check-ins section displays locations where you've checked in recently.

>> **Interests:** There are actually multiple interest boxes for things like Music, Movies, Books, and so on. In theory, these are filled out naturally as you add information to your posts. For example, if you post that you're reading *The Great Gatsby,* and tag that book using the @ symbol, *The Great Gatsby* is added to the Books box.

>> **Application Activity:** Applications are websites, games, and other programs that allow you to integrate some aspect of Facebook into using them. For example, Spotify is a music-streaming program that you can add to your computer. You can also integrate Facebook into Spotify so your friends can see what you are listening to.

Many applications may have some aspect of automatic sharing, so after you sign up, every time you take a certain action — reading articles on *The Washington Post,* watching a TV show on Hulu — that activity will be added to your Timeline. This sort of activity gets its own box with info about the application you used.

Adding to your Interest sections

Interest sections are a part of the Timeline that can be really fun way to let your friends know the music, movies, television shows, books, and other things that really define you. Most of you have at least one book that's your favorite, and maybe another that you're reading right now and would really like to talk about with someone.

You can share both books you have read and your favorite books with your Facebook Friends following these steps:

1. **Navigate to the expanded Books section of your Timeline by clicking the More link beneath your cover photo and selecting Books from the drop-down menu.**

TIP

Although I'm using Books as an example, the same applies to the other Interest sections.

This takes you to the expanded Books section of your Timeline, shown in Figure 5-11. There are three subcategories of books that you can add to: Read, Want to Read, and Likes.

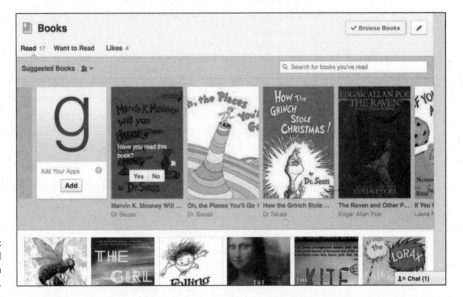

FIGURE 5-11:
An expanded Books section on your Timeline.

2. **Click into the section you want to be adding books to.**

By default, you will be in the Read section.

3. **Type the name of the book you want to add into the search box.**

Facebook will attempt to autocomplete as you type. When you see the book you want to add, click it or press Enter. You may also be able to click from a selection of suggested books that Facebook displays.

4. **Repeat Step 3 until you add every book you've read ever.**

Or, you know, until you get bored.

5. **Click the Want to Read or Likes section to add books that are on your list or that you want to actively recommend to people.**

TIP

Adding books in those sections is exactly the same: Search for the ones you want to add and then click them to select them.

Editing sections

You can decide which sections are part of your Timeline. Click the More tab beneath the cover photo and select Manage Sections at the bottom of the menu that opens. This opens the Manage Sections box. You can check and uncheck your sections to decide which ones appear as part of your Timeline.

To edit the privacy of any individual section, navigate to that section (for example, select Movies from the More menu to go to the Movies section). Click the pencil icon in the upper right corner of the section to open a menu of options.

» **Hide Section:** Select this if you want to hide the Movies section from appearing on your Timeline.

» **Activity Log:** Click this to be taken to Activity Log and see all activity related to movies that could appear in the Movies box. Activity Log gets a little more attention in Chapter 6.

» **Edit Privacy:** Click this to edit who can see all the movies you have liked on Facebook.

Your Friends and Your Timeline

Your Timeline is what your friends look at to get a sense of your life, and it's also where they leave public messages for you. In this way, your friends' posts become part of your history (just like in real life). Think about all the things you learn about a friend the first time you meet his parents, or all the funny stories you hear when your friend's significant other recounts the story of how they met. These are the types of insights that your friends may casually leave on your Timeline, making all your friends know you a little better.

When friends visit your Timeline, they'll also see a version of the Publisher (shown in Figure 5-12). This Publisher allows them to post some text or a photo to your Timeline. Check out the posts on your friends' Timelines. Chances are that you'll see a few "Hey, how are you, let's catch up" messages; a few "That was an awesome trip/dinner/drink" messages; and maybe a few statements that make so little sense, you're sure they must be inside jokes.

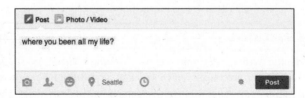

FIGURE 5-12:
Leave a public message for a friend on his Timeline.

If you're on a friend's Timeline around his birthday, you're sure to see many "Happy Birthday" posts. There aren't many rules for using Facebook, but one tradition that has arisen over time is the "Happy Birthday" post. Because most people see notifications of their friends' birthdays on their Home pages, the quickest way to say "I'm thinking of you" on their special day is to write on their Timeline.

TIP

Although I think that the back and forth between friends is one of the delights of the Timeline, some people find it a little hard to let go. If you're someone who doesn't like the idea of a friend being able to write something personal on your Timeline, you can prevent friends from being able to post on it within your Settings page. You can also limit who can see the posts your friends leave. From the Settings page, go to the Timeline and Tagging section and look for the settings related to who can post on your Timeline and who can see what others post on your Timeline.

REMEMBER

The best way to get used to the Timeline is to start using it. Write on your friends' Timelines, post a status update or a link on your own, and see what sort of response you get from your friends. After all, that's what the Timeline is all about — sharing with your friends.

IN THIS CHAPTER

Navigating the many privacy options on Facebook

Protecting yourself online and on Facebook

Deciding what to share and when

Chapter 6

Privacy and Safety on Facebook

When people talk about privacy online — and on Facebook in particular — I like to remind them that there's a spectrum of privacy concerns. On one end of the spectrum are true horror stories of predators approaching minors, identity thefts, and the like. Hopefully (and most likely), you will never deal with these issues although I do touch on them at the end of this chapter. On the other end of the spectrum are issues I usually categorize as "awkward social situations" — for example, posting a photo of your perfect beach day that your coworkers can see on a day when you called in "sick" (not that you would ever do something like that). Somewhere in between are questions about strangers seeing your stuff and security issues like spamming and phishing. All these privacy-related topics are legitimate, though you'll probably deal with the awkward end of the spectrum more often than anything else.

Regardless of where on the spectrum your particular question or problem falls, however, you should be able to use your privacy settings to make things better. I can't promise that you'll be able to prevent 100 percent of the situations that make you annoyed or uncomfortable or leave you with that sort of icky feeling, but I can tell you that you should be able to reduce how often you feel that way. The goal is to get as close to 100 percent as possible so you can feel as comfortable as possible sharing on Facebook.

Of course, there's also a spectrum of what "being comfortable" means to different people. That's why talking about privacy can get kind of confusing: There are a lot of options, and what makes me comfortable might not make you comfortable. This chapter is meant to be a guide to all the privacy options Facebook offers so that you can figure out the right combinations that make you comfortable sharing on Facebook.

Your own common sense is going to be one of the best helpers in avoiding privacy problems. Facebook status updates aren't the right place to post Social Security numbers or bank passwords. Similarly, if you're thinking about sharing something that, if the wrong someone saw it, could lead to really bad real-world consequences, maybe it's not meant to be shared on Facebook.

Know Your Audience

Before getting into specifics about all the privacy controls, you need to understand some basic parts of the Facebook vocabulary. These terms are related to how Facebook thinks about the people you may or may not want to share with. For most pieces of information, the privacy options are related to the audience who can see what you're sharing. The first two options in this list — Public and Friends — are the most basic settings that are shown by default whenever you go to change your privacy. An example of the menu used to change your audience for a post is shown in Figure 6-1. Note that only Public and Friends are displayed as options. The rest of the audience selections described in the following list are considered to be more advanced options and are therefore hidden behind the More Options selection.

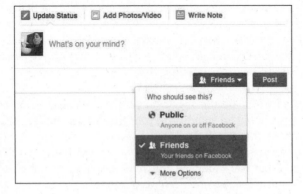

FIGURE 6-1:
The Audience options for your posts.

» **Public or Everyone:** By setting the visibility of something you post or list to Public, you're saying that you don't care who, on the entire Internet, knows this information about you. Many people list their spouse on their Timeline, and, just as they'd shout this information from the treetops (and register it at the county courthouse), they set the visibility to Public. This is a totally reasonable setting for innocuous pieces of information. In fact, some information is always available as Public Information that everyone can see. This includes your name, profile picture, cover photo, and gender.

Now, just because everyone *can* see something doesn't mean everyone *does* see everything. Your posts, information, friendships, and so on, populate your Friends' News Feeds (assuming that your Friends can see this information), but never the News Feeds of people you're not Friends with (unless you allow followers to see your public posts). When I think about who will see the information I share as Public, I imagine someone like you searching for me by name and coming to my Timeline. Although (hopefully) that might be a lot of people, it isn't anywhere close to the number of people who use Facebook. By default, much of your Timeline and all your posts are publicly visible. This chapter covers how to change these settings if you want to.

» **Friends:** Any information for which you set visibility to Friends will be accessible only by your confirmed Facebook Friends. If you trust your Friends, this is a reasonably safe setting for most of your information. If you feel uncomfortable sharing your information with your Friends, you can use Custom privacy, or you can rethink the people you allow to become your Friends.

TIP

Think of friending people as a privacy setting all on its own. When you add someone as a friend, ask yourself whether you're comfortable with that person seeing your posts.

» **Friends Except Acquaintances:** Even though I always recommend adding Friends only if you're comfortable with them seeing your posts, this setting forces me to acknowledge that sometimes you have not-quite-friends on your Friend List. These may be distant family members, professional contacts, old friends from way back when, or that super-friendly neighbor whom you maybe just wish wouldn't stop by quite so often. No matter who they are, you can add them to the Acquaintances list and then use this setting to limit what they can see about you.

» **Only Me:** This setting is basically a way of adding something to Facebook but then hiding it from being seen by other people. I can't think of many times I've found this setting useful, except when I start something like adding a photo album, and want to come back later to finish it, and don't want it to be seen until I've added all my tags and captions.

» **Custom:** If you have very specific needs, customized privacy settings may help you feel more comfortable sharing on Facebook. The Custom privacy option allows you to choose specific people (or lists of people) who can see something, or choose specific people (or lists of people) who can't see something.

>> **Lists:** Lists are ways to sort your friends into various categories. There are two types of lists: Smart Lists that Facebook creates on your behalf, and lists that you create for yourself. For example, Facebook creates the Family list based on information you enter about your family relationships. I've created a "Dummies" list to keep track of the various editors and co-authors I've had over the years. Often, you may want to share something with one particular list of people, in which case, you can choose the name of that list as your privacy setting.

Privacy on the Go

Privacy on Facebook isn't a one-time thing. Because you are constantly adding new status updates, photos, and content to Facebook, constantly interacting with friends and reaching out to people, privacy is actually an ongoing affair. To that end, one of the most common places you should know your privacy options is in the Publisher, also known as the Share box.

The *Publisher* is the blank text box that sits at the top of your Home page and under your cover photo on your Timeline. It's where you go to add status updates, photos, links, and more to Facebook. The part of the Publisher that's important for this chapter is the Privacy menu, right next to the Post button. You can see this in Figure 6-1.

Whenever you're posting a status or other content, the *audience,* or group of people you've given permission to see it, is displayed next to the blue Post button. The audience you see displayed is always the audience you last shared something with. In other words, if you shared something with the Public last time you posted a status, it displays Public the next time you go to post a status.

Hovering your mouse over this word turns it into a button. Click that button to reveal the drop-down menu. It shows the two main audience options: Public and Friends. Click the setting you want before you post your status, link, or photo. Most of the time, I share my posts with Friends. As a result, I don't actually change this setting that often. But if you do share something publicly, remember to adjust the audience the next time you post something.

Sometimes, you may find that you want to share something with only a portion of your friends. To do that, choose More Options from the Privacy menu. The Extended Privacy Menu appears, as shown in Figure 6-2.

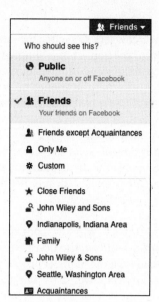

FIGURE 6-2:
Lots of options
for sharing.

The Extended Privacy menu includes many of the options discussed in the Know Your Audience section: Friends Except Acquaintances, Only Me, Custom, and Friends Lists.

Selecting Custom opens the Custom Privacy window, shown in Figure 6-3. This window appears any time you choose Custom as a privacy setting for any type of information. Customized privacy has two parts: those who *can* see something and those who *can't*.

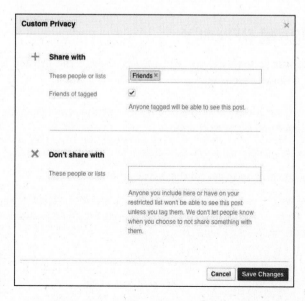

FIGURE 6-3:
The Custom
Privacy window.

The top part of the Custom Privacy window lets you enter the names of friends or Friend Lists that you definitely want to see something. Simply type the name of the person or list into the text box to make something visible to them. Additionally, a check box allows you to choose whether the friends of any people you tag can see your post. Remember, tagging is a way of marking who is in a photo, who is with you when you check in someplace, or whom you want to mention in a post. For example, say that I'm going to spend a day at the park with one of my friends. I might post a status that says "Taking advantage of the nice weather with **Kate**." The name of my friend links back to her profile. By default, Kate's friends will be able to see this post, even if they aren't friends with me. If I deselect this box, Kate's friends will no longer be able to see that post.

The lower section of the Custom Privacy window controls who can't see something. Similar to the top part of the window, the Don't Share This With section has a blank text box where you can type the name of people or lists of people. When you add their names to this box, they won't be able to see the content you post.

REMEMBER

Whatever customized audience you create for one post will be the audience next time you go to post something. Make sure you check the audience the next time you post!

WARNING

A post's privacy icon (Public, Friends of Friends, Friends, or Custom) is visible to anyone who can view that post. People can hover over that icon to get more information. Friend Lists appear as Custom privacy unless the viewer is a member of a list you shared the post with. Members of a Friend List can see other people included on the list, but are unable to see the name of the list.

Changing privacy

After you post something, you can always change the privacy on it. From your Timeline, follow these steps:

1. **Hover your mouse over the privacy icon at the top of the post whose audience you want to change.**

   Every post displays the icon for Public, Friends, or Custom.

2. **Click the button to reveal the Privacy menu.**

   You'll see the usual options: Public, Friends, and More Options. You need to click More Options to see choices like Friends Except Acquaintances, Only Me, Custom, or specific Friend Lists.

3. **Click the audience you want.**

   A change to Public, Friends, Friends Except Acquaintances, or a specific Friend List is automatically saved. Changing to Custom requires you to make selections within the Custom Privacy window again.

Privacy Shortcuts

There are actually so many settings related to privacy on Facebook that it can sometimes feel overwhelming. That's why I am such a fan of the Privacy Shortcuts menu, which helps direct you to the settings you'll want most often by asking the questions you'll ask most often:

>> Who can see my stuff?

>> Who can contact me?

>> How do I stop someone from bothering me?

To open the Privacy Shortcuts menu, click the lock icon in the big blue bar at the top of any Facebook page. The Privacy Shortcuts menu is shown in Figure 6-4. Click any of these three options to expand more privacy options.

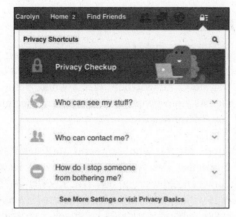

FIGURE 6-4: You can find the answers to your most common privacy questions here.

Who can see my stuff?

You can adjust the privacy for each status or post you make, which means that over time you might find yourself asking, "Wait, who can see all of this? Who can see what I posted yesterday? Last week? What about if I post tomorrow?" Well, the answers can be found here. (The earlier "Privacy on the Go" section of this chapter covers the privacy options when you're sharing something.)

Facebook offers you one setting you can adjust here, named Who Can See My Future Posts. This is the exact same control that can be found in the Publisher. It's described this way to emphasize that whatever you select here will be the default going forward, until you change it again. Click the little arrow to change this setting. You will see the same options you see from the Publisher: Public, Friends, and More Options.

Additionally, the Who Can See My Stuff section offers you two links to help you double-check and understand what people can see. The first is a link to Activity Log, which is a granular summary of everything you've done on Facebook and who can see that thing. It ranges from the status updates you write to the content you like or comment on. As you look through your Activity Log, you can change who can see it, or remove the content entirely. I go over how to navigate and edit your Activity Log in more depth in the "Privacy Tools" section later in this chapter.

Finally, the Who Can See My Stuff section offers you a link to another privacy tool, the View As tool. This tool allows you to look at your Timeline as though you are another person. I like to use this to double-check what people see when they search for me on Facebook — in my case, they mostly see my biographical information and none of my posts.

Who can contact me?

A common Facebook problem that sends people scurrying to their privacy settings is getting a Friend Request that they don't want to get. It might be from a spammer or just someone you don't know (there was a whole point in time when I regularly got friend requests from people in Turkey). This section is to help you control who can send you Friend Requests.

There are only two options for the Who Can Send Me Friend Requests setting: Everyone and Friends of Friends. Everyone means that everyone who searches for you or finds your Timeline can request you as a friend. Friends of Friends means someone has to be friends with one of your friends before he's allowed to request you. As a personal anecdote, when I worked at Facebook, I received a lot of Friend Requests from people who wanted me to pass a message along to the CEO or something like that. I found this irritating, so I changed this setting to just Friends of Friends. When I moved to a new city, I realized the people I met were unable to add me as a friend. I changed my setting back to Everyone to make it easier for friends to find me.

How do I stop someone from bothering me?

Sadly, sometimes a friendship isn't really a friendship. If someone is bothering you, harassing you, bullying you, or in any way making your Facebook experience terrible, blocking might be the solution to the problem. Blocking is different than unfriending someone because someone who is not your friend might still wind up interacting with you on Facebook. For example, if you have mutual friends, you might wind up both commenting on the same post. Blocking someone means that as much as possible, neither of you will even know that the other person is on Facebook. You won't see each other's comments, even if that person is on the same person's photo. Blocked individuals won't be able to send you messages, add you as a friend, or view your Timeline (all things they would likely be able to do even if you unfriended them).

TIP

If you're the parent of a teen, this can be a very handy setting to know about. Unfortunately, bullying can sometimes spread to Facebook from the classroom, and blocking can be a useful tool in terms of keeping your child safer on Facebook.

Privacy Settings

In addition to the privacy shortcuts, there are several more granular privacy settings located within the Settings page. You can get to these settings from the Privacy Shortcuts menu (click the link on the bottom that says See More Settings).

The Privacy Settings and Tools section of the Settings page is shown in Figure 6-5. The left side of the Settings page is a menu of different settings you can adjust here. The settings that are relevant to privacy are in the second section: Privacy, Timeline and Tagging, and Blocking. Additionally, I go over the Apps and Ads settings sections because people commonly have questions about how their information is used in these locations.

Privacy

The Privacy section of the Settings page is shown in Figure 6-5. It's broken into three sections: Who Can See My Stuff, Who Can Contact Me, and Who Can Look Me Up.

FIGURE 6-5:
Start here to set privacy options.

Who Can See My Stuff?

The Who Can See My Stuff section should look mostly familiar if you read the section on privacy shortcuts. There are three settings here, two of which are redundant with the Privacy Shortcuts menu.

>> **Who can see your future posts?** This setting shows you your current setting for when you create posts. This is who can see all your future posts (unless you change it). You can change this setting by clicking the Edit link on the right side of the page. A sample Publisher appears where you can select a new privacy setting.

>> **Review all your posts and things you're tagged in.** This setting provides a link to Activity Log. Activity Log is a granular list of absolutely everything you've done on Facebook. I cover how to use Activity Log in the "Privacy Tools" section later in this chapter.

>> **Limit the audience for posts you've shared with Friends of Friends or Public.** This setting is one you probably won't need too often, but it could come in handy once in a while. Remember, this setting is needed only if at any point, you shared posts with Everyone or with Friends of Friends. If you've shared only with Friends (or an even smaller subset of people), this setting won't change anything. Use it to change the privacy settings of all items that were previously public to be visible only to friends.

This setting might be useful if, for example, you're job hunting and you don't want potential employers to find your public posts about the most recent election. Once you make this change, it can't be undone. In other words, those posts will always be visible only to Friends unless you go back and individually make them public.

To use this setting, click the Limit Past Posts link on the right side of the page; then click the Limit Old Posts button that appears.

Who Can Contact Me?

The Who Can Contact Me section should also be familiar, as it is the same setting found in the privacy shortcuts menu. This setting lets you choose between allowing anyone on Facebook to send you a friend request or only allowing people who know your friends to send you a friend request. Click Edit and then use the Privacy menu to change your setting.

Who Can Look Me Up?

This section concerns how people can find you on Facebook. When you signed up for Facebook, you entered an email address and possibly a phone number. The first two settings ask if people who search by that information will be able to find you. If you're someone who has a slightly different name than your real name on your Timeline (for example, if I were to go by Carolyn EA on Facebook rather than my actual name, Carolyn Abram), I absolutely recommend leaving these settings set to Everyone. Limiting it limits your potential friends' ability to find you.

To change this setting for either your email address or phone number, click Edit on the right side of the page and use the Privacy menu to select whether Everyone, Friends of Friends, or only Friends can search for you by email or phone number.

The third setting here concerns search engine indexing. Search engines like Google or Bing use web crawlers to create indexes they can search to provide results to users. So when someone searches for your name on Google, by default, a link to your Facebook Timeline appears. If you deselect this setting, that will no longer be true.

To change this setting, click Edit on the right side of the page and deselect the check box labeled Let Other Search Engines Link to Your Timeline. A pop-up window will ask if you're sure you want to turn off this feature. Click the Confirm button.

REMEMBER

Even if you deselect the search engine indexing check box, people will still be able to search for you by name on Facebook itself. With the exception of someone you have blocked, people will always be able to search for you and get to your Timeline from Facebook Search.

Timeline and tagging

The Timeline, as I describe in Chapter 5, is basically where you collect all your stuff on Facebook. That means photos, posts, posts Friends have left you, application activity, and so on. Your Timeline allows you to look through your history and represent yourself to your Friends.

Tags on Facebook are a way of labeling people in your content. For example, when uploading a photo, you can tag a specific friend in it. That tag becomes information that others can see as well as a link back to your friend's Timeline. In addition, from your Friend's Timeline, people can get to that photo to see her smiling face. You can tag people and pages in status updates, photos, notes, check-ins at various places, comments, and really any other type of post. And just like you can tag friends, friends can tag you in their photos and posts.

This section of the settings page allows you to control settings related to people interacting with you on your Timeline and tagging you in posts. For controlling the privacy on things *you* add to your Timeline (that is, your posts), you use the Privacy menu in the Publisher. The Timeline and Tagging Settings section is shown in Figure 6-6.

FIGURE 6-6:
Edit your settings
for tags.

Who Can Add Things to My Timeline?

This section focuses on other people adding things like photos, posts, or tags to your Timeline.

REMEMBER

>> **Who can post on your Timeline?** In addition to being a place where you add posts, your Timeline is a place where your Friends can leave you messages or posts. If you don't want your Friends leaving these sorts of public messages (if you're using Facebook for professional or networking reasons, for example), you can set this to Only Me.

By default, only Friends can post on your Timeline. This setting means no one can post to your Timeline except you.

To change this setting, click Edit on the right side of the setting and use the drop-down menu that appears to select Only Me.

>> **Review posts Friends tag you in before they appear on your Timeline.**
Timeline Review allows you to review the tags people have added of you
before they are displayed on your Timeline. In other words, if I tag you in a
photo, that photo won't appear on your Timeline until you log in to Facebook
and approve the tag.

To change this setting, click Edit on the right side of the setting and use the
drop-down menu that appears to toggle between Enabled and Disabled. By
default, tags of you are automatically approved, and this setting is set to
Disabled or Off.

Who Can See Things on My Timeline?

There's a difference between *adding* things to your Timeline, which the preceding
settings control, and simply *looking* at your Timeline, which the settings in this
section control. Three settings here concern what people see when they look at
your profile.

>> **Review what other people see on your Timeline.** This isn't so much a
setting as a link to the View As privacy tool (which I cover in detail in the
"Privacy Tools" section later in this chapter). The View As tool allows you to
look at your Timeline as though you're someone else, thus double-checking
that your privacy settings are actually working.

>> **Who can see posts you've been tagged in on your Timeline?** After you've
approved tags (or if you leave Timeline Review off), you can still decide who
can see the content in which you're tagged on your Timeline. In other words, if
your Friend tags you in a photo, you can control who sees that photo on *your*
Timeline. The idea behind this setting is that, although you will never post
anything embarrassing to your Timeline, a Friend might (accidentally, I hope)
do so. Making sure that not everyone can see that post (except other, more
understanding friends) cuts down on any awkwardness.

To change this setting, click the Edit link on the right side of the page and
then use the drop-down menu that appears to choose who can see this
information.

>> **Who can see what others post on your Timeline?** Another way to control
the "embarrassing friend on your Timeline" problem is to limit who can see
the posts your friends leave.

To change this setting, click the Edit link on the right side of the page and use
the drop-down menu that appears to select who can see these posts.

How Can I Manage Tags People Add and Tagging Suggestions?

Although tagging has been mentioned in many of these Timeline settings, these settings refer to very specific use cases of tagging that you maybe never thought about before.

>> **Review tags people add to your own posts before the tags appear on Facebook.** This setting controls tags your friends add to content you've uploaded. For example, if I upload a photo of 20 people to Facebook and don't tag anyone in it, my friends might choose to add tags. This setting lets me choose to review the tags my friends add before the tag is visible to other people.

To change this setting, click Edit on the right side of the page; then use the drop-down menu that appears to select whether Tag Review is Enabled or Disabled. By default it is Disabled (Off).

>> **When you're tagged in a post, who do you want to add to the audience if they aren't already in it?** This setting sounds very complicated, and it is a little bit complicated. Say that I'm friends with Eric and Dave, but Eric is not friends with Dave (hmmm, this is starting to sound like a middle school math problem). Now, say that Eric adds a photo of me (meaning he has tagged me in it), and his privacy settings share that photo with his friends. Because Dave and Eric aren't friends, Dave cannot see that photo unless this setting allows my friends to be added to the audience of that photo.

To change this setting, click Edit on the right side of the page and use the drop-down menu that appears to select who is added to the audience of a post you're tagged in. There are only three options for this setting: Friends, Only Me, and Custom. By default, this setting adds your friends to the audience of a post you're tagged in.

>> **Who sees tag suggestions when photos that look like you are uploaded?** Facebook employs some facial recognition software to help people tag photos. So if a Friend is uploading 50 photos and you appear in 30 of them, Facebook might recognize your face and suggest to your friend that you be tagged in those 30 photos. This is to save your friend time while he's adding photos, and to encourage people to add more tags to Facebook. You can choose not to appear in the suggestions Facebook gives your friends by disabling this setting.

To change this setting, click Edit on the right side of the page and use the drop-down menu that appears to select whether Friends or No One will see tag suggestions.

Blocking

Most of your privacy settings are preventative measures for making yourself comfortable on Facebook. Blocklists are usually more reactive. If someone does something on Facebook that bothers you, you may choose to block him or block certain actions he takes from affecting you. The Blocking section of the Settings page is shown in Figure 6-7. You can manage six blocklists here: Restricted List, Block Users, Block App Invites, Block Event Invites, Block Apps, and Block Pages.

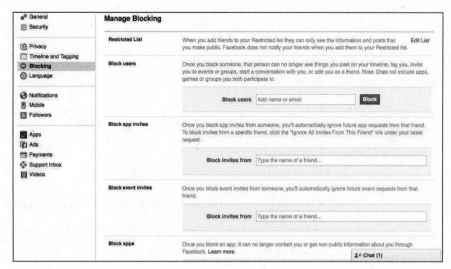

FIGURE 6-7:
Edit your
blocklists here.

Using the Restricted List

The Restricted List is a list you can create that's not quite as serious as blocking someone outright but that is also slightly more serious than simply adding the person to your Acquaintances list. For example, say that you receive Friend Requests from Veronica and Logan. You accept the Friend Requests and add Veronica to the Acquaintances list, and Logan to the Restricted list. Whenever you add a post that is visible to Everyone, both can see it. When you add a post that is visible to Friends Except Acquaintances, neither can see it. However, when you add a post that is visible to Friends, Veronica will be able to see it, but Logan won't be able to. Make sense?

To add someone to this list, click Edit List on the right side of the page. A pop-up window appears, as shown in Figure 6-8. If you've already added people to this list, they appear here, and you can remove them from the list by hovering over their pictures and clicking the x that appears in the right corner of the photos.

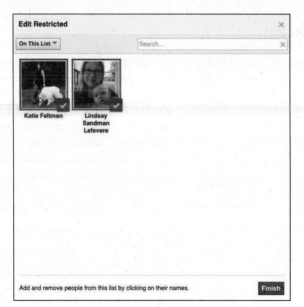

FIGURE 6-8:
Add people to the
Restricted List.

To add people to the list, follow these steps:

1. **Click the button in the top left of the box named On This List.**

   A menu of two options appears: Friends and On This List.

2. **Click Friends.**

   A grid appears showing all your friends listed alphabetically by first name.

3. **Select friends to add to the restricted list by clicking their pictures or by searching for them by name in the upper right corner and then clicking their pictures.**

4. **When you're done, click the Finish button in the lower right corner of the box.**

Blocking users

Blocking someone on Facebook is the strongest way to distance yourself from someone else on Facebook. For the most part, if you add someone to your Block list, he can't see any traces of you on Facebook. You won't show up in his News Feed; if he looks at a photo in which you're tagged, he may see you in the photo (that's unavoidable), but he won't see that your name has been tagged. When you write on other people's Timelines, your posts are hidden from him. Here are a few key things to remember about blocking:

» **It's almost entirely reciprocal.** If you block someone, she is just as invisible to you as you are to her. So you can't access her Timeline, nor can you see anything about her anywhere on the site. The only difference is that if you blocked the relationship, you're the only one who can unblock it.

» **People you block are not notified that you blocked them.** Nor are they notified if you unblock them. If they are savvy Facebook users, they may notice your suspicious absence, but Facebook never tells them that they have been blocked by you.

» **You can block people who are your friends or who are not your friends.** If you are friends with someone and then you block her, Facebook also removes the friendship. If, at some point in the future, you unblock her, you will need to re-friend her.

WARNING

Blocking on Facebook doesn't necessarily extend to apps and games you use on Facebook and around the Internet. Contact the developers of the apps you use to learn how to block people within games and apps.

To add people to your blocklist, simply enter their names or email addresses into the boxes provided. Then click the Block button. Their names then appear in a list here. Click the Unblock link next to their names if you want to remove the block.

Blocking App Invites

An *app* is a term used to describe pieces of software that use Facebook data, even when those apps weren't built by Facebook. As friends use apps and games, they may want you to join in on the fun and send you an invite to join them. This is all well and good until you find that certain people send you wayyyy too many invites. Rather than unfriend or block the overly friendly person who's sending you all those invitations, you can simply block invitations. This option still allows you to interact with your friend in every other way, but you won't receive application invites from him or her.

To block invites from a specific person, just type the person's name in the Block Invites From box, and click Enter when you're done. That person's name then appears on the list below the text box. To remove the block, click Unblock next to that name.

Blocking Event Invites

Similar to App Invites, you may have friends who are big planners and love to invite all their friends to their events. These may be events that you have no chance of attending because they're taking place across the country, and your friend has chosen to invite all his friends without any regard for location. Again, your friend is cool; his endless unnecessary invitations are not. Instead of getting rid of your friend, you can get rid of the invitations by entering his name here.

To block event invites from specific people, just type their names into the Block Invites From box, and click Enter when you're done. Their names then appear on the list below the text box. To remove the block, click Unblock next to their names.

Blocking Apps

Occasionally, an app behaves badly once you start using it. By "behave badly," I mean things like spamming your friends or using your information in ways that make you uncomfortable. If an app is doing so, you can block it to prevent it from contacting you through Facebook and getting updated Facebook information about you.

To block an app, type its name in the Block Apps text field and press Enter. The name of the app appears on the list below the text box. To remove the block, click Unblock next to its name.

Blocking Pages

Pages are basically Timelines for non-people (things like businesses, brands, famous people, pets, anything that isn't covered by the term "person"). Pages can often interact in many of the same ways as regular people on Facebook (for example, commenting on or liking your posts), which means you might find yourself in a situation where you need to block one. When you block a Page from interacting with you, it will no longer be able to interact with you or your posts, and you won't be able to interact with that Page via message or post. It also automatically includes un-liking and unfollowing the Page.

To block a Page, type its name into the Block Pages text field and press Enter. The name of the Page appears on the list below the text box. To remove the block, click Unblock next to its name.

Apps

An *app* is a term used to describe pieces of software that use Facebook data, even when those applications weren't built by Facebook. You may use apps as games, websites, and useful tools, all of which make use of the data you already share on Facebook. To make it easier to get people using these applications, they import the data from Facebook. I cover the specifics on using applications in Chapter 14. For now, keep in mind that the apps you see on this page are those you chose to interact with. You won't see random applications appear here without you giving them some permissions first.

This section, shown in Figure 6-9, is where you go to edit how apps, games, and websites interact with your Timeline.

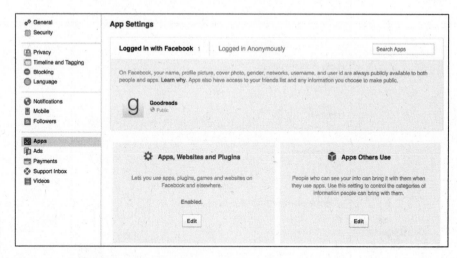

FIGURE 6-9:
App settings.

Logged In with Facebook

The Logged In with Facebook section at the top of the App Settings page shows all the apps you've used, including websites where you've used Facebook to log in. Next to each app's name in this list is the audience that can see that app on your Timeline. Click on the privacy icon or the pencil icon that appears when you hover your mouse over the app's name to open the Edit App menu.

Figure 6-10 shows the Edit App menu, where you can review and edit the information that the app can access as well as how the app can interact with your Facebook usage.

There are several sections of this menu (including a few that you need to scroll down to see). Some of these sections have options you can change, and others are merely informative.

>> **App Visibility and post audience:** The Privacy menu here has the same options as any other Privacy menu. You can choose who can see both that you use a given app as well as any posts that app makes on your behalf. For example, I keep my Kickstarter app visible to friends because I like them to know what projects I'm supporting. I make my Hulu app visible to Only Me because I'm ashamed of how much reality television I watch.

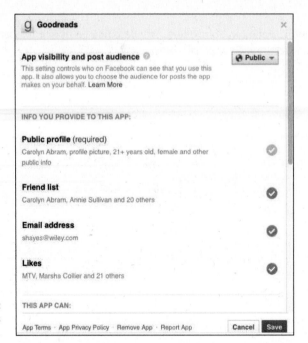

>> **Info You Provide to This App:** This list of information shows what information from your Facebook account is currently being shared with the app in question. In addition to the information type (for example, Friend List or Education History) you can see examples of that information (for example, Oliver, Felicity, John; Tufts and Phillips Academy) as well as how recently that app has accessed that info. With the exception of your Public Profile (which includes your name, profile picture, age, gender, and any other publicly available info), you can stop sharing other types of info with an app by unchecking the blue circle next to it in this menu.

>> **This App Can:** This section lets you control whether or not an app can post to your Timeline on your behalf, and whether it can send you notifications. For the most part, apps only post to your Timeline when you have taken an action within the app (for example, adding a new book to your Goodreads list). If you don't want the app to do this anymore, uncheck the blue circle. If you are receiving too many notifications from a particular app, you can use the menu here to make that stop. Simply use the menu next to *Send you notifications* to switch from Yes to No.

>> **Learn More:** This section provides links to learn more about different aspects of using apps. It also provides links to contact the developers of the app you are using. Remember, Facebook isn't always the company that has built an

app, so if you are having trouble using that app or want your info deleted, you will need to contact that company, instead of contacting Facebook.

>> **Links:** At the bottom of the Edit App menu, next to the Cancel and Save buttons, are a few links that may come in handy:

- **App Terms:** This link takes you to the app's Terms of Service.

- **App Privacy Policy:** This link takes you to the app's Privacy Policy.

- **Remove App:** If you want to sever all ties with an app, you can click this link to remove it entirely from your Facebook experience. It won't be able to access any of your info going forward.

- **Report App:** You can use this link to report an app for things like spamming, abusive behavior or content, or for using your information inappropriately.

Apps, Websites, and Plugins

This setting is like a big giant "kill" switch for using Apps, Websites, and Plugins with your Facebook account. If you are sure that there is no way you will ever want to use any sort of app under any circumstance, you can choose to disable Facebook Platform. If you do so, any apps you have used will be removed, and their posts will be deleted from your Timeline. You won't be able to log in to external websites with your Facebook credentials, and your friends won't be able to interact with you through their apps. If you're sure that this is what you want, click Edit to open the Turn Platform Off menu, then click the blue Disable Platform button.

Apps Others Use

Even if you don't use applications, your friends may. Similar to the way that you may not add photos to Facebook but your friends may add and tag photos of you, your friends may also pass on information about you to applications. You can restrict what applications can see by using the check boxes pictured in Figure 6-11.

Old Versions of Facebook for Mobile

If you've never used Facebook on a mobile phone or are certain you're using the most recent Facebook app on an iPhone or Android phone, this setting doesn't apply to you. But if you're using a version of Facebook for Mobile that doesn't allow you to change your privacy for each post you create, you can use this setting to control who sees posts you make from your phone. Click the Privacy menu at the bottom of this box to make your selection.

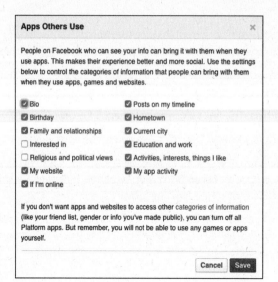

FIGURE 6-11:
What can your
friends share with
apps and games?

Ads

Facebook is free for you to use. Instead of charging its users money, Facebook pays the bills by selling ads. These ads are then shown to you. So, in a way, looking at ads is the way you pay for using Facebook. Facebook has a number of different ways that it chooses which ads to show to you, and the settings here give you a few options to control how your information gets used alongside ads and in what ads get shown to you. Keep in mind that no matter what settings you choose on this page, you will still see ads. These settings just control certain types of ads or allow you to express ad preferences. You can't turn ads off.

The first setting on this page is for Ads Based on Your Use of Websites and Apps. Facebook can choose to show you ads based on other websites you have visited. It calls these ads *online interest-based advertising.* You can choose to turn these ads off. Remember, this doesn't turn ads off, it simply means you won't see online interest-based ads.

The second setting, Ads with my Social Actions, concerns how your Facebook information may appear alongside ads on Facebook. Facebook differentiates its ads from other ads on the Internet by pointing out that their ads are "social." In other words, if my friend likes something, there's a good chance I will like it, too. So in its ads, whenever possible, Facebook includes social information. You can see an example of this in Figure 6-12.

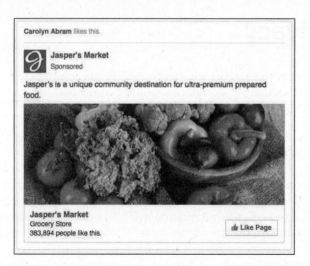

FIGURE 6-12:
An ad with social information.

Personally, I'm comfortable with my friends seeing things that I've liked, or public events I've attended, or places I've checked in, being paired with an ad for that thing, event, or place. If you aren't comfortable with this, that's okay, too; you can prevent it from happening here.

To prevent your friends from seeing any information about you next to an advertisement, click Edit on the right side of the page. Use the drop-down menu that appears (below all the text) to toggle between Only My Friends and No One. Click the Close link when you're done.

REMEMBER

Even if you don't change this setting, only your Friends ever see information about you next to ads. If we're not Friends, you'll never see a notice that "Carolyn Abram likes this movie" next to an advertisement for a popular film.

The third setting related to ads is Ads based on my preferences. Clicking Edit to the right of this setting and then clicking Visit Ad Preferences brings you to a page where you can view and edit the preferences Facebook uses to show you ads. Preferences are the same words that advertisers might use to choose who sees an ad. You might see something that is obviously pulled directly from your profile. For example, if you listed yourself as a democrat in your About section, you might see that a preference is US Politics (Liberal). Other preferences might seem more obscure or unclear how they wound up in the list. If you see a preference that you don't agree with, or that reflects certain ads you no longer want to see, hover over that item and click the X on the right side of it to remove it.

REMEMBER

Removing all your preferences from this page won't mean you stop getting ads. It only means that you're likely to see more generic, less specific ads.

Timeline Privacy

In addition to the content you post — which was covered earlier in the "Privacy on the Go" section — you can control the information that you've entered in the About and Interests sections of your Timeline.

All about privacy

This information, such as where you went to school or your relationship status, changes infrequently, if ever. You can edit the privacy for this content in the same place you edit the information itself. To get there, go to your Timeline and then click the Update Info button in the lower right corner of your cover photo.

The About page has several sections, each representing a different information category. So, for example, all your work and education information appears in the Work and Education section. When you hover your mouse over any item, a privacy icon appears signifying who can see that piece of information. By default, most of this information is set to Public and visible to Everyone, although contact information is visible only to Friends by default.

Figure 6-13 shows me editing the privacy for a piece of information — in this case, my current city in the Living section of my About page. Clicking the privacy icon to the right of the field opens up an interface for editing that information as well changing who can see it. Use the privacy menu to change the privacy and click Save Changes when you're done. Rinse and repeat for any other pieces of information in the About section.

FIGURE 6-13:
Edit privacy for every piece of information on your Timeline.

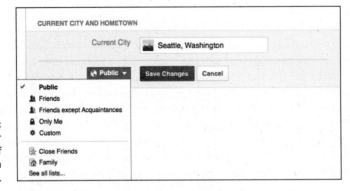

Timeline information is one of the places where the Only Me setting might come in handy. For example, lots of people don't like sharing their birthdays on Facebook, but Facebook requires you to enter a birthday when you sign up. By making it visible only to you, it effectively hides your birthday from everyone.

** Click Save Changes when you're done editing privacy settings. Otherwise, the new settings won't stick.

Interested in privacy

On your Timeline, interests are sorted into categories like Movies, Music, Books, and so on. For your TV Shows section, for example, you can add TV shows that you've watched, TV shows that you want to watch, and TV shows that you like. Each time you add a TV show to the list of shows you've watched or want to watch, you can also control who sees that you've added that particular show to that list. Figure 6-14 shows me editing who can see that I've watched the television show *Arrow*. I opened this Privacy menu by clicking the privacy icon beneath the image representing the show.

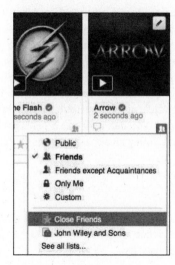

FIGURE 6-14: Selecting who can see what I've watched.

Additionally, I can control who can see what TV shows I like. Unlike the Watched and Want to Watch sections, where I can edit this individually, I decide who can see *all* the shows I've liked. To edit who can see what you've liked, follow these steps:

1. **Make sure you're looking at the correct section on your screen.**

   In this case, I'm looking at the TV Shows section.

2. **Click the pencil icon button in the upper right corner of the box.**

   A menu of options related to this section appears.

3. **Click Edit Privacy.**

   A pop-up window opens.

4. **In the section of the box labeled Likes, click the Privacy menu.**

   This opens the Privacy menu with familiar options: Public, Friends, Friends Except Acquaintances, Only Me, Custom, or Lists.

5. **Choose whom you want to see the TV shows you have liked.**

6. **Click Close to save the changes.**

Privacy Tools

Okay, that was a lot. A lot of settings, a lot of information. What if you don't want to worry about these small settings and who tagged what when? What if you just want to make sure that your Timeline looks the way you want to your friends and that people who aren't your friends can't see anything you don't want them to see? Well, the good news is that the View As tool allows you to do just that, and the Activity Log tool allows you to keep track of everything that's been happening recently and to make any needed adjustments without trying to figure out which setting, exactly, needs to be changed. You can also run a privacy checkup to make sure that your expectations of what your privacy is matches the reality.

View As

You can get to the View As tool from the Privacy Shortcuts menu. Click the lock icon next to your name in the left sidebar to open the menu up. In the Who Can See My Stuff? section, click the link to View As.

Clicking that link brings you to your Timeline. Except, it's probably not the way you usually see your Timeline. The black bar running across the top of the page lets you know that you're currently viewing your Timeline as someone who is not your friend (also known as *everyone* in the Public bucket of people). You can click through to the various sections of your Timeline. (Photos tends to be a section that people like to check, double-check, and triple-check.)

Note that no matter how much you've hidden your information and posts, everyone can see your cover photo and profile picture, gender, current city, and Friend List. Anything else the public can see can be hidden, if you so choose.

In the black bar on top of this view of your Timeline, there's a white bold link labeled View as Specific Person. If you want to check on, for example, what acquaintances or people you've added to your Restricted list can see, click this link and enter a friend's name into the text box that appears. If you're surprised by what that friend can see, you can go change the privacy on any content you don't want her to see. (If you've forgotten how to change the privacy on a post, head back up to the "Privacy On the Go" section.)

Activity Log

As you've probably noticed, a lot happens on Facebook. You take all sorts of actions: liking, commenting, posting, and so on. And people take all sorts of actions that affect you: writing on your Timeline, tagging you in photos, and inviting you to join groups. If you want to know, line by line, everything that could possibly be seen about you by someone on Facebook, Activity Log is for you.

You can get to Activity Log from a few places. You can get there from the Privacy Shortcuts menu or from your own Timeline. On your Timeline, simply click the Activity Log button, located under the right corner of your cover photo. This takes you to Activity Log (see Figure 6-15).

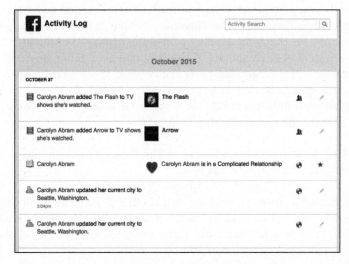

FIGURE 6-15: Here's everything you've done on Facebook recently.

When you're looking at Activity Log, notice that there's a menu on the left for viewing only certain types of posts. For example, you can choose to view all the posts you've been tagged in, or all the photo posts, or all the app-related posts.

When you're looking at an individual line item, you see several columns of information. First is an icon and sentence explaining what you did (or what a Friend did). This might be something like "Carolyn wrote on Dana's Timeline" or

"Carolyn was tagged in Dana's photo." Then there is a preview of that post, photo, comment, or whatever it is related to. For example, if you commented on a photo, the preview will show you that photo and the comment that you made.

To the right of the preview is an icon representing who can see that item. Hover your mouse over the icon to see text explaining who can see it. This might be the usual privacy options, or it might be members of a group you belong to, or in the case of a post to a Friend's Timeline, it will be that person's friends. For posts that you create, you can change the audience by clicking the icon, which opens the Privacy menu.

However, you'll find you can't change the privacy on lots of content. For example, a comment on someone else's post isn't something you can change the audience for. If you realize a comment you made or something you liked is visible to more people than you'd want, your only option is to delete that content.

You can delete content using the final icon to the right side of each item in Activity Log. This little pencil icon can be found all over the site and generally indicates that you can edit something. When you hover over the icon here, it explains that the item is allowed on Timeline. This means that people may see that item — possibly as its own post, possibly as a summarized item in recent activity, possibly in an app box when they visit your Timeline. Clicking the Edit button reveals a menu of options for changing whether something appears on Timeline. For some items, such as likes or comments, the only option is to unlike the content or delete the comment. For others, like posts you've made or posts you've been tagged in, there are more options that allow you to hide something from the Timeline or edit it on your Timeline (these are the same options that appear when you go to edit or highlight something on your Timeline).

REMEMBER

When I say something is visible on Timeline, I also mean that your Friends might see that item in their News Feed.

Personally, I find Activity Log useful in that it helps me understand all the ways I participate on Facebook and all the things my friends might see about me and my life. But I've found that I don't actually change the privacy or the Timeline settings on items here all that often.

Privacy Checkup

Privacy Checkup is a tool Facebook built to make it easier for you to make sure that everything is on the up-and-up privacy-wise. Especially if you've been using Facebook for a long time, you can start to feel uncertain about who can see what. Privacy Checkup is designed to make it easy to become certain and feel comfortable sharing.

To use Privacy Checkup, open the Privacy Shortcuts menu, and click on Privacy Checkup. This opens the Privacy Checkup window, which has three sections:

» **Posts:** The first section concerns your posts, and lets you change the default setting for who can see the posts you make.

» **Apps:** The second section shows your apps and lets you make choices about who can see the apps you use. In other words, the same things found in the Apps section of your settings page.

» **Profile:** The third section shows some of the contact and basic information from your Timeline, and lets you double-check who can see each piece of information. You can edit your privacy for any of this information directly from the Privacy Checkup window.

One of the hardest moments to hear about from frustrated Facebook users is when they say, "But I thought no one could see that!" Privacy Checkup is a great way to make sure that what you think matches the reality of your privacy settings.

Remembering That It Takes a Village to Raise a Facebook

Another way in which you (and every member of Facebook) contribute to keeping Facebook a safe, clean place is in the reports that you submit about spam, harassment, inappropriate content, and fake Timelines. Almost every piece of content on Facebook can be reported. Sometimes you may need to click an Options link to find the report link.

Figure 6-16 shows an example of someone reporting an inappropriate photo.

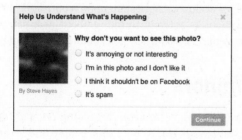

FIGURE 6-16: Reporting inappropriate content.

The reporting options vary depending on what you're reporting (a group as opposed to a photo, for example). These reports are submitted to the Facebook User Operations team. The team then investigates and takes down inappropriate photos, disables fake accounts, and generally strives to keep Facebook clean, safe, and inoffensive.

When you see content that you don't like — for example, an offensive group name or a vulgar Timeline — don't hesitate to report it. With the entire Facebook population working to keep Facebook free of badness, you wind up with a pretty awesome community.

REMEMBER

After you report something, Facebook's User Operations team evaluates it in terms of violating Facebook's Statement of Rights and Responsibilities. This means that pornography gets taken down, fake Timelines are disabled, and people who send spam may receive a warning or even have their account disabled. However, sometimes something that you report may be offensive to you but doesn't violate the Statement of Rights and Responsibilities and, therefore, will remain on Facebook. Due to privacy restrictions, User Operations may not always notify you about actions taken as a result of your support, but rest assured that the team handles every report.

Peeking Behind the Scenes

Facebook's part in keeping everyone safe requires a lot of manpower and technology power. The manpower involves responding to the reports that you and the rest of Facebook submit, as well as proactively going into Facebook and getting rid of content that violates the Statement of Rights and Responsibilities.

The technology power that I talk about is kept vague on purpose. I hope that you never think twice about the things that are happening behind the scenes to protect you from harassment, spam, and pornography. Moreover, I hope that you're never harassed or spammed, or accidentally happen upon a pornographic photo. But just so you know that Facebook is actively thinking about user safety and privacy, I talk about a few of the general areas where Facebook does a lot of preventive work.

Protecting minors

This section is purposefully vague to avoid becoming *Gaming Facebook's Systems For Dummies.* In general, I want you to note that people under the age of 18 have special visibility and privacy rules applied to them. For example, when a user under the age of 18 (in the United States) posts something and chooses Public from the Privacy menu, that post won't truly be public until she turns 18. Until then, that post will be visible only to friends of her friends.

Other proprietary systems are in place that are alerted if a person is interacting with the Timelines of minors in ways they shouldn't, as well as systems that get alerted when someone targets an ad to minors. Facebook tries to prevent whatever it can, but this is where some common sense on the part of teens (and their parents) can go a long way toward preventing bad situations.

REMEMBER

You must be at least 13 years old to join Facebook.

Preventing spam and viruses

Everyone can agree that spam is one of the worst parts of the Internet, all too often sliming its way through the cracks into email and websites — and always trying to slime its way into Facebook as well, sometimes in the form of messages to you, or Timeline posts, or groups, or events masking as something it's not to capture your precious attention.

When you report a piece of content on Facebook, "It's spam" is usually one of the reasons you can give for reporting it. These spam reports are incredibly helpful. Facebook also has a bunch of systems that keep track of the sort of behavior that spammers tend to do. The spam systems also keep track of those who message people too quickly, friend too many people, post a similar link in too many places, and do other such behaviors that tend to reek of spam. If you end up really taking to this Facebook thing, at some point you may get hit with a warning to slow down your messaging. Don't take it too personally, and just follow the instructions in the warning — this is the spam system at work.

Preventing phishing

Phishing is a term that refers to malicious websites attempting to gain sensitive information (like usernames and passwords to online accounts) by masquerading as the sites you use and trust. Phishing is usually part of spamming: A malicious site acquires someone's Facebook credentials and then messages all that user's friends with a link to a phishing site that looks like Facebook and asks them to log in. They do so, and now the bad guys have a bunch of new Facebook logins and passwords. It's a bad cycle. The worst part is that many of these Facebook users get locked out of their own accounts and are unable to stop the spam.

Just like spam and virus prevention, Facebook has a series of proprietary systems in place to try to break this cycle. If you do have the misfortune to get phished (and it can happen to the best of us), you may run into one of the systems that

Facebook uses to help people take back their Timelines and protect themselves from phishing in the future.

The best way to protect yourself from phishing is to get used to the times and places Facebook asks for your password. If you just clicked a link within Facebook and suddenly there's a blue screen asking for your information, be suspicious! Similarly, remember that Facebook will never ask you to email it your password. If you receive an email asking for something like that, report it as spam immediately.

TIP

If you want to stay up-to-date with the latest scams on Facebook, or want more information about protecting yourself, you can like Facebook's Security Page at www.facebook.com/security. This provides you with ongoing information about safety and security on Facebook.

One Final Call to Use Your Common Sense

No one wants anything bad to happen to you as a result of something you do on Facebook. Facebook doesn't want that. You don't want that. I definitely don't want that. I hope that these explanations help to prevent anything bad from happening to you on Facebook. But no matter what, *you* need to take part in keeping yourself safe. In order to ensure your own safety on Facebook, you have to make an effort to be smart and safe online.

So what *is* your part? Your part is to be aware of what you're putting online and on Facebook. You need to be the one to choose whether displaying any given piece of information on Facebook is risky. If it's risky, you need to be the one to figure out the correct privacy settings for showing this information to the people you choose to see it — and not to the people you don't.

REMEMBER

Your part is equivalent to the part you play in your everyday life to keep yourself safe: You know which alleys not to walk down at night, when to buckle your seatbelt, when to lock the front door, and when to toss the moldy bread before making a sandwich. Now that you know all about Facebook's privacy settings, you also know when to use the various privacy options, and when to simply refrain from posting.

I'M HAVING A PRIVACY FREAKOUT; WHAT DO I DO?

I cannot tell you how many times I've gotten a frantic email from a family member or friend saying something like, "Oh my gosh, my friend just told me that his friend was able to see these photos that I thought only my friends could see and now I'm freaking out that everyone can see everything; do you know what to do?"

The first step is to take a deep breath.

After that, the next best thing to do is to go to the Privacy Shortcuts menu and click the View As tool.

That allows you to click around your Timeline as though you're someone who isn't your Friend. If you think that person is seeing too much, I recommend using the Limit the Audience for Past Posts setting on the Privacy section of the Settings page. This pretty much changes anything that used to be visible to more than just friends to be visible only to Friends. After you do that, usually you can begin the process of adjusting your settings so that, going forward, you won't have any more freakouts.

IN THIS CHAPTER

Learn how to use the Facebook app on your phone

Sending messages to friends using the Messenger app

Discovering the entire suite of Facebook apps

Exploring Facebook via the mobile web and via SMS

Chapter 7

Facebook on the Go

had an existential argument with myself about this chapter as I sat down to write it. I wasn't sure it needed to exist. Not because you'll never use mobile features, but the opposite. Using Facebook on a mobile phone is so integral that it is virtually indistinguishable from using it on the computer.

In part, that's by design. Any actions you take on Facebook on the web are visible on Facebook on your phone and vice versa. You can start a comment thread on your phone and pick it up on your computer. You can post a photo from your computer and check on how many likes it received while you're on your phone at a coffee shop later. The Facebook app is designed to look and feel like Facebook, so that without even thinking about it, you'll likely be tapping on the link or button you need instinctively.

Personally, I use Facebook more from my phone than I do from my computer. It's when I'm out and about that I see things happening that I want to share. I take photos on my phone and want to get them out into Facebook-world immediately. When I'm out and about is also when I tend to have time to kill: waiting for a doctor's appointment to start, sitting on a bus, pacing back and forth with a screaming baby. These are the times when I most want to read about my friends, catch up on interesting links and articles, and generally know what's going on around me.

In this chapter, I make a foolish assumption: I assume that you have a mobile phone and know how to use its features. In addition, for the bulk of this chapter, I assume that you have an iPhone or Android phone where you can use apps, or at least browse the web from your mobile browser. If you have a mobile phone that can send and receive text messages but can't use apps or browse the web, skip over the bulk of this chapter to learn about Facebook Texts.

The Facebook App

The Facebook app exists for iPhones and Android phones, as well as special versions for Windows phones. I am an iPhone user, so the steps and figures in the upcoming section are based on my experiences using Facebook for iPhone. If you are an Android user, worry not; the functionality is largely the same, and many of the numbered steps will likely be very similar to what you see on your phone. The biggest differences will be in the locations of certain buttons or links.

Before you can get started with the Facebook app, you need to download the app to your mobile phone. For Android phones, that means doing so from Google Play, and for iPhone users, that means doing so from the App Store. The app is free to download and use. Once it has been downloaded, you will need to log in to your Facebook account (shown in Figure 7-1). You will only need to log in the first time you use the Facebook app; after that, your phone remembers your login info.

FIGURE 7-1:
Log into the Facebook app for iPhone.

Layout and navigation

The bulk of the Facebook app's Home page (shown in Figure 7-2), much like the Home page on the web, is News Feed. You can use your finger to swipe News Feed up and down in order to browse your friends' posts (a bit more on News Feed in a little bit). A News Feed icon in the bottom menu ensures you are always able to return to this Home page from wherever else you are on Facebook.

FIGURE 7-2:
Facebook for
iPhone home.

The other parts of Facebook you see in your web browser — the left sidebar, the Publisher, and the blue bar on top — are distributed between menus at the top and bottom of the screen.

TIP

For Android users: Instead of menus at the top and bottom of the screen, the Facebook app for Android has two menu bars at the top of the screen, one blue and one white.

Search

The app does have a blue bar on top, but it has only two items. A Search box and a People icon. The search box can be used to find your friends and also to search for trending topics. When you tap into the search box the keyboard interface appears, as well as recent searches and trending topics.

If you want to search for something that doesn't appear in your search history or as a trending topic, simply type your query and tap Search. Facebook auto-completes when you type, so the items you see beneath the search box will shift as you type. If you're just typing in a friend's name in order to get to their Timeline, simply tap on their face when you see it in order to go there.

Facebook Search allows you to search not just for people but for places, Pages, posts, and other types of Facebook content. The search results page has an extra menu bar at the top of the page. Tap on any of the filters to see only results of that type.

Chat

Tap the people icon in the blue bar on top of the screen to see a list of your friends. Your friends are listed by how often you message with them on Facebook. A mobile phone icon next to their name indicates that they use Facebook from their phone, and you may also see how long ago they logged in to Facebook. A green dot next to their name indicates they are currently logged in to Facebook. Tap on any of these friends' names to open the Messenger app and send a message to them.

Tapping a friend's name opens the Messenger app (or prompts you to add the Messenger app), which Facebook uses for all chatting and messaging from your phone. Tap on the left side of the screen (where you can see part of News Feed) to return to News Feed.

Requests/Messages/Notifications

When you use Facebook on the web, the blue bar on top of the screen contains icons to represent incoming Friend Requests, Notifications, and Messages. Those same icons are represented on the mobile app at the bottom of the screen. When you have new requests, messages, or notifications, small red bubbles above the relevant icon appear. Tap on any of these icons to see your requests, messages, or notifications. Keep in mind that tapping on the messages icon opens up the Messenger app.

Tapping on the requests icon brings you to a Friend Requests page. There, you can tap to Confirm or Delete any incoming friend requests. It also shows you people you may know, and you can tap to add anyone as a friend or remove people from the display.

Tapping on the notifications icon brings you to the notifications page. This displays the same info that displays in the notifications menu on the site. Tap on any notification to go to the content it's referring to. For example, tapping on a birthday notification brings you to your friend's Timeline, where you can leave a Happy Birthday wall post. Tapping on a notification about people liking your status brings you to that status post.

More

The More [. . .] icon at the bottom of the screen is basically where all the links normally found on the left sidebar can be found. Tapping the More icon brings you to a menu, shown in Figure 7-3.

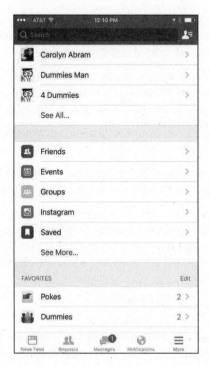

A brief refresher on some of these links:

>> **<*Your Name*>:** This menu option takes you to your own Timeline. In general, Timelines are organized into the same format as Timelines on the regular site, with a few stylistic changes to make sure all the information can fit on the screen. Click the Post button beneath your profile picture to add something to your Timeline.

>> **<*Pages*>:** If you admin any Pages, they appear here. You can tap on them to view their Timelines.

>> **Friends:** The Friends section of the iPhone app should resemble your phone's contact list. You can scroll through your friends from A to Z or search for them from the Search box at the top of the list.

- **>> Events:** This lets you view any events you've RSVP'd to. This is incredibly useful when it turns out neither you nor your significant other remembers the exact street address of the dinner you're going to.

- **>> Groups:** This lets you interact with any groups you are a part of. This way, you don't miss out on discussions when you're out and about.

- **>> Saved:** You can save links, articles, and videos for later viewing from your News Feed. When you decide you have time to look through these saved items, tap on this option.

- **>> Favorites:** Any apps, groups, or Pages you interact with frequently appear in this section. You may also see links to view certain friend lists, nearby friends, and nearby places. Tap on any item to visit that group, app, Page, list, or feed.

- **>> Settings:** Tap on settings to go to your Account Settings, News Feed Preferences, or Activity Log.

- **>> Privacy Shortcuts:** Tap on Privacy Shortcuts to view the same privacy shortcuts you can access from the blue bar on top of any Facebook page on the web.

- **>> Help and Support:** If you ever have a question that I can't answer, tap on Help and Support to visit the Help Center. You can also report a problem with Facebook (either that something is broken or that you are seeing something you think is abusive or illegal).

- **>> Log Out:** Tap this to log out of the Facebook app.

To navigate around Facebook using the app, simply tap on what you want to see more of. See a photo thumbnail that looks interesting? Tap it. You want to see a person's Timeline? Tap his face or name. You can navigate back from wherever you go by tapping the back arrow or x in the upper left corner of whatever you wind up looking at. You can also always tap on the News Feed icon in the bottom menu in order to go back to News Feed and your Home page.

WARNING

You might see slightly different or additional items in the More section. These may be links to other features or applications within Facebook. Facebook is tailored to you so what you see may be a bit different from what I see.

News Feed

Use your finger to scroll down News Feed and see what all your friends have to say. If new stories appear while you are reading News Feed, a "New Stories" bubble appears at the top of the screen. You can tap that bubble to speed all the way back to the top of News Feed without having to manually scroll all the way back up.

A News Feed story in the app looks more or less exactly the same as a News Feed story on the web, and you can interact with it the exact same way. Tap to like, comment, or share. You can also tap on the down arrow in the upper right corner of any story to bring up the News Feed menu, where you can hide certain posts or unfollow a friend whose posts you don't want to see anymore. You can also tap on that menu to save a post for later.

TIP

One thing to look for in News Feed stories is a small lightning icon in the corner of article previews. This doesn't appear for all articles, just for ones that have their content hosted on Facebook's servers. Articles with this icon will load nearly instantaneously when you tap on the article. Articles without this icon may take longer to load.

Posting from the app

Much like on the website, you can post content from the top of your News Feed. Tap on Status or in the What's on Your Mind? box to open up the mobile Publisher, shown in Figure 7-4.

FIGURE 7-4:
iPhone status updates start here.

The mobile Publisher has all the same options as the Publisher on the web, the main difference being the location of some of these items. Instead of the Post button and Privacy menu being at the bottom of the Publisher, these are at the top. Tap where there is a To: field (like an email) to change your privacy. By default, your post will be visible to whomever your last post was visible (in Figure 7-4, that is Friends). You can tap to select a different audience, including specific friends or lists.

REMEMBER

You can change your privacy every time you create a new post.

The Post button is at the top right of the mobile Publisher. When you finish typing your status and adding any photos, tags, links, activity info, or location info, tap that button to post your status to Facebook.

There are five icons at the bottom of the mobile Publisher, representing things you can add to your status post:

>> **Photos (camera icon):** Adding a photo to your post will require you to give Facebook permission to access the camera roll on your phone. I go over some of the editing options in the next section on posting a photo from your phone.

>> **Tags (person + tag icon):** Tapping this opens a menu for searching and selecting friends to tag. Tap on a person's name to tag her.

>> **Links (chain link icon):** Tapping this allows you to search the web for an article or link you want to add to your status. I generally think it's easier to simply copy a link into your post, but this is a neat little shortcut to know about.

>> **Activity (smiley face icon):** Tapping this opens a menu for selecting from different activity and emotion words you can use to describe what you are doing, thinking, or feeling.

>> **Location (location pin icon):** Tapping this opens a menu for selecting where you are. You may need to turn on Location Services from the Settings menu of your phone in order for this to work automatically. You can also search for locations if you don't see the correct place appear in the list.

Photo posts

Given that so many photos live on phones these days, chances are you may want to use Facebook to share them. Sharing photos can be incredibly easy, but there are also a lot of advanced options. First, let's go over the basic photo sharing post:

1. **Tap the Photo button at the top of News Feed.**

   This brings up your phone's camera roll, which you can use to select photos.

2. **Tap on the photos you want to select.**

Facebook highlights selected photos in blue and counts how many photos you have selected (shown in Figure 7-5).

TIP

Tap photos in the order you want them to appear.

FIGURE 7-5:
Share photos
from your
phone's camera
roll.

3. **Tap Done in the upper right corner.**

This brings you back to the Publisher, with the photos you have added now displayed.

4. **Tap Post in the upper right corner.**

This brings you back to News Feed, where you can see your new post being added as a new story.

Those are the basics. Just a few taps and you've shared a moment of your life with your friends. Now, if you want to be a bit more advanced about it, including a few photo editing options, read on:

1. **Tap the Photo button at the top of News Feed.**

This brings up your phone's camera roll, which you can use to select photos.

2. **Tap on the photos you want to select.**

   Facebook highlights selected photos in blue and counts how many photos you have selected (shown in Figure 7-5).

3. **Tap Done in the upper right corner**

   This brings you back to the Publisher, with the photos you have added now displayed. You can scroll down using your finger to get to each individual photo for editing.

4. **Tap on people's faces to tag them.**

   Facebook automatically puts boxes around faces it detects in the photos; simply tap on a box to add a name to the face.

5. **Tap on the Edit button in the bottom left of any photo to edit it.**

   To remove a photo at this point, click the x in the upper right corner of the photo you want to remove. You don't *have* to edit any of your photos, or you can edit all of them. You can see a few of the editing options in play in Figure 7-6. You can edit photos in any of the following ways:

   - *Filters:* Filters are ways to change the overall color or tone of the photo. For example, you can convert a photo to black-and-white.

FIGURE 7-6:
Make your
photos awesome.

- *Tag:* Tags are ways to mark who is in a photo. Tap on a face to open a tagging box. This highlights the face in question and opens a text box where you can type in the name of that person. Facebook autocompletes as you type; tap on the correct name when you see it appear.

- *Crop:* You can crop photos by using your fingers to move the proposed border of a photo. You can also find a button here to rotate a photo (no sideways photos for you!) and to automatically crop a photo into a square instead of a rectangle.

- *Text:* You can add a caption beneath a photo in Step 7, or you can add text that gets displayed on top of the photo. Tap to type the text you want to add, then use your finger to drag the text to where you want it in the photo.

- *Stickers:* You can also add a sticker to the top of a photo. You can select from a basic set of stickers that Facebook provides or download various "sticker packs" such as mustache shapes or holiday-related stickers. After you select the sticker you want, you can use your finger to drag it to where you want on the photo.

- *Doodle:* You can also doodle a little drawing on the top of any photo. When you select doodle, a small color chart appears on the right side of the screen. Put your finger down on the color you want to select, and wait for a small dot in that color to appear to the left of your finger. Drag your finger up and down to change color, and to the left or right to change the thickness of your line. Once you are at the right color and thickness, release your finger. Then you can draw your doodle, using your finger, on top of your photo.

6. **Tap Done in the upper right of the page when you are done editing.**

Repeat Step 5 as needed for each photo you are sharing.

7. **Add photo captions.**

If you are only adding one photo, that means tapping into the Say Something About This Photo field and writing a comment. If you are sharing more than one photo, tap beneath each photo where it says *Add a Caption.*

8. **Tap the Album icon to add a photo to an existing album or create a new album.**

Tapping the Album icon brings you to a menu of your previously created albums. Tap on the one you'd like to add to, or tap to create a new album. When you have named your album, you return to the mobile Publisher, and the name of the album is displayed at the top of the screen.

9. **Tap the Location icon to add location info.**

Just like any other post, you can add location info so people can know where a photo was taken.

10. **Double-check who can see your photos at the top of the post.**

At the top of every post is information about privacy. At the top of the Publisher a To: field is prefilled with your most recent privacy choice. You can change the privacy for this post by tapping and selecting new privacy options from the menu that opens.

11. **Tap Upload or Post in the upper right corner.**

This brings you back to News Feed, where you can see the News Feed story that has been created about your new photos.

Check-ins

Whenever you post something to Facebook, you can add location information, also known as a *check-in* to your post. This is true on the website as well as when you are using the Facebook app on your phone. When you are using the app, Facebook expects that you are going to be more likely to want to check in someplace, so it makes it really easy to check in from the app.

When you check in, you see a list of locations based on the location information shared by your phone (you may have to grant Facebook permission to access this information). These might be restaurants or parks or buildings. When you select a location by tapping on it, you *check in* to that location. Checking in basically means actively telling Facebook that you're there. Facebook won't share your specific location unless you check in (it does frequently include general location information like the name of the city you are in).

You can tag friends in your check-ins or add photos or a few words about what's going on. After you check in, your friends can see where you are in their News Feeds. If they're out and about and also using Facebook on their phones, they can see if they are near you by tapping Nearby from the Facebook menu.

Checking in leads to all sorts of nice serendipitous encounters. When I was in Boston recently, I checked in to a few different restaurants. An old friend I hadn't seen in ten years sent me a message asking how much longer I'd be in town. I didn't even know she had moved to Boston. We had brunch the next day.

To check in, follow these steps:

1. **Tap Check In at the top of News Feed.**

A list of nearby places appears. These places may range from official businesses (Peet's Coffee) to people's homes (Carolyn and Eric's Place) to shared spaces (Dolores Park, San Francisco Airport Terminal 2).

2. **Select the name of the place you'd like to check in to.**

   If you don't find what you're looking for, type the name of the place you want to check in to in the search bar above the list of suggested locations. If it's not found, you can click the blue Add < *place name* > to fill out place info and create a new place where everyone can check in. The Create a Place page is shown in Figure 7-7.

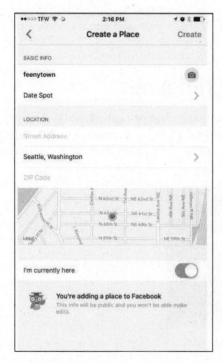

FIGURE 7-7:
The Create a Place page.

3. **(Optional) Type a comment into the Publisher.**

   The Publisher looks like it usually does, only the location information is appended to your post.

4. **(Optional) Tap the Person icon to tag friends.**

   Your list of friends appears. Tap the ones you want to tag.

   Some people are very private about their location information, so it's considered polite to ask people before you tag them.

   REMEMBER

5. **Tap Done when you're done tagging.**

6. **Double-check your privacy in the top of the Publisher.**

   At the top of every post is information about privacy. At the top of the Publisher a To: field is prefilled with your most recent privacy choice (usually Public or Friends). You can change this by tapping and selecting new privacy options from the menu that opens.

7. **Tap Post in the upper right corner.**

   This officially marks you as "here." The check-in is added to your Timeline and your friends' News Feeds, where they can comment or like your check-in, or maybe even pop by to say hi.

Checking out Timelines

Like News Feed, Timeline in the Facebook app should look pretty familiar, if a bit narrower than you're used to. Figure 7-8 shows a mobile Timeline. Your cover photo sits across the top of the screen, with your profile picture in the center.

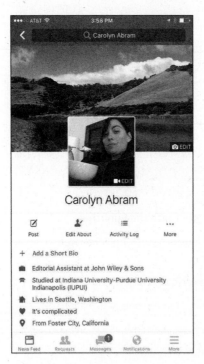

FIGURE 7-8:
Your Timeline in the Facebook app.

Beneath your profile picture are links to post, edit the About section of your Timeline, view your Activity log, and More. Tapping More gives you options to change your profile and cover photos or go to your privacy shortcuts. Underneath these links is your biographical information like where you work and live, your relationship status, and where you went to school.

Use your finger to scroll down the page. As you do, you'll pass by the mobile Publisher, thumbnails of recent photos, as well as a preview of your friends. Beneath that are your actual posts. Most recent posts appear first, and you can keep scrolling back to the very beginning, if you so choose.

When you are viewing posts, you can tap on the tiny down arrow in the upper right corner of the post to see options related to that post (see Figure 7-9). Depending on the type of post you will see different options, but in general this is where you can go to hide a post from your Timeline, edit the content of a post, or change the privacy settings on a post.

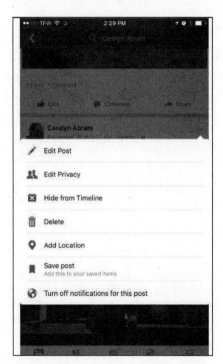

FIGURE 7-9:
Post options.

Profile Videos

One mobile-only feature you can add from the Facebook app is a profile video. Profile videos are meant to be like a profile picture just, you know, in motion. Profile videos are up to seven seconds long and play on a loop when people are looking at your

Timeline from their phone. A still image from the video will then appear as your profile picture in thumbnails around the site. Follow these steps to record a profile video:

1. **From your Timeline, tap on the Edit link at the bottom of your existing profile picture.**

   This brings up a menu of options: Take a New Profile Video, Upload Video or Photo, Select Photo on Facebook, or View Profile Picture.

2. **Tap Take a New Profile Video.**

   This opens your phone's camera interface (you may have to tap to allow Facebook access to your camera).

3. **Tap the red button to begin recording.**

   Remember, you have a maximum of seven seconds to work with.

4. **Tap the red button again to stop recording.**

   You automatically go to a preview of your new profile video.

5. **If you're happy with your video, tap Next in the upper right corner.**

   To record a new video, tap the back arrow in the upper left corner.

6. **Choose a thumbnail from your video to be your profile picture.**

   To select from the various thumbnails within your video, move your finger along the video "reel" at the bottom of the screen. The main part of the screen will change, frame by frame. When you see a frame you like, stop moving your finger.

7. **Tap Save in the upper right corner.**

   This brings you back to your Timeline, where you can see your profile video in its natural habitat.

REMEMBER

Profile videos are visible to anyone who visits your Timeline, just like your profile picture and cover photo. Thumbnails from your profile video appear in News Feed and anywhere else on Facebook you might see a profile picture.

Life Events

The Publisher on your Timeline works the same as the Publisher at the top of your mobile News Feed. You can use it to add a status update, photo, link, location, and so on. In addition, you can use the Publisher on your Timeline to add life events.

TIP

For Android users: The mobile Publisher on your Timeline isn't expanded with a Write Something box. It's just three buttons: Status, Photo, and Life Event. Tapping on any of these buttons opens the full Publisher for sharing.

1. **From the Publisher on your Timeline, tap Life Event.**

   This opens a menu of options for life events, with the most common events listed as suggestions.

2. **Tap on the life event you want to add.**

   This opens a Publisher similar to the one you would use to add a status post or share a photo. The main difference is that the life event headline (and associated icon) is listed at the top of the post.

3. **Type in any details about the event.**

   You can tap on the event's headline to change how the headline reads, as well.

4. **(Optional) Add photos, tags, or location info.**

   Just as you would for a status update, tap on the Camera icon, Tagging icon, or Location icon, respectively, to add this info.

5. **Tap on the Clock icon if you want to change the date of the life event.**

   By default, the life event will be dated as happening on the day you post it.

6. **Double-check your privacy setting at the top of the screen.**

   The mobile Publisher displays your audience in a To: field at the top of the post.

7. **Tap post.**

   The life event appears on your Timeline.

Using Groups

You can use Facebook groups to communicate with a group of friends about anything in the world. Groups are covered in detail in Chapter 10, as is the Facebook app that's *only* for groups (named, aptly enough, Groups). However, you can access and interact with any groups you belong to through the Facebook app (see Figure 7-10).

1. **From the Facebook app, tap the More icon at the bottom of the screen.**

   This brings you to a list of apps and favorites you might want to visit from your phone.

   TIP

   For Android users: Often your groups appear listed on this page, instead of on a separate Groups page, in which case you can skip to Step 3.

2. **Tap Groups.**

   This brings you to the Groups page, shown in Figure 7-9. Each group is represented by a circle that you can tap on to visit. This page is broken into a few sections: Favorites, Recently Viewed, and Create New Group.

FIGURE 7-10:
The Groups home
on your phone.

3. Tap on the group you want to go to.

This brings you to your group's mobile Home page.

Unsurprisingly, your group's home looks a lot like its home on the website (shown in Figure 7-11). You see the cover photo on top; links to Add Members, Search, and get Info; mobile Publisher; and any recent posts displayed in the group's Timeline.

Tap into the mobile Publisher (the Write Something box) to post something to the group. You can post links, articles, text, or photos, and it will be available to all members of that group.

TIP

Just as you can on the website, you can search within a group's posts for particular information. Tap the Search icon (beneath the cover photo) to bring up a search interface. You can then enter a search term (or terms) into the Search box in the blue bar on top. The search results you see come only from the group you are currently viewing.

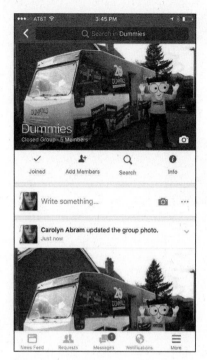

Events

I'm not going to pretend that Facebook Events is the feature you use most when you are out and about. But I will say that when you want to view an event on the Facebook app, it's because you *really* need to see that event. You either need an address, or a start-time, or a number to call, and the only place you know for sure you can find it is from that event's page. To get to a particular event, follow these steps:

1. **From the Facebook app, tap the More icon at the bottom of the screen.**

   This brings you to a list of apps and favorites you might want to visit from your phone.

2. **Tap Events.**

   This brings you to the Events page, shown in Figure 7-12. This page shows you upcoming events that you have been invited to, as well as upcoming public events that are popular in your area, and upcoming birthdays.

3. **Tap on the event you are looking for.**

   This brings you to that event's page, where you can see information about the event and its guests, as well as publish a post to the event.

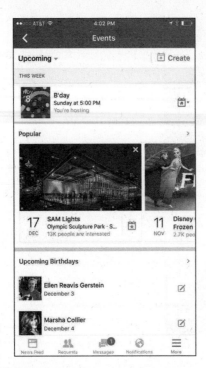

Facebook Messenger

The Facebook app is designed to let you do everything you can do on Facebook from your phone. One big part of using Facebook is communicating with your friends. Communication can happen through comments and posts, but a big piece of talking to friends is talking to them directly using Facebook messages (the details of using Facebook messages are covered in Chapter 9). Because getting in touch directly with a friend is sometimes more important when you're out and about than, say, checking out his latest photos, Facebook has built a separate app for messages. If you use the Facebook app and ever try to send a message, you will be asked to add the Facebook Messenger app as well.

Messenger handles all the chats and messages between you and your Facebook friends when you are on your phone. As a stand-alone app, you can easily get to it and use it to communicate on the go, without getting distracted by the rest of Facebook. My husband and I actually use Messenger as our chief means of communication during the day while we're at work. It's just as immediate as texting but doesn't incur any additional texting charges on our phones, and it's easy to switch from a chat on the computer screen to a chat in Messenger without losing any of what we were talking about. Messenger has all the same functionality as sending Facebook messages: You can message one person or multiple people, send photos, videos, stickers, and GIFs, and conversations are easily grouped in one place.

The Messenger app described and shown in this section is being used on an iPhone. There might be a few slight differences between it and the Android version.

Navigating Messenger

Opening the Messenger app brings you to your recent messages, shown in Figure 7-13.

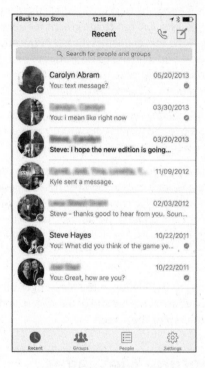

FIGURE 7-13:
Your Messenger inbox.

The bulk of the page is taken up by your messages, organized by conversation, with the most recent one at the top. Each conversation shows the profile picture of the friend (or friends) you are conversing with. Any conversations that have unread messages appear in **bold.** Each conversation has a time or date next to it reflecting the last time anyone on that thread sent a message. Use your finger to scroll down to older conversations. Tap on any conversation to open it up and view its contents or add to the conversation.

At the top of the screen is a search bar that lets you search for people and groups you might want to message. In the upper right corner are two icons. The phone icon allows you to start a phone call to a friend. The paper and pencil icon allows you to start a new message to a friend.

REMEMBER

When you use Facebook messages, new messages simply get added to any previously sent messages, sort of like your text messages on your phone. They don't get sorted by subject matter or date, only by who is talking to one another.

At the bottom of the screen are four icons.

>> **Recent (clock icon):** Tapping this brings you back to your recent messages.

>> **Groups (people icon):** Tapping this brings you to a page where you can access and create groups for easy messaging. Groups in this context are meant to function like email lists. You can create groups for things like family members or teammates — the sort of people who will frequently want to get in touch with one another — and then use those groups to send messages. Once you've created a group, messages to that group will appear with the group's name, instead of with the names of all the participants.

>> **People (bullet list icon):** This brings you to a list of your friends who also use Messenger. You can also tap to see friends who are currently active on Facebook, either from the web or from their phone.

>> **Settings (gear icon):** This brings you to a settings page where you can adjust settings for your notifications, for whether you want to sync Messenger with your phone's contact list, whether you want to give Messenger permission to access your phone's camera and photos, and settings related to making payments via messenger. You can also find links here to report a problem or search for help.

TIP

For Android Users: The locations of the menus in the Messenger inbox are swapped. Search, Phone, and New Message are at the bottom of the screen, and Recent, Groups, People, and Settings are at the top of the screen.

Viewing and sending Messages

Figure 7-14 shows how a message thread or conversation looks inside the Messenger app. It looks a lot like a text message thread, with each message contained in a speech bubble. Your messages appear on the right side, in blue bubbles, messages from other friends appear on the left side, in gray bubbles. The most recent message is at the bottom of the screen and you can use your finger to scroll up to view older messages. Your entire history of messaging with this friend can be found here. It doesn't matter whether you were messaging from phones or computers; you can go back to the beginning of it all.

At the top of the screen you can tap ‹ Recent to go back to your recent messages, and tap either the phone icon or video player icon to start a phone or video chat, respectively.

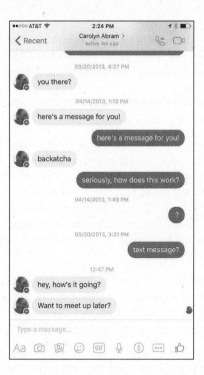

FIGURE 7-14:
A message thread
between friends.

At the bottom of the screen is a space for typing your message. Use the keyboard to enter your message and then tap the Send button on the lower right of the text you've entered.

Underneath the space for text you may notice a series of icons that show off the variety of content you can append to a message:

>> **Aa icon:** By default, when you open a message, you land in a text box where you can type your message. If you ever tap on some of the other icons but want to get back to regular old words on a screen, tap the Aa icon.

>> **Camera icon:** Tap the camera icon to open your phone's camera and take a photo or video to send to your friend. You may have to authorize Facebook Messenger to access your camera the first time you do this.

>> **Photos icon:** Tap the photos icon to attach photos that already exist in your camera roll. You can browse through your camera roll using your finger, then tap the photo you want to send. You can choose to edit a photo or send it immediately. Editing options are adding a text overlay or adding a doodle to it. Remember to tap Send (in the upper right corner) when you're done editing. You can learn more about photo editing in Chapter 11.

» **Smiley icon:** Tap the smiley face icon to add a sticker to your message. There are thousands (perhaps more) sticker options you can add. Tapping the smiley icon brings up recently used stickers; simply tap to select one. If you want to search more widely, look for the magnifying glass icon at the bottom of the screen (after you have tapped the smiley icon). This is the search icon and it allows you to browse through stickers by category.

» **GIF icon:** A *GIF* is a file format that has, over time, come to describe short (really short, often only a second or two), looped video. GIFs are used to capture emotions or sentiments that can be hard to express in words (or easy to express in words, but more fun to describe in a short motion). For example, you might choose to tell someone that something she said is exciting, or you might choose to send a GIF of a unicorn shooting a rainbow out of its horn. You can browse through GIFs by tapping the GIF icon and tapping on the GIF you want to send to your friend.

» **Microphone icon:** Tap this icon to record an audio message to send to your friend. Tap the red button that appears to start recording, then let go when you're done recording. Keep in mind that you won't be given a chance to review your recording; it just gets sent as soon as you're done.

» **Coin icon:** Tap on the coin icon to access Facebook's payments platform and send money to your friend. I go over how payments work in Chapter 9, where I discuss messages.

» **More [. . .] icon:** Tap this More icon to see apps that can integrate into Messenger, such as apps for drawing pictures to send to friends or apps that give you more options for GIFs and emoji.

» **Like icon:** Tap this to send your friend a Like, which appears as a thumbs up in the message thread.

The Facebook Family of Mobile Apps

In addition to the basic Facebook app and the Messenger app, Facebook has created a whole suite of apps that are meant to appeal to different types of Facebook users (and, often to compete with other company's apps). Some of these apps might be relevant to you, others might not be so useful. All apps can be found by searching for their name in your smartphone's app store. All are free to use. I list them here in order of how likely you are to use them.

Groups

If you use groups to communicate with friends and family, the Facebook groups app may just be for you. Much like the Messenger app bundles all the features related to messaging friends off to a stand-alone app, the Groups app provides an easy way to get directly to your groups. You can then post to any of your groups, keep up with any group discussions, and receive group notifications in one place on your phone. I belong to a group on Facebook that's made up of local parents, and I love being able to get notifications whenever parents post to the group that they are heading over to the park, so I can go meet up with them. I go over how to use Groups, including some information about the Groups app, in Chapter 10.

Moments

The Moments app is a great app for people who take a lot of photos on their phones, but only want to share them with a small number of people. Like, only the people who are in them. It provides an easy way to sync photos from a particular event with other people who were there. Instead of publishing photos to Facebook, as you might do from the Facebook app itself, Moments lets you more or less send photos from your phone to other Facebook users. You get the benefit of Facebook's photo tools, such as facial recognition, but you don't have to create big albums or share your photos more widely if you aren't comfortable doing so.

Paper

The Paper app is designed for people who just can't get enough news. News from Facebook friends, news from magazines, news from blogs, news about the world, news about celebrities, news about the arts. If you are the type of person who just wants to keep reading articles on your phone, Paper is for you. Paper provides an alternate view of your Facebook News Feed, as well as a way to subscribe to feeds about a variety of topics where you can easily browse headlines and quickly get to articles you want to read and images you want to see.

Hello

The Hello app is a pretty recent addition to the Facebook family (introduced in April 2015) and is currently only available to Android users. Hello is basically an app that connects your Facebook info to any phone calls you send or receive. In other words, even if you've never added a friend's number to your phone book, if you receive a call from him through Hello, his Facebook info will be used to identify him to you. You can also easily block calls from certain people or phone numbers.

Rooms

The Rooms app is an app for creating community spaces around topics or interests. There's obviously a lot of overlap between a room and a group, so in general I'd say Rooms helps you connect with people you might not interact with in real life. Groups tend to have some sort of real-world counterpart, whereas a room might be based entirely around sharing photos and videos from concerts, or sharing quotes on top of pictures. They are more similar to public message boards than to the sorts of groups you are most likely to belong to on Facebook. Rooms lets you take advantage of Facebook's photo-sharing features (like adding emoji) with a broader audience than just your friends. Right now, Rooms is only available on the iPhone.

Slingshot

The Slingshot app is a way to share snippets of your life with friends and prompt them to share back. You can "sling" a photo or video to a group of friends, and friends will not be able to see it until they "sling" something back to you. This creates a collaborative space for sharing the goofy, the profound, and the mundane more directly with specific Facebook friends.

Riff

The Riff app lets you make collaborative videos with your friends. The classic example of this being useful is in making a "Happy Birthday" video with your friends to celebrate someone else's birthday. Without having to collect a whole bunch of videos, you can assemble a whole bunch of well wishes, one after another, into a very happy birthday message.

Facebook on Your Mobile Browser

Viewing a web page from your phone can be extremely difficult because the information that is normally spread across the width of a monitor must be packed into one tiny column on your phone. Facebook is no exception to this, which is why the very first tip in this section is: Never go to www.facebook.com on your mobile phone. You'll regret it.

But fear not, you still have a way to carry almost all the joys of Facebook right in your purse or pocket. On your mobile phone, open your browser application and navigate to m.facebook.com — a site Facebook designed specifically to work on a teeny-tiny screen.

The first time you arrive at m.facebook.com, you're asked to log in. After that, you never (or rarely) have to reenter your log-in info unless you explicitly log out from your session, so be sure you trust anyone to whom you lend your phone.

WARNING

If you plan to use the Facebook Mobile site frequently, I recommend you have an unlimited data plan that allows you to spend as much time on the Mobile Web as you like for a fixed rate. The Facebook Mobile site is nearly as comprehensive and rich as the computer version. You can spend hours there — and if you're paying per minute, spend your life savings, too.

Mobile Home

After you log in, you see the mobile version of the Facebook Home page, shown in Figure 7-15. The design of the mobile site closely resembles the design of the regular website, with some minor differences. Some differences exist simply because of less space; the mobile site must cut to the chase while allowing you to get more information on a particular topic.

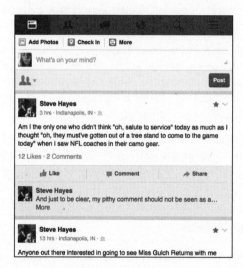

FIGURE 7-15:
Facebook Mobile Home.

TIP

To follow along with this section, you can navigate to m.facebook.com on your web browser. Just imagine what you see on about one-tenth of the screen.

In this section, I detail what you see on the Mobile Home page; I cover the other pages in the following sections.

From `m.facebook.com` you'll see these items in your Mobile Home page:

>> **Blue bar on top of the page:**

Much like on the regular website, the blue bar contains many of the links you will need most often for navigating Facebook:

- **News Feed:** Tap the newspaper icon in the blue bar on top at any time to see or refresh your News Feed. News Feed itself takes up the bulk of your mobile Home page.

- **Friend Requests, Messages, and Notifications:** The three icons across the top of your screen are used throughout the Facebook experience: Friend Requests, Messages, and Notifications. New or unread actions are marked by a red flag in each category, just like when you log in to your Facebook account from a PC. Tap any of these icons to review that category.

- **Search:** Tap the magnifying glass icon to open a search page where you can search for friends, Pages, posts, and trending topics.

- **More:** The icon with three horizontal lines opens a menu with links to the things usually found in your left sidebar: your profile, events, groups, favorites, apps, and so forth.

>> **Mobile Publisher:** Facebook makes it easy to update your status, share photos, and check in so you can spread the news the moment you're doing something you want people to know about. The mobile Publisher has the same privacy options; just tap or select the people icon on the left side of the Publisher to change who can see your post.

>> **News Feed:** News Feed itself takes up most of the space on the Mobile Home page. Scroll down to keep seeing stories from your friends. Just like on the regular site, you can like, comment on, or share your friends' posts.

Mobile Timelines

Timelines on Facebook appear more or less the same as Timelines on the regular site, except there is only one column of stuff instead of two. As you scroll down a mobile Timeline, here's what you'll see:

>> **Profile picture and cover photo:** Just a smaller version of the profile picture and cover photo you see on the regular site.

>> **Action buttons:** If you are looking at a friend's Timeline, you will see blue links indicating that you are friends and are following that person. If you aren't yet friends with that person, you'll see links to Add Friend or Message her.

Buttons labeled About, Photos, and Friends let you jump to those sections of your friend's Timeline.

>> **Publisher:** Use the mobile Publisher to leave a post on a friend's Timeline or share a photo there. Remember, things you post on a Timeline are visible to your friend's friends.

>> **Photos and Friends:** Before you start seeing your friend's posts on her Timeline, you can see thumbnails of recent photos she's added or been tagged in, as well as a preview of her friend list.

>> **Timeline:** As on the regular site, the star of the show is your friend's Timeline, where you can see her most recent posts, whether that's a status update or a photo. You can also see how many people liked or commented on her posts, and you can add to those counts yourself by doing the same.

Mobile Inbox

The Mobile Inbox functions the same as the Inbox on the regular site, but in a more compact view. In the Mobile Inbox, your most recent messages appear first. You can see the name and profile picture of the people on a given thread, as well as a preview of the most recent message sent.

Tap on a message preview to open it. When you open a mobile thread, similar to regular Facebook, the newest message is at the bottom with the Reply box beneath it. You can access a drop-down menu with action links by selecting the envelope with an arrow icon in the upper right corner (below the blue bar). You can Mark Read/ Unread, Delete, Delete Selected, Archive, Block Messages, or Report Spam or Abuse. The Mark as Unread option is particularly handy because often you read a message on your mobile phone, but don't have time or energy to type a response right then. Marking it as Unread reminds you to respond when you return to your computer.

Facebook Texts

Much of this chapter assumes you have a smartphone, or at least one with some capacity to use a browser. However, if you don't have a phone like that, you can still use Facebook via text message. To get started with Facebook Texts, you first need to enter and confirm your phone number in the Settings page from your web browser:

1. Choose Settings from the Account menu (down arrow) in the upper right corner of the big blue bar on top.

2. Click the Mobile tab on the left side of the page.

3. **Click the green Add a Phone button.**

   You may be prompted to reenter your Facebook password. When that's all squared away, the Confirm Your Number dialog box appears.

4. **Choose your country and your mobile carrier.**

   If your carrier isn't listed, you may be out of luck using Facebook Texts from your mobile phone.

5. **Click Next.**

   This brings you to Step 6, which you actually have to do from your phone.

6. **From your phone, text the letter F to 32665 (FBOOK).**

   FBOOK texts you back a confirmation code to enter from your computer.

   This can take a few minutes, so be patient.

7. **Enter your confirmation code into the empty text box.**

8. **If you see the Share My Phone Number with My Friends check box, choose whether you want your phone number added to your Timeline.**

   I find it very useful when friends share their mobile numbers on Facebook because it allows me to use Facebook as a virtual phone book. If you're not comfortable with that, simply deselect the check box. If you don't see this check box, skip to Step 10.

9. **If you see the Allow Friends to Text Me from Facebook check box, select whether you want friends to be able to text you from Facebook.**

   Again, I find this useful, so I leave this check box selected. If you don't want people to be able to text you through Facebook, simply deselect the check box. If you don't see this check box, skip to Step 10.

10. **Click Next.**

    This confirms your phone.

After your phone is confirmed, Facebook Texts are the most basic way to use Facebook on your phone. You don't need a camera on your phone or a smartphone to use Facebook Texts. Using just a simple Short Message Service (SMS) or text message, you can update your status to let people know where you are and what you're up to.

Here are the various actions you can take on Facebook via SMS; all messages get sent to 32665 (FBOOK):

>> **Update your status:** Type any sort of phrase into a text message. Your status will appear on your Timeline and in your friends' News Feeds.

>> **Add a new Facebook friend.** Send the word **add** followed by the person's email address or the word **add** followed by the person's phone number. Using your phone to immediately friend a person you meet is less formal than exchanging business cards, less awkward (and more reliable) than exchanging phone numbers, and gives you more flexibility later for how you want to get in touch.

Friending someone from your phone has all the same implications as friending someone from your computer, so friend wisely.

REMEMBER

>> **Subscribe to a friend's status updates.** Send the word **sub**, followed by your friend's name. If you have a few friends whom you like to hear absolutely everything from, this is a great way to keep up on the go.

If you subscribe to a lot of friends' statuses, make sure you have unlimited texting; otherwise, charges could pile up quickly.

WARNING

>> **Unsubscribe from a friend's updates.** Send the word **unsubscribe** followed by the friend's name. This is different from unfollowing or hiding someone in News Feed. Subscribing is different than reading News Feed since you have to elect each subscription individually. Unsubscribing is simply a way to stop getting updates sent to your phone. Your News Feed on your web browser will be unaffected by either subscribing or unsubscribing to a friend's updates.

If you realize you want fewer people's statuses sent to your phone, just unsubscribe from the ones you don't want to see regularly.

TIP

>> **Stop getting texts.** Text the word **stop**.

>> **Restart getting texts.** Text the word **on**.

Mobile settings

Once you've started using Facebook Texts, there are a number of settings you can adjust to better suit your texting lifestyle. Figure 7-16 shows your Mobile Settings tab after texts are turned on. You can get here on the regular Facebook website by clicking the Account menu (the down arrow on the right side of the big blue bar on top), selecting Settings from the menu that opens, and then selecting Mobile on the left side of the page that opens.

>> **Text Messaging:** Decide which phone number you want your texts to be sent to. You need to change this setting only if you have more than one mobile phone number listed for your account.

>> **Mobile PIN (not pictured):** Creating a mobile PIN is a security precaution you can take to keep someone from accessing any part of your Facebook account by spoofing your phone number or borrowing your phone. If you choose to create a PIN, you will need to start all texts to Facebook with that PIN.

FIGURE 7-16:
Set your
preferences for
receiving texts on
your mobile
phone.

>> **Facebook Messages:** Click Edit to open a drop-down menu where you can specify which messages warrant a text. You can choose to receive a text whenever someone sends you a Facebook message from either his computer or his mobile phone, or never.

>> **Daily Text Limit:** The Daily Text Limit allows you to modify the number of text messages you receive per day.

WARNING

If you have a mobile plan for which you're charged per text message (and you're exceedingly popular), use the settings that limit the number of messages Facebook sends you per day. Otherwise, you may have to shell out some big bucks in text message fees.

Remember to click Save Changes after updating this setting.

>> **Time of Day:** You can choose to only get texts from Facebook at certain times of the day, so that your phone doesn't bother you when you're sleeping (or while you're at work, perhaps).

Mobile notifications

Just when you thought you were done with Facebook Texts settings, I introduce a whole 'nother bunch of settings to further fine-tune your Facebook Texts experience. To get started, head to the Notifications tab of the Settings page and click Edit next to the Text Message section.

From this section, you can change the following settings:

>> **Turn text notifications on or off.** Fairly self-explanatory, although it's worth noting that even if you turn off these notifications, you can continue to use the SMS commands I describe earlier in this section to update your status, add a new friend, and so on.

>> **Decide which actions are text-worthy.** Choose up to three categories to be notified about via text: be notified when someone comments on your posts or status updates, when you receive a Friend Request or have a Friend Request you sent confirmed, and whether to receive texts about everything else, which encompasses actions like being tagged in a photo or receiving an Inbox message.

>> **Receive text notifications from friends only.** This check box controls whether you want to receive a text only when you receive an Inbox message from a friend. This means that if, for example, a non-friend sends a message to your Inbox, you will not be notified by text.

3

Connecting with Friends on Facebook

IN THIS PART . . .

Finding and adding friends

Sending messages

Managing your inbox

Creating groups

Sharing with groups

Chapter 8

Finding Facebook Friends

Hundreds of sayings abound about friendship and friends, and most of them can be boiled down into one catch-all adage: friends, good; no friends, bad. This is true in life and also true on Facebook. Without your friends on Facebook, you find yourself at some point looking at a blank screen and asking, "Okay, now what?" With friends, you find yourself at some point looking at photos of a high school reunion and asking, "Oh, dear. How did that last hour go by so quickly?"

Most of Facebook's functionality is built around the premise that you have a certain amount of information that you want your friends to see (and maybe some information that you don't want *all* your friends to see, but that's what privacy settings are for). So, if you don't have friends who are seeing your posts, what's the point in sharing them? Messages aren't that useful unless you send them to someone. Photos are made to be viewed, but if the access is limited to friends, well, you need to find some friends.

On Facebook, the bulk of friendships are *reciprocal,* which means if you add someone as a friend, he has to confirm the friendship before it appears on both Timelines. If someone adds you as a friend, you can choose between Confirm and Delete Request. If you confirm the friend, *Congrats!* You have a new friend! And if you don't, the other person won't be informed.

If you're low on friends at the moment, don't feel as though you're the last kid picked for the team in middle-school dodge ball. There are many ways to find your friends on Facebook. If your friends haven't joined Facebook, invite them to join and get them to be your friends on Facebook as well as in real life.

What Is a Facebook Friend?

Good question. In many ways, a *Facebook Friend* is the same as a real-life friend (although, to quote many people I know, "You're not real friends unless you're Facebook friends"). These are the people you hang out with, keep in touch with, care about, and want to publicly acknowledge as friends. These aren't people you met on Facebook. Rather, they're the people you call on the phone; stop and catch up with if you cross paths at the grocery; or invite over for parties, dinners, and general social gatherings.

In real life, there are lots of shades of friendship — think of the differences between acquaintances, a friend from work, an activity buddy, and best friends. Facebook gives you a few tools for negotiating these levels of friendship, which I cover in the "Managing How You Interact with Friends" section of this chapter. But by default, most friendships are lumped into a blanket category of "friend."

Here are the basics of what it means to be friends with someone on Facebook, though you'll notice that each of them comes with a few caveats on how it can be adjusted by either person in the friendship.

>> **They can see all the stuff on your Timeline (like your posts and other information) that you have set to be visible to Friends.**

Remember, this is what happens by default. You can actually control which friends can see which posts more specifically by learning about your privacy options (which you can do in Chapter 6), and about Friend Lists, which I go over later in this chapter.

>> **They see new posts you create in their News Feeds on their Home pages.**

Again, the information your friends see in their News Feed depends on the audience you've chosen to share each post with. It may also depend on your friends' News Feed settings.

>> **You can see their posts and other information on their Timelines.**

This, of course, depends on their own privacy settings, but in general, you'll be able to see more as a friend than you did before you became friends.

>> **You see new posts from them in your News Feed on your Home page.**

This depends on your friend's sharing settings, but more importantly, you can control whose posts you see in your News Feed through managing your own News Feed settings and preferences. I cover how to do this later in this chapter.

>> **You'll be listed as friends on one another's Timeline.**

This is a small detail, but it's important in understanding the difference between becoming friends with someone and simply following someone. Lots of people, especially public figures or people who have a business of some sort, allow you to subscribe to their posts without becoming friends. In these cases, you see their posts on your Home page, but they won't see your posts unless they choose to subscribe to you.

Adding Friends

Facebook has some unique verbiage that it has created over time. One of the most important Facebook verbs is "to friend." *Friending* is the act of adding someone as a friend. You may overhear people use this casually in conversation: "Oh, you won't believe who finally friended me!" And now, you too, will be friending people.

Sending Friend Requests

Now that you know what a friend is, it's time to send some requests, and maybe even accept some pending ones. For the purposes of this example, I searched for the Timeline of Carolyn Abram using the search box in the blue bar on top. I cover using Search to find friends later in this chapter, so for now just remember that as you type, Facebook tries to autocomplete what you're looking for, meaning search results will appear below the search box as you type, as shown in Figure 8-1.

When you see the person you think you want to add, click on her face; this takes you to her Timeline. At the bottom of her cover photo, sort of in the middle of the page is an Add Friend button. To add this person as a friend, all you need to do is click the Add Friend button. You can see this button in Figure 8-2. Clicking this button sends a Friend Request. When she accepts, you'll become friends.

TIP

Depending on people's settings, you might not see an Add Friend button. If you can't send a friend request, you can usually send the person a message or follow his public posts without becoming friends first.

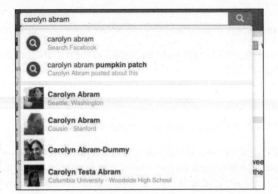

FIGURE 8-1:
The search
results for
Carolyn Abram.

FIGURE 8-2:
A Timeline before
I become a friend.

REMEMBER

You won't be friends with someone until she confirms your Friend Request. After she confirms, you're notified by a red flag appearing above the notifications icon in the blue bar on top.

So what does your potential friend see after you send a request? That is a brilliant segue into the next topic, accepting Friend Requests.

Accepting Friend Requests

When you receive a new request, a little red flag appears over the Friends icon in the big blue bar on top of each page. You may also be notified in your email or on your phone. Figure 8-3 shows an example. The number in the red flag indicates how many Friend Requests are waiting for you.

FIGURE 8-3:
Someone wants
to be your friend!

Clicking this icon opens the Friend Requests menu, as shown in Figure 8-4.

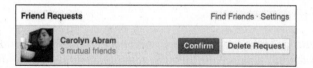

FIGURE 8-4:
Click Confirm or
Delete Request.

To accept the Friend Request, click the Confirm button. You now have a friend. To reject the request, click Delete Request. When you click Delete Request, you will have the option to mark that request as Spam if you suspect it is from a fake profile.

TIP

Some people worry about clicking that Delete Request button. If you're not sure what you want to do, you can always leave the request untouched. But never hesitate to click Delete Request for someone you really just don't want to be friends with. Facebook won't notify her that you ignored her request.

Choose your friends wisely

Generally, you send Friend Requests to and confirm Friend Requests from only people you actually know. If you don't know them — *random Friend Requests* — click Delete Request. Accepting a Friend Request from random people has a tendency to ruin the Facebook experience — it puts random content in your News Feed, exposes your own content to people you don't know, and is generally a bad practice. Remember the lecture you got about choosing good friends when you were in high school? It's every bit as true now.

If there are people you don't know personally but find interesting (such as a celebrity or public figure), you may be able to subscribe to their posts without becoming friends with them (more on that in the "Following" section near the end of this chapter). If that's not a possibility, you could add them as friends and then add them to your Acquaintances or Restricted Friend List, if you use these lists to control your privacy.

It's quality, not quantity

Another common misperception about Facebook is that it's all about the race to get the most friends. This is very, very wrong. Between the News Feed and privacy implications of friendship, aim to keep your Friend List to the people you actually care about. Now, the number of people you care about — including the people you care about the most and those you care about least — may be large or small. I don't think it matters how big or small your list is as long as the people you care about most are on it. In fact, one of the reasons for a number of the Friend List management tools that I cover in this chapter is because, over time, people's Friend Lists tend to bloat.

As you change jobs or cities or start a new hobby, you add more and more friends, but that doesn't displace the fact that you care about friends from your past. The Friend List management tools aim to help you keep track of the people you care about most, and not get distracted by the more distant friends.

Finding Your Friends on Facebook

How do you get to the people you want to be your friends? Facebook is big, and if you're looking for your friend John, you may need to provide some more detail. Facebook has a couple of tools that show you people you may know and want as your friends, as well as a normal search-by-name functionality for finding specific people.

Import your friends

If you're someone who uses email to communicate with your friends and family, an easy list of people you'd probably want to add as Facebook friends already exists — your email address book. Facebook has a tool, which I refer to as *Friend Finder*, that matches email addresses from your email address book to people's Timelines on Facebook. Because each email address can be associated with only one Facebook account, you can count on such matches finding the right people.

With your permission, when you import your address book, Facebook also invites people who don't have a Facebook account but whose email addresses match those in your address book to join Facebook. Sending invites this way causes Friend Requests to automatically be sent to those people. If they join based on an invite you send, they find a Friend Request from you waiting when they join.

To add your email contacts, you need to give Facebook your email address and email password. Facebook doesn't store this information. It just uses the information to retrieve your contacts list that one time.

Chances are that you came across the opportunity to add your personal contacts when you first set up your account. The following steps make several assumptions — namely, that you use web-based email (Hotmail, Yahoo! Mail, and so on), that you haven't already imported your contacts, and that the address book for the email has a bunch of your friends in it.

Here's how to add your email contacts to your Friend List:

1. **Click the Friends icon on the big blue bar on top.**

The Friend Request menu opens.

2. **At the top-right corner of the menu, click the Find Friends link.**

Figure 8-5 shows the Add Personal Contacts section of the Find Friends page. It's usually on the right side of the page.

FIGURE 8-5:
An unfilled Friend
Finder.

3. **Select the email or instant message service you use by clicking its icon.**

This may be Windows Live Hotmail, AOL, iCloud, or Skype.

4. **Enter your email address in the Your Email field.**

5. **Enter your email password (not your Facebook password) in the Email Password box and then click Find Friends.**

TIP

These instructions are meant for first-time users of the Friend Finder. If you've used it before, or if you're currently logged in to your webmail client, you may see some fields prefilled or additional pop-up prompts asking you for your permission to send information to Facebook. Don't worry if what you see on the screen doesn't match the figures here at the beginning.

If Facebook finds matches with the emails in your address book, you see a page that looks similar to Figure 8-6. (If Facebook doesn't find any friends, go to Step 6.) These people are the ones Facebook thinks you may know.

6. **Click the check box to the right of anyone's name and photo to add him as a friend.**

   Everyone you select receives a Friend Request from you.

   After you click either Add as Friends or Skip, you land on the Invite Friends portion of Friend Finder. Here you find a list of contact names and email addresses. These emails or phone numbers are those that don't have matches on Facebook.

7. **(Optional) Invite people to join Facebook and become your friends.**

   Any of your contacts who have not yet joined Facebook can be invited to join. If they do join, when they sign up they will receive a friend request from you. By default, all the contacts on your list are selected. You can:

   - *Invite all these contacts:* Make sure the Select All/None box is checked and click Send Invites.

   - *Invite none of these contacts:* Make sure the Select All/None box is unchecked and click Skip.

   - *Invite some of these contacts:* Uncheck the Select All/None box and then use the check boxes to the left of their email addresses to choose which ones you want to invite to join Facebook. Selected check box = invite sent; deselected check box = no invite sent.

   After you make your selections, click Send Invites or Invite to Join. If you don't want to send any invitations, click Skip.

After taking all these steps, I hope you manage to send at least a few Friend Requests. Don't be shy about adding people you know and want to keep up with; it's not considered rude to add people as your friends. Your friends need to confirm your requests before you officially become friends on Facebook, so you may not be able to see your friends' Timelines until those confirmations happen.

If the whole experience yielded nothing — no friends you wanted to add, no contacts you wanted to invite — you have a few options. You can go through these steps again with different email addresses. You should probably use any email address that you use for personal emails (from where you email your friends and family). If that's not the problem, you have more ways to find friends.

People you may know

After you have a friend or two, Facebook can start making pretty good guesses about others who may be your friends. Facebook primarily does this by looking at people with whom you have friends or networks in common. In the People You May Know box, you see a list of people Facebook thinks you may know and, therefore, may want as friends. People You May Know boxes appear all over the site — on the Find Friends page, on your Home page, and sometimes on your Timeline or on the right side of a group. Usually the boxes include a list of names, profile pictures, and some sort of info like how many mutual friends you have or where the other person attended school. These little tidbits are meant to provide context about how you might know that person.

Anytime you find yourself looking at the People You May Know list and you do, in fact, know someone on the list, simply add that person as a friend by clicking the Add Friend button or link by the person's name. If you're not sure, you can click a name or picture to go to that person's Timeline and gather more evidence about whether and how you know that person. Then you can decide whether to add that person as a friend. If you're sure you don't know someone, or if you do know someone but are sure you don't want that person as your Facebook friend, mouse over the person's picture and click the X or Remove button that appears. After you do that, she stops appearing in your People You May Know list. As you add or remove people from the list, more pop up to take their places. This fun can last for hours.

Find classmates, co-workers, neighbors, and mutual friends

Especially when you are just getting started on Facebook, it can be helpful to look for large groups of people you might want to become friends with. A common assumption is that you are likely to be friends with your friends' friends, as well as with people you've gone to school with and worked with over the years. To find these people, use the Search for Friends box, located beneath the Add Personal Contacts box on the right side of the Find Friends page.

The Search for Friends box, shown in Figure 8-7, lets you isolate potential friends along a variety of criteria. You can mix and match these criteria or just use one at a time.

>> **Name:** You can search for an individual by name by entering the name into the Search for Someone box.

>> **Mutual Friend:** You can browse for friends by looking at your existing friends' friends. Facebook displays the names of three friends, and you can view their friends by selecting the check box next to their name. You can also enter a friend's name into the Enter Another Name box in order to add him to this list. One good way to hone in on the people you most likely want to be friends with is to select at least two names from your existing Friend List. If two (or three, or four . . .) of your friends are friends with the same person, the chances are even greater that you want that person to be your friend.

>> **Hometown:** If you've previously listed your hometown on your Timeline, you can select it here to view people with the same hometown. If you haven't, or if you have another city you consider a hometown, you can enter a city name into the Enter Another City box to view potential friends from the old stomping grounds.

>> **Current City:** If you've previously listed your current city on your Timeline, you can select it here to view other people who live there. If you haven't, or if you have another place you consider to be where you *really* live, you can enter a city name into the Enter another City box to view potential friends from the current stomping grounds.

>> **High School:** If you've previously listed any high schools you attended on your Timeline, you can select them here to view other people who went there. You can also use the text box to enter in a high school name and look for people who went there.

>> **College or University:** Any colleges you listed as having attended appear here. Select any of them to see people who went there as well, or enter a college name into the text box to search for people who went there.

>> **Employer:** Any employers you've listed on your Timeline appear here. Click the check boxes to select or use the text field to search for a different employer.

>> **Graduate School:** If you've listed a graduate school you attended on your profile, you can click here to select it. You can also enter any school's name into the text field to see people who went there.

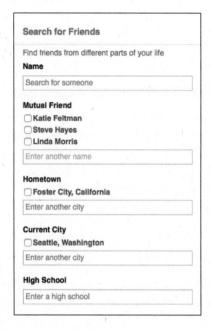

Search for Friends

Find friends from different parts of your life
Name

Search for someone

Mutual Friend
☐ Katie Feltman
☐ Steve Hayes
☐ Linda Morris

Enter another name

Hometown
☐ Foster City, California

Enter another city

Current City
☐ Seattle, Washington

Enter another city

High School

Enter a high school

FIGURE 8-7:
Use the check boxes to find your friends.

REMEMBER

When you select more than one check box, it actually shows you *fewer* people because now Facebook is looking for people who both worked at Mom's Pizza *and* went to Hamilton High School. To find more people, select only one check box at a time.

Find what you're looking for: Search

When you're just starting on Facebook, you want to find everyone you know as quickly as possible and build out your Friend List. After you build it a bit, though, what if you find other people who may want to be your friends? Facebook Search offers you the capability to seek out certain friends by name.

WARNING

The search box in the blue bar on top lets you search a whole lot of things on Facebook: pages, groups, events, even things your friends have posted. But most of the time, you use it to search for people. It may be people you're already friends with and you just want to go to their Timelines. Sometimes it will be people you aren't friends with yet but whom you want to reach out to.

Basic Search can be a little confusing because Facebook autocompletes the names that you type and assumes you're trying to get to your friends' Timelines. If you're the type of person who is used to pressing the Enter key to begin a search, this can lead you landing on friends' Timelines when you meant to search for someone *else* named Waldo.

You'll wind up using Search two basic ways. The first way is if the name of the person you're looking for (or at least someone with the same name) appears in the autocomplete menu. You can accomplish that sort of search following these steps:

1. **Begin typing the name you're looking for in the search box.**

   Pay attention to the people who appear in the autocomplete menu. Facebook displays first your friends and then friends of friends. There's a good chance that you may find the person you're looking for in this menu.

2. **If you see the name in the autocomplete menu, use your mouse or arrow keys to highlight the person you're looking for.**

3. **Click the name or press Enter.**

   This brings you to the person's Timeline, where you can verify that you know the person and add him as a friend.

If you don't see the person you're looking for, don't despair; you can get more results by typing the person's full name into the search box and selecting the Search option from the auto-complete menu. This brings you to a search results page, where you can see all matches for the name you just searched for.

TIP

If you know you have the right name but there are too many search results, try going to the Find Friends page and using the Name field in the Search for Friends box. When you get the results, you will then be able to add more details like where that person is from or where they went to school to help you find your friend.

Managing How You Interact with Friends

After you do all the work of finding and adding your friends, at some point, you may find that things are feeling a little out of control. Chances are you may be seeing posts from someone you find uninteresting; you might not be sure who, exactly, can see your own posts anymore. At this point, it's a good idea to get acquainted with the way Facebook automatically helps you end the madness, as well as some of the more specific and manual things you can do.

Friend Lists

Friend Lists are subsets of your giant list of friends. Friend Lists are a way of organizing your friends into lists to make your Facebook experience even easier and more personalized to you and your types of friends. Organizing your friends into lists allows you to share different types of information with different sets of friends. For example, your best friends may get to see your party photos, and your family may get to see your wedding photos. This is a custom privacy setting you can use all over Facebook.

Pre-fab lists

Facebook creates three lists for you when you join that you can choose to add people to:

>> **Close Friends:** You can add your best friends to your Close Friends list. Adding them to this list signifies to Facebook that you want to see a lot more of them in your News Feed. You can also then select this list as a custom privacy setting when you are posting something to Facebook.

>> **Acquaintances:** The opposite of the Close Friends list. This list is meant to be a place where you can cordon off the people you don't know as well. They may be perfectly nice people, but they aren't necessarily the people you want to share everything with. Anyone you add to this list won't appear as often in your News Feed.

>> **Restricted:** This list is for people you want to add as friends but don't want to see posts that are visible to friends. In other words, people on this list see only posts that you choose to make public.

By default, these lists will be empty. In other words, Facebook creates lists that get special treatment for certain parts of Facebook, but it's up to you to let Facebook know who belongs on any of them. To learn how to add and remove people from these lists, you can skip a few pages ahead to the "Managing lists" section.

Smart Lists

Smart Lists are the lists that Facebook both creates and populates on your behalf. These lists are created automatically based on shared characteristics of your friends. Here are some common Smart Lists:

>> **Family:** Based on information you've entered about your family, they may show up on this Smart List.

>> **<Your High School>:** If you've caught up with a lot of old friends on Facebook, a Smart List might be created so you can post photos from the reunion or share memories just with them.

>> **<Your college/university/workplace>:** Similar to a high school list, depending on the information your friends have listed on their profiles, additional Smart Lists may be created for these groups. For example, I have Smart Lists for Stanford (where I was an undergraduate), CCA (where I was a graduate student), and Facebook (where I used to work).

>> **<Your current/former city> area:** Depending on the info you and your friends have listed on their profiles, Facebook creates lists people who live in or near your current city.

TIP

You can change the radius on a location-based list. From that list's page, click the Manage List button and then select Edit Radius from the menu that opens. You will then be able to change the radius of who is included from as small as 5 miles to as large as 200 miles.

Although Facebook is smart, it's not perfect. Although these lists will be mostly accurate, you may find that you have to do some editing to them. The accuracy of the lists may also depend on how you want to use your lists. For example, you may want your Family list to make it easy to share with just your immediate family and, therefore, need to remove the more distant members. Or you want it to be a giant family reunion all the time, in which case, you need to add some of the third and fourth cousins once removed to the mix.

Creating your own Friend Lists

Smart Lists can usually help you figure out whom you want to share your own posts with. But sometimes you may want a specific list that Facebook can't figure out. This might be a sub-sub-group, like all the people you played Frisbee with in college. In these cases, you can create your own list.

To create a Friend List, follow these steps:

1. **From the Home page, hover your mouse over the Friends item in the left sidebar and click More.**

   This brings you the Friend Lists page, which displays a list of your friends.

2. **Click the Create List button at the top of the page.**

   The Create New List window appears, as shown in Figure 8-8.

3. **In the List Name box, type the name of your list.**

   Maybe something like **Dummies** for the Dummies Team.

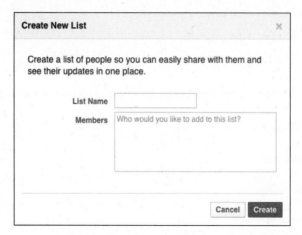

FIGURE 8-8:
Creating a Friend
List.

4. **Add friends who belong on this list by typing their names in the Members box.**

   Facebook autocompletes as you type. Press Enter when you highlight the correct friend's name.

5. **Click Create.**

   Now, wherever Friend Lists appear on Facebook, including where you set privacy, you have access to the new list you just created.

REMEMBER

Friend Lists you create are private, so even if the list you're messaging is known in your mind as *Annoying Co-Workers*, all that your annoying co-workers see is a list of names. Members of Smart Lists are able to see the name of a list they've been added to.

Managing lists

Regardless of the type of list, adding and removing people from a list follows the same steps:

1. **Click Friends in the left sidebar.**

   The Friend Lists page appears.

2. **Click on the list you want to manage.**

   For example, clicking on Close Friends opens the Close Friends page. If you already have friends on this list, you will see a feed of stories only from friends on this list. If you don't have any friends on this list yet, you'll see a big blank space where a feed would normally appear. On the right side of the page is an On This List box, shown in Figure 8-9.

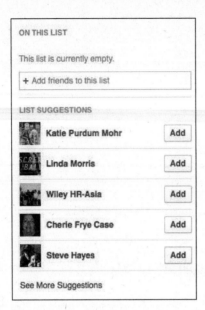

3. **To add people to a list, enter their names in the text box in the On This List section.**

    Facebook autocompletes as you type. Select your friends' names when you see them. You can also click the Add button next to any of the names Facebook suggests to add them to the list.

To remove people from a list (starting from the list's page), follow these steps.

1. **Click the Manage List button in the upper right corner of the list's page.**

    A menu appears.

2. **Select Edit List.**

    A pop-up window displays the names and pictures of all members of the list.

3. **Hover over the person you want to remove.**

    A small X appears in the upper right corner of the person's picture.

4. **Click the X.**

    Repeat Steps 3 and 4 for each person you want to remove.

5. **Click the Finish button when you're done.**

TIP

Updating lists on the go

After you create and start using your lists, you can continuously add people to them at the same time you add them as friends.

When you're the one sending a Friend Request, follow these steps to also add the person to a particular Friend List:

1. **From his Timeline, after you've added him as a friend, click the Friend Request Sent button.**

   A menu appears asking you if you want to add that person to any of your Friend Lists. By default, your most commonly used lists will appear at the top.

2. **Click the list you want to add your friend to.**

   You may need to select Add to Another List to see your full menu of lists.

If you're the one receiving the Friend Request, you can follow these steps to add someone to a list as you accept the request:

1. **From the Friend Request menu, click Confirm.**

   This adds the person as a friend. The Confirm button changes to a Friends button.

2. **Click the Friends button that appears.**

   A menu with options related to becoming this person's friend appears.

3. **Click the list you want to add this person to.**

   You may need to select Add to Another List to find the list you want.

If at any point you remember, *Hey, I meant to add So-and-So to the Teen Girl Squad list*, simply visit that person's Timeline and click the button that says Friends at the lower right of the cover photo. The menu covered in the preceding steps appears, which you can use to add So-and-So to the right list.

Groups

Groups are, in many ways, a more public version of Friend Lists. Instead of your friends not knowing which list they're on, friends are always notified when they're added to a group. In turn, they can add their friends to the group if they think the information shared there is relevant to them. Groups are extremely useful for sharing information that only a specific group of people might care about. For example, a funny video from a family gathering that perhaps only members of your crazy family will understand is a good candidate to be shared via a family group. I cover Groups in great detail in Chapter 10.

News Feed options

In addition to News Feed views, you can use News Feed options to help you control which friends' posts you see when you log in to Facebook. For example, if one of your friends changes her profile picture back and forth between two photos all week long, it might start to clutter up your News Feed. Similarly, I've heard lots of complaints about reading political screeds you disagree with during the election season. Chapter 4 covers controlling your News Feed and which posts you see from which people in great detail.

Following

Following is a way of saying you really really want to see someone's posts. On some social media sites, following is the primary way of interacting with other people. On Facebook, following is baked into friending someone or liking a page. However, you actually can follow someone you are not friends with. In fact, by default when you add a friend, you follow them, even before they've accepted your friend request. The catch here is that following someone without becoming their friend means you only see their public posts in your News Feed.

Occasionally, certain people (usually public-ish figures) have allowed people to follow their public posts without requesting friendship. Following someone is as easy as — actually, it's easier than — adding someone as a friend. Navigate to that person's Timeline and click the Follow button. To unfollow her, click that same button (it now says Following) to open a menu of options. Select the Unfollow option (the last item on the menu).

If you're someone who plans on posting lots of public updates or are a public figure (locally or nationally), you can allow people to follow you instead of becoming your friend (they'll also be able to add you as a friend, but you won't have to accept their requests for them to see your posts). Follow these steps to allow people to follow you:

1. **Click the upside-down triangle in the upper-right corner of the big blue bar on top.**

   A menu of options appears.

2. **Select the Settings option.**

   The Account Settings page appears, which has a menu running down the left-hand side.

3. **Select Followers from the left menu.**

   The Follower Settings page appears.

4. **Use the privacy menu to choose who can follow you.**

   You can toggle between Everybody and Friends. If you choose Everybody, congrats! People can now follow your public posts. Once you opt into this feature, more settings appear on the page. These settings allow you to specify how followers can find and interact with your Timeline. This is also where you can connect a Twitter account so your tweets will also be imported to Facebook.

Unfriending

It happens to everyone: After a while, you start to feel like a few people are cluttering up Facebook for you. Maybe you just feel like you have too many friends, or maybe you and a friend have legitimately drifted apart. Maybe you had a big falling-out and just need a break. Don't worry; Facebook friendships are not set in stone. You can *unfriend* just like you friend people.

To unfriend someone, do the following:

1. **Go to the person's Timeline.**

2. **Click the Friends button.**

   A menu appears that is for assigning people to Friend Lists. The last item in this list is Unfriend.

3. **Click the Unfriend link.**

   A window pops up asking if you're sure you want to remove this friend.

4. **Click the Remove from Friends button.**

   Take a moment of silence. Okay, that was long enough.

TIP

People aren't notified when you unfriend them, but people who care about you (that is, family, close friends) have a tendency to notice on their own that, hey, you're not in their list of friends anymore. This can sometimes lead to awkwardness, so it might be worth using your privacy settings to further limit these people's knowledge of your life *before* you unfriend them.

Lots of people go through periodic friend-cleaning. For example, after changing jobs or moving, you may notice that you want to keep in touch with some people from that chapter in your life; others, you just don't. Unfriend away.

Chapter 9

Just between You and Me: Facebook Messages

C hances are that you're someone who communicates with other people online. You may use email all the time or use instant messaging programs like AIM or Skype. If you have a smartphone, you probably check email and text messages on it as well. Facebook has similar functionality and integrates into all these programs. In other words, Facebook Messages stitches together email, texting, and instant messaging with a Facebook twist.

One special component of Facebook's messaging system as opposed to other systems is that you no longer have to remember email addresses, screen names, or handles. You just have to remember people's names. The other benefit is that your entire contact history with specific people is saved in one place. I refer to this ongoing conversation as a *conversation* or *thread*.

If this sounds confusing to you, think of it as mirroring the fact that usually you don't simply stop speaking to someone in real life. You may have asked a friend about getting lunch next week, but then you pick up the conversation again a week later to figure out where you want to go for lunch, or to let her know that you're running 30 minutes late. Even after the lunch is over, chances are one of you will want to meet up again soon.

Instead of splitting all of these up into discreet emails, texts, or phone calls, Facebook thinks of your communication as one long, ongoing discussion that lasts the entirety of your friendship.

Sending a Message

Figure 9-1 shows the basic New Message chat window. I generated this by clicking the Messages shortcut in the big blue bar on top (it looks like two overlapping word bubbles) and clicking the Send a New Message link from the menu. A New Message chat window opens from the bottom of the page. This interface, with the message window floating over the Facebook in the background, is designed to look like an instant messaging service. Remember, on Facebook there's no real distinction between chats (instant messages) and messages. Everything gets saved to your message history. Anytime you click on a Message button or link from a friend's Timeline or Timeline preview, a new message window opens, with that friend's name pre-filled in the To: field.

FIGURE 9-1:
The New Message chat window.

The New Message chat window has only two fields for you to fill out: a To: field and a message box where you type the text of your message. Unlike emails, this chat window has no spaces for CC, BCC, or a subject line.

To address your message, simply start typing the person you're messaging into the To: field. Facebook autocompletes as you type, and you'll see that it tries to fill in the names of friends as well as friends of friends. In other words, it assumes you are messaging someone you know somehow. When you see the name you want, highlight it and click or press Enter. You can type more than one name if you want to have a conversation with more than one person at the same time.

After you enter a friend's name, you can click in the Type a Message field to start typing your message. Enter your message in the message box. There are no rules around what goes here. Messages can be long or short, fat or skinny, silly or serious — whatever you have to say. Press Enter to send your message (or Shift + Enter to create a paragraph break). If you have an existing message thread already started with that person, you see that your new message simply gets added to the bottom of the conversation.

Figure 9-2 shows a chat window between friends. It is designed to look somewhat like the text message interface on your phone. A profile picture of your friend is shown on the left side of the chat window, next to the white speech bubble that contains her message. Your own messages appear in blue anchored to the right side of the chat window. You can scroll up to see older messages.

FIGURE 9-2:
A conversation between friends.

Sending links

If you want to add a link to a website or article to a message, you can copy and paste it into the message box. Facebook then generates a preview of the article so your friend has more info before clicking the link. You can remove this preview by clicking the X in the upper right corner of the preview. If you ever choose to share a link from another website (many news sites have links to share articles, for example) you can select to share it in a private message and accomplish the same thing: sending the link and a preview to a friend, as well as explaining why you are sending it.

Sending photos

To add photos to your message, click the camera icon at the bottom of the chat window. Doing so opens up an interface for navigating your computer's hard drive, so make sure you know where your photo is saved. If you want to share a photo that is already on Facebook, the easiest way to share it is to navigate to that photo, tap the share link at the bottom of the photo, and choose to share it in a private message.

Sending stickers

Stickers on Facebook are a lot like the stickers you might have once used to adorn a school notebook or a letter from summer camp, except, you know, digital. There are virtually infinite sticker options you can send to friends, from smiley faces to ones related to various holidays to ones created by specific artists.

Clicking on the smiley face icon at the bottom of a chat window opens the Search Stickers menu, shown in Figure 9-3.

FIGURE 9-3:
Selecting stickers.

You can browse through the various categories of stickers here. Click a category name to see stickers in that category, then scroll down to see the full collection. As soon as you click on a sticker, it is sent to your friend.

Along the top of the Search Stickers menu are recently used sticker collections you have used. You can also click on the plus sign here to go to the sticker store. In the sticker store you can browse through sticker option and choose to add them to the options you see when you go to send a sticker. After you have added a sticker collection (by clicking the green Free button), close the sticker store by clicking the x in the upper right corner. Then, when you reopen the Search Stickers menu, you'll see your new sticker pack along the top of the menu.

Sending GIFs

A *GIF* is a file format that supports animated images. But when people talk about GIF, they are usually referring to how gifs are used on the Internet: as ways to share a clip, usually on a loop, that captures a funny moment, emotion, or thought. So, for example, if someone tells you something that exasperates you, you could send a gif of a famous person rolling his eyes to communicate that you are, in fact, rolling your eyes as well.

You can click on the GIF icon at the bottom of the chat menu to browse through gifs that you can send to a friend. By default, Facebook shows you trending gifs (in other words, gifs that other people have been sending). You can search for the type of gif you are looking for using the Search box at the top of the GIF menu. As soon as you click on a gif, it is sent to your friend.

Sending payments

You can use Facebook to send money to friends. This may or may not be a feature that you find useful. It requires both you and your friends to enter debit card info into Facebook, which it stores securely in its systems. Facebook does not charge a fee to send payments between friends.

If you've never sent money before, follow these steps the first time you want to send money to a friend:

1. **Tap the $ icon in the bottom of a chat window with your friend.**

   A payment interface appears, shown in Figure 9-4.

2. **Type the amount of money you want to send into the payment field.**

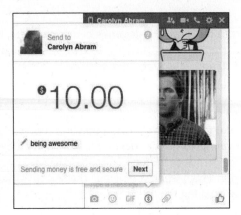

FIGURE 9-4:
Sending money
to friends.

3. **(Optional) Type in the reason for the payment in the "What is this payment for?" field.**

4. **Click the Next button.**

   A window opens for entering your debit card info for making the payment.

5. **Enter your debit card info into the relevant fields.**

6. **Click the Pay button.**

   The money has been sent to your friend. He will need to enter a debit card into Facebook in order to receive the money.

REMEMBER

Payments only work with debit cards. Using debit cards allows you to pay directly from your bank account, and allows your friend to put money directly in her bank account. Make sure when you enter your card info, it is for a debit card, not a credit card.

WARNING

Once you've sent money, you can't cancel the payment. Be sure that you are okay with the money leaving your account before you click the Pay button.

Sending attachments

Much as it does in many email programs, the paperclip icon signifies attaching files to a message. Clicking the icon opens an interface for searching and selecting files from your computer's hard drive. You can attach photos, videos, documents, and so on.

Video chat

Video chat is a pretty cool way to talk with friends via video (assuming you both have webcams). Keep in mind that you can video chat with only one friend at a time. Here's how to begin a video chat:

1. **Begin a conversation with a friend.**

2. **Click the video icon to begin video chat.**

If you've already set up video calling, this step begins the call. A pop-up window appears, letting you know that Facebook is calling your friend.

If you haven't yet used video calling, a pop-up window appears, asking you if you want to set up video calling.

If you aren't asked to set up video calling, skip to Step 4.

TIP

3. **Click Set Up or Install.**

A file download initiates. Each web browser and operating system may have slightly different instructions. In general, you need to save the file to your hard drive and run it to complete the setup.

After the setup is complete, a new pop-up window appears telling you that Facebook is calling your friend. In the future, you'll be able to skip Step 3 and go straight to Step 4 when you want to use Video Chat.

4. **Wait for your friend to pick up.**

When he does, a video of him appears in a new window above Facebook. A video of you (what your friend is seeing) appears in the upper corner of this window.

5. **To end the call, close the window.**

REMEMBER

Video chat assumes both people have webcams either built in or installed in their computers. If you don't have a webcam, Video chat isn't really for you.

Message Options

Chances are if you send out a message, pretty soon you'll get a reply. Depending on your settings and whether you're logged in to Facebook, when you receive a new message, you see either a new chat window open up (like you're receiving an IM) or a little red flag on your Home page over the Messages icon in the big blue bar on top. Click the flag to open the Inbox preview; then click the message preview to open the conversation in a chat window at the bottom of your screen.

At the top of each chat window is a blue bar displaying the name of the person you're chatting with and several icons.

>> **Add Friends:** This icon, which shows the outlines of two people and a plus sign, allows you to add someone to a conversation you are having with a friend. Click this to open up a text field where you can enter a friend's name. Remember to click the Done button when you have finished adding names. This opens a new conversation among all of you, and will appear as a separate conversation in your Recent Messages.

>> **Start Video/Voice Call:** Assuming your computer is up to the task, you can click on the video camera icon or the phone icon to start a video or voice call, respectively, with your friend.

>> **Options:** Click the gear icon to view a full menu of options related to your conversation:

- **See Full Conversation:** Selecting this option brings you back to the Inbox view of your entire conversation history.

- **Add Files:** Just like when you're sending a message from the Inbox, you can select this option to search your computer for files you want to share.

- **Add Friends to Chat:** If you're discussing something with a friend and think that you need the opinion of someone else, you can add her to the chat, which opens a new group chat window.

- **Turn Off Chat for <*Friend*>:** Friends may be more likely to chat with you when they see that you're online. If any friend in particular is popping up a little too often, you can turn off chat for that individual person. From that point on, she will no longer see you in the Chat menu.

- **Mute Conversation:** Just like with the Inbox, you may find a chat thread growing annoying or irrelevant. You can mute the conversation to stop being notified whenever someone replies.

- **Delete Conversation:** Deleting a conversation is permanent. It deletes the entire history of your messages with a friend. Keep in mind that deleting it only deletes it for you. Your friend will still be able to see the message history if she so chooses.

- **Block Messages:** You can prevent someone from sending you messages by choosing to block messages from her. If people are harassing you on Facebook, you might also consider blocking them entirely or reporting them for harassment.

- **Report as Spam or Abuse:** If you're getting odd messages from a friend promoting something he wouldn't normally promote, there's a chance his account was *phished,* meaning someone who shouldn't have gained access to it. Report the spam messages to protect yourself, your friend, and other users from having the same thing happen to them.

» **X:** Clicking the X in the upper right corner of your chat window closes the chat. Remember, everything you've said remains saved in your message history, so never worry about closing a window.

Inbox

After you're comfortable sending and receiving messages to and from your friends, it's time to find out about the Inbox, where all your messages are collected for easy viewing at any time. Facebook's Inbox is organized a bit differently from traditional email Inboxes. Most significantly, messages you receive from people you aren't friends with and are unlikely to know are separated from the conversations you're having with friends.

To understand how Facebook Messages works, take a look at how your Messages Inbox is organized on the page. First, navigate to the Messages Inbox from your Home page by clicking the Messages icon (it looks like two overlapping word bubbles) in the big blue bar on top. This opens a preview of your Inbox. Click on See All at the bottom of the preview to view your Inbox. Figure 9-5 offers a snapshot of a sample Inbox.

FIGURE 9-5: Welcome to Facebook Messages.

The main portion of this page, the center area, is where conversations appear. As you click different conversations on the left, the contents of that conversation — messages, photos, links, and files — appear in the main portion of the screen.

The left side of your Inbox displays your messages. Each conversation gets its own line in the Inbox. Like your email Inbox, these conversations are organized from most recent near the top to older ones toward the bottom of the page. As you scroll down, Facebook will continue to load your conversation history.

Figure 9-6 shows a close-up of two conversation previews. The top one is a one-on-one conversation with a single friend. That friend's profile photo and name is displayed. The bottom one is a conversation between more than one person; those friends' photos and names are displayed. On the right side of each is the conversation's timestamp. And below the name of the person or people you're talking to is a preview of what was most recently said.

FIGURE 9-6: Conversation previews in the Messages Inbox.

When you hover your mouse over a particular conversation, two icons appear in the lower right corner:

» The **little circular button** allows you to mark a conversation as read or unread. The button appears filled when the message is unread and unfilled when the message is read.

» The **little X icon** allows you to archive a conversation. *Archiving* conversations allows you to move them to a different part of your Inbox until a later time, when they become relevant to you again.

Conversations in the Inbox

In Figure 9-7, you can see a conversation as it appears in the Inbox.

The most important thing to notice is that all the content here is the same content you would see in a chat window. Facebook doesn't care where you wrote a message from, all of it goes into your message history. The most recent message is on the bottom of the page. Scroll up to see older messages.

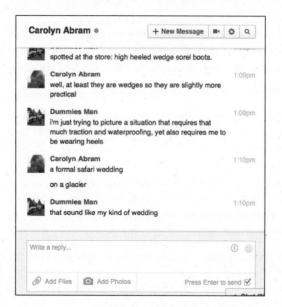

FIGURE 9-7:
A conversation in
the Inbox.

Unlike a chat window, which looks more like a text message interface, messages viewed from the inbox tend to look a bit more like an email thread. Your friend's name and photo appears above their message, and you can see your own name and photo appear above the messages you sent.

At the bottom of your conversation, below the most recent message, is the message composer. The message composer is similar to the one you use in the chat window, though it lacks a button for sending GIFs. You can click the Add Files or Add Photos button below the composer window to add files or photos. Click the gray money icon or smiley icon on the right side of the composer to send payment or stickers, respectively.

One additional option you have from the composer is Press Enter to Send. The Press Enter to Send option, located next to the Reply button, allows you to send messages simply by pressing Enter. Some people love this; other people hate it. To turn it on, check the Press Enter to Send box. If you need a paragraph break in whatever you're writing, press Shift+Enter. Deselect the box to turn it off. When it is turned off, a Reply button appears. You can then click that button to send your message.

At the top of your conversation page are four buttons: the New Message button, the Start Video Call button (video camera icon), the Actions button (gear icon), and a Search button (the magnifying glass).

The New Message button opens a blank conversation with a blank To: field and an empty message box.

Clicking the Search icon (the magnifying glass) opens a Search box you can use to search the entire conversation for something. Trust me, after a few back and forths between you and your friend, when you need to remember something she said a while ago, this comes in handy.

The Actions button features a drop-down list. Many of the options are the same as the ones detailed in the "Message Options" section of this chapter. In addition, from here you can:

>> **Open in Chat:** Opening a message thread in Chat allows you to send messages back and forth with your friend while you're browsing Facebook. It opens a small chat window at the bottom of the screen. You can then chat with your friend even when you leave the Inbox.

>> **View Photos in Thread:** Choosing this allows you to view all the photos that have been shared in a given thread. Click on any photo to enlarge it, which then gives you a chance to download that photo to your computer or forward that photo in to other people in new messages.

>> **Mark as Unread:** Choose Mark as Unread to mark the conversation as having unread messages (makes sense, right?). After you choose this option, the main Messages Inbox appears, and the conversation is highlighted in blue.

>> **Archive:** Choose Archive to save your conversation in the Archives of your Inbox. You won't see the conversation when you look at your Inbox, but you will be able to go view it at any time. If one of you starts talking to the other again, the conversation will reappear in your Inbox.

>> **Mute Conversation:** Muting a conversation means you will no longer be notified about incoming messages. In other words, Chat windows won't open up while you're browsing Facebook, and you won't get any alerts on your phone about new messages (related to this particular conversation). You can choose to mute a conversation for one hour, until tomorrow morning, or until you choose to Unmute it.

>> **Delete Conversation:** Deleting a conversation deletes the entire message history. You won't be able to see it or search through it ever again, so make sure you really want to delete it. Remember, the person (or people) you are talking to will still be able to see the entire conversation unless they choose to delete it as well.

>> **Delete Messages:** This option allows you to delete some (or all) of the messages from any given conversation. After a message is deleted, you can never get it back.

REMEMBER

Just because you've deleted a message doesn't mean your friend has deleted it. So if you send some private information and then delete the message, your friend can still see that information unless he deletes it as well.

>> **Block Messages:** You can choose to block messages from a certain person if he is bothering or harassing you. This option only prevents him from messaging you; if you want to entirely keep him from interacting with you on Facebook, you will need to block him from the Blocking section of the Settings page.

>> **Report Spam or Abuse:** If you're getting odd promotional messages or abusive messages or messages asking for your password or other information a friend would not need to ask for, click to report spam or abuse. Even if these messages are coming from a friend, there's a chance her account has been accessed by a spammer and reporting it will help prevent them from doing more damage in your friend's account.

>> **Keyboard Shortcuts:** This option opens a window with keyboard shortcuts that do . . . nothing. As far as I can tell, it's a practical joke on the part of Facebook. Well played, Facebook. Well played, indeed.

>> **Feedback:** This option takes you to the Help Center, where you can submit specific feedback to Facebook for improvements to Messages.

Conversations with lots of people

You can message more than one person at a time. Doing so creates a new conversation among all the people you message. Everyone can see and reply to the message. So if you send a message to Mike, Jenny, and Steve, a new conversation is created. When you're looking at that conversation, you can see all the messages that have been sent by all the people involved.

Much like the individual conversation, you can read this exchange from top to bottom, with the most recent message appearing at the bottom of the page. You can scroll up to read earlier messages.

TIP

Below the most recent message is a box for replying. The main thing to remember about group conversations is that you cannot reply individually to members of the conversation. When you reply, all members of the conversation see your reply.

As you're reading, you can see who said what by looking at the names and profile pictures identifying each message. Each message is separated and has a timestamp so you can see when it was sent. At the top of the page, just like with a one-on-one conversation, is the New Message button, the Actions button with a drop-down list, and a Search button for searching through the content of the conversation.

Along with the options found for a conversation between you and one friend, some additional options exist for group conversations:

>> **Add People:** If you feel that someone has been left out of the conversation, or if you suddenly realize he should be part of the conversation, choose this option to add him. You're asked to enter the name(s) of the person you want to add. The person added can see the entire conversation history, even though he wasn't added until the middle of the conversation.

>> **Edit Participants:** You can select this option to view all the participants on a given thread and click to remove them if their presence is no longer needed. Keep in mind that other members of the conversation will be able to re-add that person if they choose, so if someone is using a message thread to harass you, you may need to leave the thread yourself and block that person to prevent her from being able to contact you in that way.

>> **Edit Conversation Name:** You can give a conversation among many people a particular title. This helps differentiate it in your Inbox, especially if you have an individual conversation happening with someone who is also in a group conversation with you. There are no rules around conversation names, but other members of the conversation will be told what name you give it.

>> **Edit Conversation Picture:** Similar to a conversation name, a conversation picture appears in the inbox and is a quick way to differentiate among different conversations that may be happening at the same time. Click to upload a conversation picture from your computer's hard drive.

>> **Leave Conversation:** If a conversation isn't interesting to you anymore, choose this option to leave it. If you do leave a conversation, the other people on the thread will see a small notice that you have left.

>> **Create Group:** If you find yourself talking with the same set of people all the time, you may want to create a group for a richer set of options for sharing. Groups make it easier to share and talk about things like links, photos, and documents. To learn more about how to use groups for sharing, check out Chapter 10.

>> **Create Event:** If the topic of conversation is about planning to go somewhere and do something, you can create an event for that something. Creating an event from a message thread will automatically invite everyone on the message thread to that event.

GROUP CONVERSATIONS

A Facebook group is a way for a group of people to connect and share in the same place on Facebook. Creating and using groups is covered in detail in Chapter 10. But it bears mentioning here that one of the useful features of Groups is the capability to start message threads and chats with the members of your group.

To start a group chat, follow these steps:

1. **Navigate to the group's page on Facebook.**

2. **On the right side of the group page, click the link that says Message.**

   A window opens that allows you to select from the group's members.

3. **Select the group members you want to be part of the chat.**

   Click the faces of all the people you want included in the message thread. If you want everyone included, click Select All at the bottom of the window.

4. **Click the Start Chat button.**

   A chat window opens at the bottom of the screen. Use it as you would any chat window.

The Chat Menu

The Chat menu is like a buddy list that you may use for instant messaging. You can always see a minimized version of the Chat menu in the lower right corner of Facebook. It is a tiny bar that says Chat (n), where n is the number of friends currently online. Click on the bar to open the Chat menu, shown in Figure 9-8.

By default, the Chat menu displays the friends you message and chat with most often, in alphabetical order. A green dot next to their names means they are active on Facebook. A mobile phone icon next to their names means they have downloaded the Facebook app for iPhone or Android and can receive your message on their phones. No icon means they aren't currently logged in or have turned off Chat. Messages you send to them will go to their Messages Inboxes.

Beneath the friends you message most often are the rest of your friends, as well as any existing group conversations you might want to participate in. Scroll down to browse your friends.

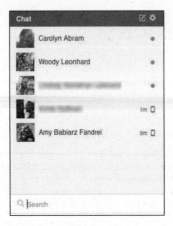

FIGURE 9-8:
The Chat menu.

At the bottom of the Chat menu is a Search bar. To quickly find the friend with whom you want to chat, or to see if that friend is even online, start typing that friend's name in the Search box at the bottom of the Chat menu. As you type, the list of online friends narrows to only those with names that match what you've typed. After you see the friend you were looking for, click the name to start chatting.

When the Chat menu is expanded, two icons appear at the top of the its window. There is a pencil and paper icon you can click to open a new message window. There is also a gear icon that, when clicked, offers these options for adjusting your Chat experience.

>> **Chat Sounds:** If Chat Sounds is on (signified by a check mark next to this option), you will hear a sound every time you receive a new chat.

>> **Block Settings:** Selecting this option brings you to the Blocking section of the Settings page. There you can block people who may be bothering you through messages from messaging you, or from interacting with you at all on Facebook.

>> **Advanced Settings:** Selecting this option reveals a pop-up window of options, shown in Figure 9-9. These options help you control who can and cannot see you as online and available in Chat.

Three options are available here:

- **Turn Off Chat for Only Some Friends:** If there are just a few friends you don't want knowing when you're online, enter their names into the box below this option, and they won't be able to chat with you. Instead, messages from them will go straight to the Inbox.

- **Turn Off Chat for All Friends Except:** This is the option if you really don't want to talk to anyone except your nearest and dearest via Chat. When you select this option, you then enter the names of people or Friend Lists that will be able to see that you're online.

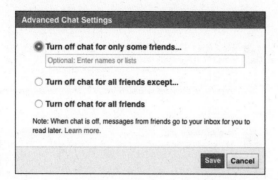

FIGURE 9-9:
Choose who can
chat with you.

- **Turn Off Chat:** This option means no one will see that you're online or be able to send you instant messages via Chat. Instead, messages sent to you will go to the Inbox.

» **Close All Chat Tabs:** If you are simultaneously chatting with lots of different people and want to close all the chat windows you have open, select this option. All your chat tabs will close (but don't worry, none of your conversations will be lost).

» **Turn Off Chat:** This is the same as the "Turn Off Chat" option found in the Advanced settings. Lots of people like to use Chat sometimes but not at other times (for example, I sometimes turn Chat off when I'm working from home). This option lets you easily toggle Chat on and off.

» **Turn Off Video/Voice Calls:** If you are okay chatting by typing, but don't want to receive any voice or video calls, use this option to toggle video and voice calls on and off.

REMEMBER

Turning off chat simply means messages won't pop up, unbidden, at the bottom of your screen. Messages will still be delivered to your Inbox and you will be able to read and respond to them there.

Messaging on the Go

Facebook integrates its messaging system seamlessly with its smartphone apps. It even has an app just for messaging: Facebook Messenger. You can see the same message three different ways in Figure 9-10. The first is a message in the Message Inbox, the second is in a Chat window, and the third is using the Facebook Messenger app for iPhone.

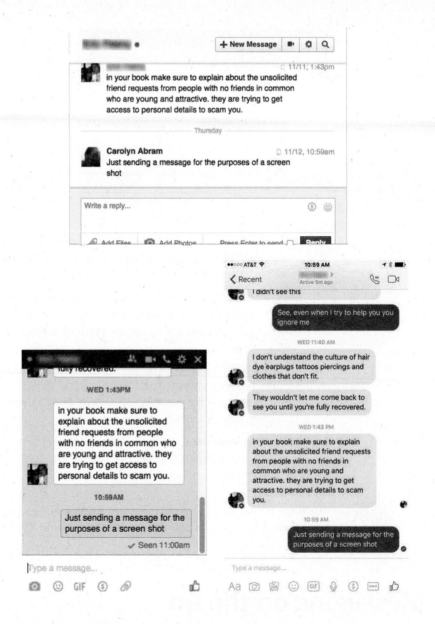

FIGURE 9-10:
The same conversation, viewed three ways.

Notice that in each view, you see the same conversation, with slight adjustments to allow for the amount of screen real estate you get.

The Facebook Messenger app is pretty simple. It displays the contents of your Inbox: a list of conversations from most recent at the top to oldest at the bottom. You can tap any conversation to open it and read it. When you're looking at a conversation, tap into the text box at the bottom of the screen to open a keyboard for typing a new message.

To start a new conversation, when you're looking at your Inbox, tap the new message icon (it looks like a pencil inside a box) in the upper right corner of the screen. This opens a New Message screen, where you can enter the names of the people you want to message and the message itself. This should feel eerily similar both to sending a text message and to sending a message on Facebook.

If you're using an app like Facebook Messenger on your phone, you will likely be notified on your phone each time you get a new message. You can adjust these settings from the app itself. If you want to know more about using Facebook from your mobile phone, check out Chapter 7.

Chapter 10

Sharing with Facebook Groups

By now, you've probably individually found and linked yourself to your friends. Hopefully, you've also started sharing with them by posting statuses and photos and links, and you're seeing your News Feed fill up with much of the same. All that is great, but as you share certain things, you may find yourself thinking, "Really, only people from work will care about this article" . . . or . . . "Really, only the people in my parent support group will find this funny." Now, you could elect to use Friend Lists to choose who can see these posts. But you also want those people to talk about it with you. *Groups* are a way to truly interact with a group of people, almost as though you were sitting in the same room.

Groups can be large or small. They may have very active participants or have many people who just sit back and watch for relevant info. Some groups may involve ongoing forums; others may exist only to achieve a goal (for example, planning a big event), and the conversations will peter out over time. Groups can be open to anyone in the world to join, or they can be more private affairs that require invites to join. This chapter covers how to use the features of groups, as well as the many options that come with using, creating, and managing groups.

Evaluating a Group

When someone adds you to a group, a notification is sent to your Facebook Home page. The next time you log in, you'll see a little red flag over the notifications icon (the globe icon in the big blue bar on top). When you click it, it will tell you what the group is and who added you; then you can go check out the group and make sure you want to be a part of it.

REMEMBER

Although your notification may explain that you were invited to join the group, these invitations work by adding you to the group until you decide to leave it. It's sort of like saying "RSVP regrets only" on an invitation to a party.

When looking at a group, you'll find a lot to pore over, as you can see by the sample group shown in Figure 10-1. Groups are designed to look a bit like a Timeline — the cover photo, the Publisher, and the recent posts from group members in the center of the page should all look familiar to you. Other parts of the group are unique, such as the members and description box on the right side of the page.

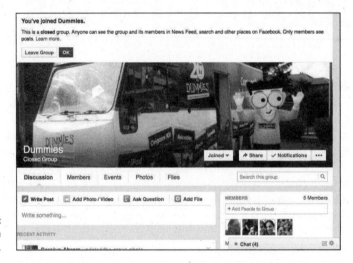

FIGURE 10-1:
Checking out a group.

When you first visit a group, before doing anything else, make sure you want to be a part of that group. Although I'd like to think I'd join any group that would have me, I, for example, wouldn't want to join one that's about garnering support for a cause I don't believe in.

The first thing I look at when I get added to a group is the privacy settings. Facebook puts a big banner at the top of the group to make sure you understand the privacy setting of the group you just joined. Facebook Groups have three privacy options:

>> **Public:** Open groups are publicly visible and available for anyone to join. In other words, anyone who uses Facebook will be able to see the posts and the members of that group.

>> **Closed:** Closed groups are only partially visible. Anyone on Facebook can see the name of the group and its members but won't be able to see the posts until becoming a member of the group. People are added to closed groups by other members, or they can request to join it.

>> **Secret:** Secret groups are the most private groups. No one other than those who have been added to it can see that it exists, who its members are, and the posts that have been made. If you're invited to join a secret group and you choose to leave it, you won't be able to add yourself again later on, because you won't be able to find it.

Once I know who can see that I joined a group and any posts I make, I go on to look at the group name and who added me. Usually that's enough for me to know if I belong there or not. For example, if a friend from my parenting group adds me to a November/December Parents group, I know I want in. When a more distant friend adds me to the I Love Puppies group, I may do a bit more research to see if I want to be a member.

If I'm unsure about wanting to be part of a group, I check out the recent posts in the center of the page. These posts are ones that group members have shared directly with this group. In other words, say that I post a funny photo of my husband mowing the lawn with the baby on his back. If I post it from my Timeline or from my Home page, all my friends will see it. It won't appear in the Recent Posts section of any of my groups. If I post it to my New Moms group, only group members will see it, and it will appear in the group's recent posts section.

Looking at the recent posts tells me a lot about what to expect from a group in the future. Are posts relevant to the group or not? Is there a lot of discussion or not? Am I interested in the posts I'm seeing? These are the sorts of things I think about when I decide whether to stay in a group.

If the group was created only recently, you may not find many posts yet. You can still learn a bit about the group by checking out the group description (shown in Figure 10-2). On the right side of the group's page (next to the recent posts) is a box that shows members of the group, as well as a description section. If it's a long description, click the See More link to view the full text.

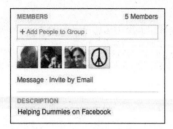

FIGURE 10-2:
About this group.

After you acquaint yourself with the group, you can decide whether you want to remain a member or leave the group. If you decide you want to leave, follow these steps:

1. **Click the Joined button at the bottom of the cover photo.**

When you click the Joined button, a drop-down menu appears.

2. **Select Leave Group from the drop-down menu.**

A pop-up window opens, asking if you are sure that you want to leave the group.

3. **Decide whether you want to prevent members of the group from adding you again by selecting or deselecting the Prevent Other Members of This Group from Re-adding You check box.**

You can leave this check box selected, which means you'll never be able to be added to the group again; or if you think maybe in the future you might want to be part of the group, deselect this check box.

4. **Click Leave Group.**

More often than not, however, you'll usually decide to stay in the group, which actually brings you to the point of sharing and communicating with fellow group members.

TIP

If you're considering leaving a group because you're being inundated by notifications about new posts, you can instead just turn off notifications from that group. From the group, click the Notifications button at the bottom of the cover photo. You can then select whether you want notifications about All Posts, Highlights (as determined by Facebook's algorithms), Friends' Posts, or None (Off).

You can get back to any particular group from your Home page by clicking its name in the left sidebar. Groups you look at frequently should be in the Favorites section, and ones you visited recently should be in the Groups section of the left sidebar. You may have to click the See More link to see a full list of your groups. Click the name of the group you want to visit.

Sharing with a Group

The whole point of creating or joining a group is to enable communication, so get started communicating! Ways that you can get involved include posting to the group, commenting on others' posts, chatting with group members, and creating files or events.

Using the Publisher

Posting to the group works the same way as posting from a Timeline or the News Feed. There is a Publisher at the top of the Recent Posts section of the page. A few sections of the Publisher appear for groups that *don't* appear on Timelines or in News Feeds: Create Poll and Add File.

REMEMBER

The important thing to remember is that when you share something from a group, you're sharing it only with the members of that group. And if you're a member of a group, you also need to remember that you may not be friends with everyone in the group. In a big group, you may actually be sharing with many people who typically couldn't see the things you post.

Although the Publisher works almost the same way across Facebook, all the options are briefly explained here within the context of groups.

Writing a post

Posts are basically like status updates that you share only with the members of a group (unless the group is open, in which case anyone can see your post). You might post an update just to say "Hi" or to start a discussion with group members. To write a post, follow these steps:

1. **Click in the Publisher (where it says Write Post at the top of the group page).**

2. **Type whatever you want to say in the box.**

   For the Dummies group, this might be something like "What do people think of the new groups?" or "Does anyone know how I can start group chat?" You can also post a link to a relevant article or website in this space. You can see a post in progress in Figure 10-3.

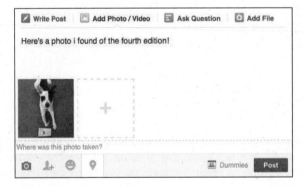

FIGURE 10-3: What's on your mind?

3. **(Optional) Add photos, tags, activity, or location information to the post.**

   Click the appropriate icon at the bottom of the Publisher to add any additional information or content.

4. **Click Post.**

   Your post appears in the group, and group members may see it in their notifications and News Feeds.

TIP

If you want to share a link, usually some sort of article, video, or other online content that you want the group to see, simply type or paste the complete link to whatever you want to share, along with your thoughts or opinions, in the Publisher.

Creating a poll

One of the added features of Groups is the Create Poll feature. Polls allow group members to gather information in a more efficient way than simply using a post and then sorting through the comments for the answers. Members can vote on polls from the Recent Posts section of the group. To ask a question and poll your group, follow these steps:

1. **Click Create Poll in the Publisher at the top of the group page.**

2. **Type your question in the Ask Something box.**

   You can see a poll being created in Figure 10-4.

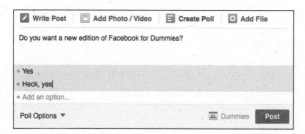

FIGURE 10-4:
You've got
questions?
Facebook has
answers.

3. **Type your first option into the first Add an Option section.**

4. **Add more options until you're finished.**

   Facebook keeps adding more boxes as you fill up these first few, so just stop when you're ready.

5. **Click on Poll Options at the bottom of the Publisher to choose whether people can add more options and if they can select more than one option.**

   The Allow Anyone to Add Options check box controls this setting. Allowing this options means people can add more answers to a poll. If before people could choose only Dog or Cat, for example, group members may be able to add Hedgehog as an option. Depending on how big your group is, this choice may or may not be significant. You can also choose, via check box, whether people have to make one selection or can choose multiple answers from the poll.

6. **Click Post.**

   The question then appears in the group and in members' notifications and News Feeds. They will be able to vote, like, or comment on the question.

Adding a file

Adding files is part of the Files and Docs feature of groups. If you're part of a group that has real-world things to accomplish — for example, a literary magazine to put out or a wedding welcome letter to create with your family — you can add files to help you collaborate on these documents. From the Publisher, you can upload files from your computer or, if you use Dropbox (an online file storage and sharing site), from your Dropbox.

I cover the different ways to add and create files in the "Files and docs" section, later in this chapter.

Reading and commenting on posts

After you create a post or see a post that someone else has created, that's when things really get interesting, because members of the group can start talking about it. On Facebook, that means commenting, liking, and following posts.

One unique feature of posts to Facebook Groups is that you can see who has read those posts. At the bottom of each post, look for a check mark icon. Next to it, Facebook displays the number of people who have seen that post. If you hover over the number, you will see a list of names. These are the people who went to the group after you posted. It doesn't necessarily mean they've read your post in depth yet.

Below each post are two links of actions you can take:

>> **Comment:** When you see something you have an opinion on, click Comment below the post and let everyone know. (This action means you'll be notified about all subsequent posts.) Often, you'll see a blank comment box already open beneath a post, just inviting you to chime in.

>> **Like:** When you like anything on Facebook, the person who created that content is notified that you like it. It's an easy and quick way to say "Good job!" when you don't have an active comment to make.

Depending on your notification settings, you may be following all posts in a group, only ones from friends, or none at all. When you comment on a post or vote on a question, you automatically start following that post. Following a post means you'll be notified every time there's a new comment on that post, which can be awesome if you're actively talking about something with group members, or kind of annoying if there are too many people commenting. If that happens and the notifications are bothering you, you can always unfollow a post by taking these steps:

1. **Hover your mouse over the post you no longer want to follow.**

   A small down arrow appears in the upper right corner of the post.

2. **Click the down arrow to open a menu of options.**

3. **Click Turn Off Notifications For This Post.**

TIP

Just as you can unfollow a post you previously commented on, you can choose to follow a post you haven't commented on. If you want to read what others have to say, but don't have anything to add at this time, follow the preceding steps for the post you want to follow. Instead of the Turn Off option, you will see a Turn On option. Select that option to be notified every time a group member adds a new comment on that post.

Chat

One of the most exciting features of Groups is the capability to talk in real time with other group members, so you can do something like ask when people are leaving for that Ultimate game.

When you chat with group members, any member of the chat can add more people — even if they aren't in the group — to that chat. The people who are added can see the entire conversation, even parts that happened before they joined in.

To chat, follow these steps:

1. **From your group, click the Message link on the right side of the page.**

    The Message link is located underneath the members displayed on the right side. When you click, a window opens displaying all the group members (as shown in Figure 10-5).

FIGURE 10-5:
Choosing the group members you want to chat with.

2. **Choose whether you want to chat with all members of the group or just specific people.**

   For example, you might want to ask everyone if there's any interest in meeting for a drink after work, or you might have a very specific question for your two editors. Select as many (or as few) people to include in a chat by clicking on people's faces.

3. **After you choose the people you want to talk to, click the Start Chat button.**

   A chat window opens at the bottom of your screen.

TIP

If you don't want to be bothered by conversations others start, you can always use the Options menu of the chat window to mute or leave the conversation. For more details on using Facebook Messages and Chat, check out Chapter 9.

Events

Your group may be based around an activity, so Facebook makes it easy for people to plan events for group members, whether it's a game of pick-up or a family reunion. To create an event, follow these steps:

1. **From your group's page, click the Events tab (it's next to the Members tab underneath the cover photo).**

   The group's Event Calendar appears. This calendar displays any upcoming group events.

2. **Click the Create Event button.**

   The Create New Event pop-up window appears, shown in Figure 10-6. If you've read Chapter 12, about planning events, these fields should look familiar.

3. **Fill out the event details.**

   Event details include the event's photo, name, location, date, and time.

   By default, a check box at the bottom of the screen notes that all members of that group will be invited.

4. **Decide whether you want to invite all group members by selecting or not selecting the Invite All Members check box.**

   Regardless of what you choose, all members will be able to view the event and RSVP. However, if you leave the Invite All Members box selected, when group members are notified about the event, they will be told that you were the one who invited them.

Create Event for Dummies

Event Photo

Add Event Photo

For best results, use a 1920 X 1080 pixel image (16:9 aspect ratio)

Event Name   Add a short, clear name

Location   Include a place or address

Date/Time   11/18/2015   9:00 PM   PST   + End Time

Description   Tell people more about the event

☑ Invite all members of **Dummies**   Cancel   Create

FIGURE 10-6:
Creating an event for group members.

5. Click Create.

The event's page appears. Here you can add an event photo and keep track of RSVPs. (I cover this type of event maintenance in detail in Chapter 11.) As the event creator, you're automatically listed as attending. The post appears in the group's recent posts and in members' News Feeds.

To RSVP to a group event, follow these steps:

1. Click the event's name in the Recent Posts section of the group.

The Event Home page appears. This page shows you more information about the event, including who has already RSVP'd.

2. Choose Join, Maybe, or Can't Go.

All these options are big blue buttons on the right side of the page. To find out more about how to interact with the event as it draws near, check out Chapter 12.

Files and docs

Other features that are particularly helpful to groups representing real-world projects are files and docs. These are ways to create and share files among group members. *Docs* are more like wikis in that they are able to be edited by all members of the groups. *Files* are more like a file-sharing system that allows people to upload and retrieve files from user to user.

Docs

To create a document that all group members can see and edit, go to the Files tab of the group and click the Create Doc button. This brings you to the New Doc page, where you can enter a title and body text. Some basic formatting options are at the top of the body section, as shown in Figure 10-7. After you enter all your text, click the Save button.

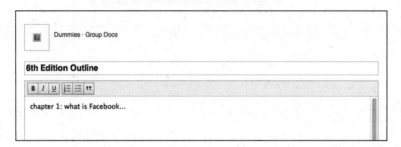

FIGURE 10-7:
What's up, doc?

After you create a doc, any member of the group can view it, comment on it as though it were any other post, and also click Edit Doc next to it in order to change it. You can always find docs that have been created by clicking the Files tab. Click on the title of the document you want to change from the list of documents displayed on the screen and then click the Edit button when you are looking at that doc. You can also leave comments on docs in order to let group members know what you liked or didn't like about them.

REMEMBER

Docs are a *collaborative* way to write something: As with a wiki, anyone who is a member of the group can edit and delete docs that have been created. (A *wiki* is a website that anyone can make changes to. Probably the most famous example is Wikipedia.) So if you've written something you don't want changed in any way, keep it on your own computer.

Files

Like docs, files are shared among group members, but unlike docs, they cannot be edited within Facebook. Instead, members upload, download, and then reupload files they want changed. Or they simply upload files they want to share, and other group members are then able to download the files to their own computers.

From the Files tab, click the Upload File button to add files from your computer. To download files that others have added, click the Download link to the right of the file.

Creating Your Own Groups

Now that you understand how to use groups, you may find an occasion to create your own group. As a group's creator, you're by default the *group administrator*, which means that you write the group's information, control its Privacy settings, and generally keep it running smoothly. You can also promote other members of the group to administrator. This grants them the same privileges so that they can help you with these responsibilities.

Here are the steps you follow to create a group:

1. In the Groups section of the left sidebar, click the Create Group link.

The Create New Group window appears (see Figure 10-8).

2. Enter a group name into the Group Name field.

Choose something descriptive, if possible, so that when you add people to it, they'll know what they're getting into.

3. Type the names of people you want to add to the group.

At this time, you can add only friends as members. Facebook tries to autocomplete your friends' names as you type. When you see the name you want, press Enter to select it. You can add as many — or as few — friends as you like. If you forget someone, you can always add him later.

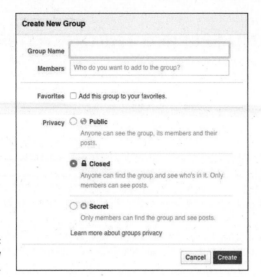

4. **Choose whether you want to add the group to your Favorites section.**

   You will always be able to get to this group from the Groups section, but if you think you'll be using it a lot, it might be convenient to have it in the Favorites section as well. Just check the "Add this group to your favorites" check box if you do want it there.

5. **Choose the privacy level for your group.**

   Groups have three privacy options:

   - *Public:* Public groups are entirely available to the public. Anyone can join simply by clicking a Join button; anyone can see all the content the group posts. This type of group is best for a very public organization that wants to make it easy for people to join and contribute.

   - *Closed:* By default, your group is set to Closed. This means that anyone can see the list of members, but only members can see the content posted to the group by its members. People can request to join the group, but admins (like you) need to approve those requests before the requesters can see group info.

   - *Secret:* Secret groups are virtually invisible on the site to people who haven't been added to the group. No one except members can see the member list and the content posted.

     People who have been added to the group can also add their friends, so if you're protecting state secrets, you might want to find a more secure method. I recommend carrier pigeons.

WARNING

6. **Click Create.**

The window changes to the icon selection window.

7. **Choose an icon from the options and click the OK button.**

Facebook tries to provide an option for lots of common group types. If you can't find anything that represents your group, click Skip.

After you choose your icon and click OK, you're taken to your group's Home page.

Personalizing Groups

After you've set up your group, there's still some work to do to help friends and potential members evaluate it and make sure they want to join.

Adding a cover photo

If your group does not yet have a cover photo, the space where the cover photo will be should have two buttons: Upload Photo and Choose Photo. Click Choose Photo to choose a photo from either photos that you have added to Facebook or photos that have been shared within your group (if your group is brand new, you likely won't have any photos in the latter category). You can browse any photos you have added to Facebook. Click on the photo you want to use to select it. This brings you back to your group, where you can click and drag the cover photo to reposition it. Click the blue Save Changes button in the bottom right corner of the photo when you are done.

You can also choose to upload a photo from your computer's hard drive. Simply click the green Upload Photo button, navigate to the photo you want to use, and click upload. You then return to the group, where you can click and drag the cover photo to reposition it. Click the blue Save Changes button in the bottom right corner of the photo when you are done.

You can change your group's cover photo at any time by hovering your mouse over the cover photo and clicking the Change Group Photo button that appears in the upper right corner of the cover photo. You can then choose where you want to select a photo from (group photos, your photos, synced photos, or uploaded from your computer).

Add a description

Remember, when people are deciding whether or not to join a group, they need to know what that group's purpose is. One way to let them know is to create a group description. To add a group description, look over on the right side of the group for the Members and Description box. Click on the Add a Description link, then type your group's description into the box that opens.

This is a good place to outline why the group exists, and maybe some do's and don'ts for the group. For example, you might want a group for discussing parenting challenges, but you might want to request parents not post photos of their children's potty training successes. You may want teammates to coordinate travel to a Frisbee game but not smack talk the other team. Be descriptive and honest. And click the blue Save button when you're done.

You can edit your group's description at any time by clicking the blue Edit link next to the Description section.

Group Dynamics

Now that you know how to create, share, and navigate your way through a group, it's time to look at some of the long-term things to keep in mind as you join groups.

Controlling notifications

Sometimes, especially in larger groups, you may find yourself a bit overwhelmed by all the notifications. To control them, you just need to get comfortable with the Notifications Settings menu, which you access by clicking the Notifications button from a group's Home page. Clicking Notifications (it's in the lower right corner of the cover photo) reveals a drop-down menu with four options, as shown in Figure 10-9.

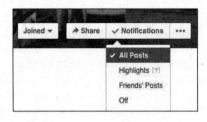

FIGURE 10-9:
Controlling
notifications.

>> **All Posts:** Because comment threads can often become very long and rambling, this option allows you to see when a new post is created, but not see comments on those posts unless you follow the post.

>> **Highlights:** This option means you'll get notifications for posts that have lots of likes and comments, and for friends' posts.

>> **Friends' Posts:** In especially large groups, you might not be official Facebook friends with everyone in the group, so a good way to filter down to the material you're most likely to care about is to pay attention only to the things your friends post.

>> **Off:** Some people may want to read the posts only when they choose to look at the group and not receive any notifications from this group. Selecting Off gives you that silence.

If you're being inundated by email notifications but still want the notifications to appear on Facebook, you can change your email notification settings from the Account Settings page. To adjust this setting, follow these steps:

1. **Click the upside-down triangle icon in the blue bar at top of any page.**

   A drop-down menu appears.

2. **Select Settings.**

   The Settings page appears. You can choose different types of settings from the menu on the left side of the page.

3. **Click Notifications on the left side of the page.**

   This opens all notifications settings. Look for the Email line in the How You Get Notifications section.

4. **Click Edit to the right of the Email option.**

   This expands to three options for email notifications: All Notifications, Important Notifications, and Only Notifications about Your Account Security and Privacy.

5. **Select either Important Notifications, or Only Notifications about Your Account, Security and Privacy.**

   This step limits how many email notifications you receive from Facebook.

TIP

If, after you change this setting, you're still getting emails about activity happening in a group, scroll to the bottom of one of the offending emails and click the Unsubscribe link. You will be asked to confirm that you want to unsubscribe from that type of email. After you confirm, you'll no longer see emails about groups.

Limiting notifications doesn't mean you won't see posts from that group in your News Feed. If you don't want to see group posts in your News Feed, you need to unfollow that group:

1. **From the group's Home page, click the Joined button in the lower right corner of the cover photo.**

   A tiny menu appears. The menu has two options: Unfollow Group and Leave Group.

2. **Choose Unfollow Group.**

   You will no longer see News Feed stories about things that happen in the group.

Searching a group

If your group is particularly active — meaning that lots of people are constantly posting content and commenting on things — you may have trouble finding something that was posted in the past. On the right side of the group's page under the cover photo is a search box. Click into it to search posts by keyword.

The search functionality here can be a bit limited, so sometimes posts will escape you entirely. The only way to find them is to keep scrolling back and back in the group's history.

Adding friends to a group

In most groups, most members can add more members at any time. This is a fast and easy way for groups to get all the right people in it even if the original creator isn't friends with everyone in the group. For example, if I'm friends with someone creating a group for our neighborhood association, but he isn't friends with my husband, I can easily add him to the group instead of him searching for my husband, adding him as a friend, and then adding him to the group. You can add friends to a group via Facebook or email, as described in the following sections.

Adding friends by name

At any time, you can type a friend's name in the box on the right side of the group that says Add People to Group. Facebook autocompletes as you type. Press Enter when your friend is highlighted, and she will be notified that she has been added to the group. Repeat as necessary.

Adding friends by email address

If you are ever starting a group from scratch and have an email list to draw from, you can easily add people to that group by their email address. If they don't have a Facebook account, they will need to create one to join the group. If they do have an account, the invitation will be sent to their account even if you aren't friends with them.

To invite friends via email, follow these steps:

1. **Click the Invite by Email link (it's at the bottom of the Members section on the right side of the page).**

An interface opens for entering email addresses.

2. **Type in each email address individually, followed by a comma.**

The email address is displayed in a light blue box once you have entered the comma. If the email address doesn't appear in a box (as shown in Figure 10-10), it has not been accepted by Facebook and will not receive an invitation.

FIGURE 10-10:
Entering email
addresses.

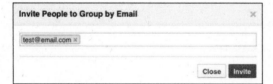

3. **Click Invite.**

A confirmation message displays all the email addresses that have received invitations to join.

Being a group administrator

If you're the creator of a group, you're automatically its *admin*, or administrator. Additionally, you can be added as an admin of someone else's group. After you have members in your group, you can use the group member list to remove (and even permanently ban) undesirable members, promote your most trusted members to administrators, or demote your existing administrators (if any) back to regular members.

Edit Settings

To get started in your career as an admin, take a look at the Edit Group Settings page, shown in Figure 10-11. You get to this page by clicking the [. . .] button on the right side of your group's page (at the bottom of the cover photo). This expands a drop-down menu with several options. Select Edit Group Settings from the menu, which takes you to the Edit Group Settings page.

Group Name	More Dummies
Group Type	+ **Pick a Group Type** Group types help people see what the group is about.
Privacy	○ **Public** Anyone can see the group, its members and their posts. ○ **Closed** Anyone can find the group and see who's in it. Only members can see posts. ● **Secret** Only members can find the group and see posts.
Membership Approval	● Any member can add or approve members. ○ Any member can add members, but an admin must approve them.
Web and Email Address	Customize your group's contact info so you can create posts using email or quickly share a link to your group. **Customize Address**
Description	This group is for dummies.

FIGURE 10-11: Editing Group Settings as an admin.

The Edit Group Settings page allows you to revisit some of the decisions you made when you were first creating your group, as well as adjust some settings that tend to be relevant only for people who are admins of large, open groups.

>> **Name:** Edit the group name here (but I don't recommend pulling the rug out from underneath people by, say, changing a group name from Yankees Fans to Red Sox Fans).

>> **Icon:** You can change your icon at any time from here.

>> **Group Type:** You can choose a group type here to provide more context to members. Keep in mind that a Buy, Sell, Trade group has additional features.

>> **Privacy:** The privacy level of the group can change here. Again, I don't recommend changing a secret group to an open group if people are sharing content they may feel is sensitive.

>> **Membership Approval:** By default, any member of a group can add other members. You can change this option by requiring admins to approve new members.

>> **Group Address:** If you want, you can create a group email address and web address. Group addresses appear as something like *groupname*@groups.facebook.com and web addresses appear as something like www.facebook.com/groups/*groupname*. Emails sent to the group email address are added as posts to the group wall.

>> **Description:** The description of your group appears in the About section of the group the first time new members visit your group page. So this is a good place to set expectations for what the group is for and how you expect to use it.

>> **Tags:** Tags are another way to let people know what your group is about. Tags can be any sort of keyword such as "television" or "hiking."

>> **Posting Permissions:** By default, all members of a group can post to it. But if you're the admin of a large group, you may want to change this setting so that only administrators can post. Keep in mind that this can really limit discussion!

>> **Post Approval:** Similarly, if you want to make sure the content of a group is appropriate and relevant, you can choose to have admins approve posts before all group members see them.

Click Save when you're done editing your group's information; otherwise, all your hard work will be lost.

Edit Members

As an admin, you can remove and ban members from the group, as well as create other admins to help shoulder the burden of admin-hood.

To edit members, follow these steps:

1. **Underneath the group's name, click the Members tab.**

The Members section of the group appears, the bulk of which is taken up by images of group members. If you are an admin, below each group member's name is a little gear icon.

2. **Click the gear icon below the name of the person you want to remove or make an admin.**

A menu with two options appears: Make Admin or Remove from Group. You can see this in Figure 10-12.

3. **To make someone an admin, click Make Admin.**

When someone is already an admin, you can remove her admin status by choosing Remove as Admin from this same menu.

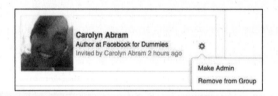

FIGURE 10-12:
Editing group
members.

4. **To remove someone from the group, choose Remove from Group.**

   You need to confirm this via a pop-up window that appears. If someone has been posting consistently offensive or abusive content, you can ban that person permanently by selecting the Ban Permanently check box; that person can never rejoin the group.

Pinning posts

If you have a large group that has a lot of activity, especially a lot of people joining over time, you may find that similar posts happen all the time. If there are posts that you think need top billing, admins have the ability to "pin" posts to the top of the page. Pinned posts appear before more recent posts. One group I belong to, for example, is entirely made up of people who no longer work for Facebook. A pinned post at the top of the discussion section details commonly needed contact addresses and forms that people need to fill out right when they leave the company.

To pin a post, follow these steps:

1. **On the post you want to pin, click the tiny upside-down arrow in the upper right corner of the post.**

   A menu of options related to the post appears, including options to save it and report it.

2. **Select Pin Post.**

   The post then appears as a pinned post at the top of the page.

Reporting offensive groups

If you stumble upon an offensive group in your travels, you should report it to Facebook so that the company can take appropriate actions. To report a group, follow these steps:

1. **Click the [. . .] icon on the right side of the group's Home page and then select the Report Group link.**

   A form appears in a pop-up window.

2. **Fill out the report by choosing a reason for the report.**

3. **Click Submit.**

Facebook removes any group that

>> Contains pornographic material or inappropriate nudity.

>> Attacks an individual or group.

>> Advocates violence.

>> Serves as advertisements or is otherwise deemed to be spam by Facebook.

REMEMBER

Many groups on Facebook take strong stands on controversial issues, such as abortion or gun control. In an effort to remain neutral and promote debate, Facebook won't remove a group because you disagree with its statements.

4

What to Do on Facebook

IN THIS PART . . .

Creating photo albums

Sharing photos and videos with friends

Creating and managing events

Interacting with Pages

Using games, websites, and apps with Facebook

Creating Pages for promotion

IN THIS CHAPTER

Looking at friends' photos and videos

Adding your own photos and videos to Facebook

Adding photos and videos from your iPhone or other smartphone

Understanding privacy for photos and videos

Chapter 11

Filling Facebook with Photos and Videos

acebook Photos is the leading photo-sharing application on the web. This may sound surprising because entire sites are dedicated to storing, displaying, and sharing photos, whereas Photos is just one piece of the Facebook puzzle. But the fact that *all* your friends are likely on Facebook and using Photos makes it a one-stop shop for tracking all the photos of you, all the photos you've taken, and all the photos of your friends.

Additionally, Facebook Photos allows you to add and share videos. Though slightly less common, videos are pretty similar to photos. If you let them languish on your hard drive or on your mobile phone, nobody gets to enjoy them. Nobody gets to tell you how cute the photos of your baby are. No one lets you know that she likes your wedding video. When you share photos and videos, they can become even more cherished, even more valuable as keepsakes.

Viewing Photos from Friends

Just by opening up Facebook and looking at News Feed, you'll find yourself looking at lots of people's photos. You'll see photos a few different ways: in your News Feed, in the photo viewer, and in an album format.

Photos in News Feed

Figure 11-1 shows an example of how a single photo appears in News Feed. Most of the screen is taken up by the photo. Running across the top is the name of the person who posted it and any description she wrote about it. There is also info about when the photo was added and how it was added (via mobile phone, for example). Underneath the photo are links to Like, Comment, and Share the photo. Beneath those links is the count of how many likes the photo has already gotten, and any comments people have already made. You may even see a blank comment box, waiting for you to add your two cents.

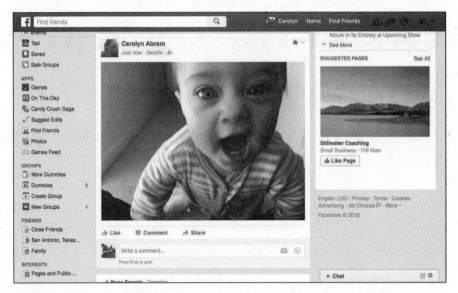

FIGURE 11-1:
Looking at a friend's photo in News Feed.

Clicking the photo expands the photo viewer, which is covered in the following section.

Figure 11-2 shows an example of a photo album preview in News Feed. It's similar to the single photo, but previews more of the photos from the album. The name of the album appears at the top of the post and tells you how many photos are in the album. Clicking any of the photos expands the photo viewer, and clicking the album title brings you to an album view.

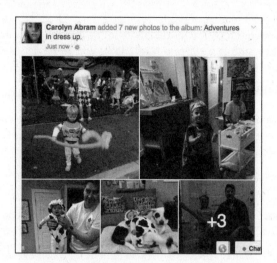

FIGURE 11-2:
Looking at a
friend's album in
News Feed.

Photo viewer

The photo viewer is an overlay on top of Facebook that allows you to quickly browse photos and leave likes and comments. Clicking a small version of a photo almost anywhere on Facebook expands the photo viewer and fades the rest of the screen to black, as shown in Figure 11-3. The left side of the viewer is where the photo appears, and the right side is where comments, likes, and info about the photo appear.

FIGURE 11-3:
The Photo
Viewer.

When you hover your mouse over the photo, more options show up in white on the photo. On either side is an arrow that allows you to navigate through a photo album. Clicking anywhere on the photo will also advance the album forward. At the bottom of the viewer, the following information appears:

>> **<Album Name>:** The album's name is usually one your friend has created, like "Summer in February!" or a descriptive name generated by Facebook, such as "Mobile uploads."

>> **Photo count:** The number of the photo you're on in the album (for example, 5 of 8) is also displayed.

>> **Tag Photo:** Clicking this allows you to add *tags* or labels for those in the photo. I cover tags in upcoming section, "Editing and Tagging Photos."

>> **Options:** Clicking this reveals a menu of options for things like downloading the photo to your computer, reporting the photo, removing a tag, or making a photo your own profile picture.

>> **Share:** Clicking this lets you post the photo to your own Timeline.

>> **Send:** Clicking this option lets you send a message to a friend with the photo attached. Keep in mind that sometimes you may be able to see photos your friend cannot see.

>> **Like:** Same as with the Like link that appears on the right side of the viewer, selecting this option lets the person who added the photo know that you like the photo.

The album view

The album view is the grid of thumbnail photos that you see when you click the name of an album or click a View Album link. Most average screens can fit about 8 to 12 photos in this view, and as you scroll down the page, more and more photos appear until you reach the end of the album. Sometimes if people add a really large album, you may want to just skim an album view to see where the parts of the album are that interest you. Clicking on any one photo brings up the Photo Viewer.

At the top of the album view is the name of the album, some info about when and where the album was added, and any general info your friend has added about the album. Beneath the last row of photos, you can see who has liked the album or commented on it. Figure 11-4 shows an example album view.

House at 6 months

Updated over a year ago · Taken in Seattle, Washington

We bought a house. And then we made some improvements

FIGURE 11-4:
An album view
of photos.

TIP

Commenting on an album is different than commenting on a single photo. Leave a comment on an album to comment on the collection: "Looks like a great trip!" "Can't wait till we see the place ourselves." Comment on a single photo when you have something to say about that photo in particular: "Did you use a fish-eye lens to get this shot?" or "OMG I was at this exact spot a year ago!"

Viewing photos on your mobile device

Chances are that if you have a smartphone or a tablet computer like an iPad, you'll wind up looking at photos using the Facebook app. Looking at photos on these devices isn't too different from looking at them on a computer screen. Tapping a photo in News Feed expands the photo and fades the rest of the screen to black. At the top of the screen are icons for closing the photo and returning to News Feed (x), tagging the photo (tag icon), and more options (. . . icon). At the bottom of the screen are buttons you can tap to like, comment, or share the photo. Tapping the count of likes or comments expands a screen where you can scroll through the comments people have made on the photo.

When someone has added multiple photos in one post, you see a preview of those photos in your mobile News Feed. When you tap on any of the photos, you are taken to an album view, where you can scroll up and down to browse through all the photos that have been added. Tap on the back arrow in the upper left corner to return to News Feed. Tap on any photo to view it in the photo viewer, and then swipe left and right to navigate through the album. The two-finger method of zooming in and out also works on Facebook photos.

Viewing tagged photos and videos of yourself

When I say *photos and videos of yourself*, I'm referring to photos and videos in which you're *tagged*. Tags are ways of marking who is in a photo — the online equivalent of writing the names of everyone appearing on the back of a photo print. Tags are part of what make Facebook Photos so useful. Even if you don't add lots of photos, other people can add photos of you. Photos you've been tagged in might be scattered across your friends' Timelines, so Facebook collects all these photos in the Photos section of your Timeline. You can get there by clicking the Photos tab underneath your cover photo.

The Photos section defaults to showing Photos of You. You can also view photos you've added (Your Photos) or albums you've added (Albums). The Photos of You section shows the most recently tagged photos at the top of the page. As you scroll down, you see older and older photos of yourself. This is a great place to take a trip down memory lane, and also to make sure that you're aware of all the photos of you that are out there.

If you've been tagged in a photo and you don't like that tag, you can always remove the tag. Then that photo will no longer be linked to your Timeline, and it won't appear in the Photos of You section of your Timeline either.

If there's a photo or video you don't want on Facebook at all, even after you've removed the tag, get in touch with your friend and ask him to remove it. If you think it is offensive or abusive in any way, you can also report the photo and ask Facebook to remove it.

Adding Photos to Facebook

Facebook is a great place to keep your photos and videos because it's the place where most of your friends will be able to see them. Whether that's a single photo you snapped on your phone or a big album detailing the latest family vacation, photos are most fun when you can share them and talk about them with your friends.

Facebook has a slight distinction between uploading photos and creating a photo album. Albums are often created to document a particular event or period of time, whereas uploads happen on an ongoing basis. Facebook assumes that uploads happen more frequently, so the Publisher on your Home page defaults to this option. Because Facebook makes this assumption, I go over all the ways of uploading photos before going into Album creation.

Uploading photos

If you have a few photos you want to quickly share, follow these steps to get them out to your friends:

1. **Click Add Photos/Video in the Publisher on your Home page.**

   A window appears allowing you to browse your computer's hard drive and select the photo you want (see Figure 11-5).

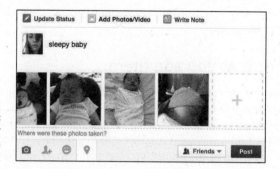

2. **Click the photo(s) you want to share.**

3. **Click Open or Choose (the wording may depend on your browser and operating system).**

   Clicking Open or Choose brings you back to Facebook. A thumbnail of that photo appears inside the Publisher (shown in Figure 11-5).

   Sometimes Facebook may be a little slow to add your photo. Blue progress bars may appear instead of thumbnails. You won't be able to post your photo until the photo has been added.

WARNING

4. **Click in the Publisher (where you see Say Something about This Photo) and type any explanation you think is necessary.**

5. **(Optional) Add tags, location info, and change the privacy of those photos from the options at the bottom of the Publisher.**

   If you've never changed your Privacy settings, by default, everyone on Facebook can see your photos if she navigates to your Timeline. I usually like sharing my photos with Friends. Of course, you can always choose a custom group of people who can and cannot see the photo.

6. Click Post.

Clicking Post officially posts the photo to Facebook. People will be able to see the photos on your Timeline and in their News Feeds (provided they're allowed by your Privacy settings to see the photo). By default, this photo is added to an album called Timeline Photos, which is basically a collection of all the photos you've ever added individually.

TIP

You can also drag and drop photo files from your desktop straight into the Publisher just like moving files around on your computer. Once you have dragged a photo into the Publisher, you can add a comment, location, tags, and change privacy like normal.

Editing photos as you add them

Uploading photos is meant to be pretty easy. In essence you click on the photos you want to share and then you click post. Voilà, shared photos. However, Facebook offers a whole bunch of cool photo-editing options that you can choose to use as you add your photos. To get to these options, hover your mouse over any of the thumbnail previews of the photos you have chosen to add (do this *before* you click Post). When you hover over the thumbnail, three icons appear. Click the X icon to remove the selected photo from the post. Click the tag icon to tag people in that photo. Click the paintbrush icon to open a photo viewer with editing options (shown in Figure 11-6).

FIGURE 11-6: Photo editing options.

WARNING

This is one of those places where what you see on-screen might be different than what's pictured in the figures in this book. Don't worry, the editing options are the same, just some of the locations (left versus right, top versus bottom) might be different.

FILTERS

Filters allow you to change the color balance of the photo you have chosen. Changing the color balance has a tendency to change the mood of the photo a bit, so a silly photo can become more romantic if it is now black and white, or a photo might appear more precious if it has a vintage filter.

TAG

You can tag people in a photo by clicking on their face and then typing their name into the text box that opens. Facebook auto-completes as you type; hit Enter to select their name when you see it highlighted. Tagging friends will notify them that they have been tagged in a photo and may allow their friends to view that photo as well.

CROP

Cropping the photo involves changing the borders of the photo. After you click Crop, guidelines appear that you can move to crop the photo. Grayed-out areas don't appear. You can also choose to change the photo between Original and Square. Since lots of photos sometimes appear as thumbnails (such as in album previews), changing to square can make them fit more nicely into those square boxes.

When you crop a photo, you can also choose to rotate it. No need to make people tilt their heads at their computer screens in order to see your photo properly. Click Rotate to rotate the photo 90 degrees. Click it as many times as you need to get it to the proper orientation.

ADD TEXT

Unlike a caption, which tends to describe a photo, text on a photo is a way of editing the photo itself to say something. Text appears overlaid on top of the photo. Click on Add Text to open a text box, and then start typing to add your text.

You can change the color of the text using the color palette on the left side of the screen. Simply drag the circle over the color palette until the text changes to the color you want, then release it. Use the Left and Centered buttons to decide whether your text should be centered in the text box or left-justified. Use the Font drop-down menu to choose a font for your text.

Click and drag the text box to move it to where you want it to appear on the photo. Click on the blue two-way arrow to change the size and orientation of the text. Drag it out to make it bigger and in to make it smaller, and drag it up or down to spin the text on its axis. Click the X at the upper right corner of the text box to delete the text entirely.

Once you're happy with what the text says and how it appears on the photo, click on another portion of the photo to remove the text box, leaving just the text behind. Click on the text again to bring back the text box and the relevant editing options. You can add more than one text box to a photo.

ADD STICKER

Stickers are pretty much exactly what they sound like: digital drawings you can stick on top of your photos. Click on Add Sticker to browse through the sticker store for the sticker you want. When you click on the sticker you want, it appears in the center of your photo with a circle around it. Hover your mouse cursor over it until the cursor turns into a four-way arrow, and then click and drag it to your desired location on your photo. Click the blue two-way arrow to rotate the sticker and change its size (drag out to make it bigger, in to make it smaller). Click the X to delete the sticker. When your sticker is the proper size, orientation, and location, simply click another part of the photo to remove the circular frame from the sticker. Click the sticker again if you want to once again change something about it. You can add as many stickers as you want to a photo.

When you finish editing your photo, click the blue Save button. This brings you back to the Publisher, where your edited photo now appears as a thumbnail. You can repeat the editing process for each photo you are adding, but keep in mind that these advanced editing options are entirely optional. Well, if your photo is upside down I strongly recommend rotating it to the proper orientation, but everything else is totally up to you.

Adding photos from your iPhone

Lots of photos you see on Facebook are added when people are nowhere near a computer. Instead, they're the photos of things that happen while you're out and about. Things that are beautiful (spring blossoms!), or weird (how did this person lose only one high heel?), or just emblematic of your day (another cute photo of the baby).

If you add the Facebook app to most smartphones, you can send photos from your phone right to Facebook. I go over how to add a photo from the Publisher of the iPhone app in Chapter 7. You can also add photo from your iPhone's camera roll.

To add a photo from your iPhone's camera roll, follow these steps:

1. **From your photo gallery, tap the photo you want to share; then tap the Send icon at the bottom left of the photo.**

   A menu of options appears, including things like email or text messages. If you previously installed the Facebook app, you should see the Facebook icon among the other options.

2. **Tap the Facebook icon.**

   A Facebook Publisher appears, as shown in Figure 11-7.

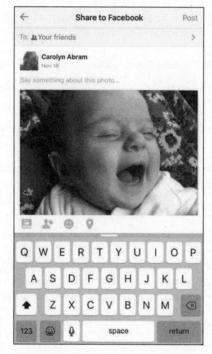

FIGURE 11-7:
Don't let your photos go unshared!

3. **(Optional) Use the keyboard to type any explanation the photo needs.**

4. **(Optional) Tap the Album icon to add the photo to an existing album on Facebook.**

   By default, Facebook adds your photo to a Mobile Uploads album.

5. **(Optional) Tap on any of the icons at the bottom of the photo to add tags, activity info, or location info, respectively.**

6. **(Optional) Tap the To: field at the top of the Publisher to edit who can see that photo.**

   Remember, by default, the audience you shared your last post with will be the people who can see this post.

7. **Tap Post in the upper right corner of the Facebook window.**

   The photo is added to your Timeline as part of the Mobile Uploads album, and it may appear in your friends' News Feeds.

Creating an album

Whereas a single photo can share a moment, an album can truly tell a story and spark conversations with your friends. To create an album, follow these steps:

1. **From the Publisher, click Create Photo Album.**

   This opens the same interface for exploring your hard drive that you used to upload a single photo.

2. **Select multiple photos by pressing the Ctrl or Command button and clicking the files you want.**

TIP

   If you use a program like iPhoto to organize your photos, create an album there first; then navigate to it and select all those photos to add to Facebook. You'll save yourself some time trying to figure out whether you want to use IMG0234 or IMG0235.

3. **When you're done, click Open.**

   The Create Album window appears, shown in Figure 11-8. The progress bar fills with blue as your photos are uploaded. You can always add more photos by clicking the Add More Photos button at the top of the Create Album window.

4. **Edit the Album info and options.**

   The left side of the screen contains all the relevant album info:

   - **Untitled Album:** Enter your album title here. Usually something descriptive does the trick: "Hawaii" or "Halloween."

   - **Say something. . .:** Click here to add an album description. You might talk about why you took these photos, or anything else you think people might want to know about your album.

   - **Where were these taken:** Click here to add location information. You may already have location information added automatically, as Facebook pulls location info from your computer and from your photos. Any locations you add get added as tags the album has.

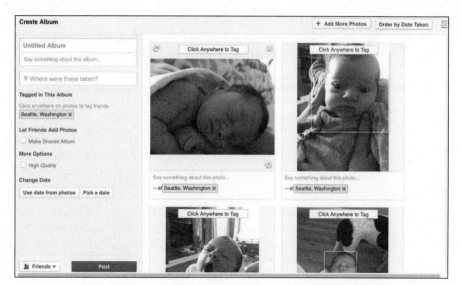

FIGURE 11-8:
Create your
album here.

- **Tagged in This Album:** As you add tags to your photos (more on that in Step 10), your friends names will appear here.

- **Let Friends Add Photos:** Often photo albums center around an event where many people took photos. You can create a shared album to allow multiple friends to add photos to the album. If you check this check box, a text field appears where you can enter the names of people you want to share the album with.

- **High Quality:** High-resolution photos obviously look a bit better, but they also take longer to upload. Unless you're a pro photographer or using a truly professional-level camera, standard quality is usually sufficient.

- **Change Date:** By default, your album will be dated from the date you upload it. If you want, you can use the date the photos were taken as the date of the album, or you can pick a date for the album.

5. **Choose who can see the album by using the Privacy menu.**

   The Privacy menu reflects the privacy setting from the last time you posted something. If you last posted something publicly, for example, the Privacy menu displays the globe icon and says "Public." As usual, the basic options are Public, Friends, Only Me, or a Custom set of people. If you are uploading a shared album, the options will be Public or Friends of Contributors.

6. **(Optional) After your photos finish uploading, add descriptions to individual photos.**

   The thumbnail of each photo has a blank space beneath it. Click into that space to add a caption or description of that individual photo.

TIP

Hover the mouse cursor over any preview and click on the rotation icon in the upper left corner that appears to rotate the photo.

7. **(Optional) Click and drag photos to reorder them in your album.**

8. **(Optional) Click friends' faces to tag them. Type the name of the friend in the box that appears.**

The tagging box is shown in Figure 11-9. You don't have to tag friends in your album. However, tagging is highly recommended. It allows your friends to learn about your photos more quickly and share in discussing them with you.

Facebook's facial recognition may automatically add tags of people it recognizes. This allows you to make sure your friend is tagged in many photos without having to enter his name a zillion times. You can remove any incorrect tags by clicking the X next to the person's name underneath the photo in question. You can remove all tags for a particular friend by clicking the X next to his name in the Tagged in This Album section on the left side of the Create Album window.

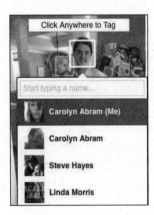

FIGURE 11-9:
Who dat?

9. **Click Post.**

Whew! That was a bit of a marathon. If you need a break or a drink of water, feel free to indulge. Then, when you're ready, jump to the "Editing and Tagging Photos" section to find out how to edit your album and the photos in it.

Editing and Tagging Photos

After uploading a photo, you can still make changes to the way it appears on Facebook. If you added a whole album, you may want to add more photos or rearrange the order of the pictures. For any photo you added from a phone or just quickly from your computer, you may want to add tags, date, or location information. Doing all of this is relatively easy using the following common editing "tasks."

Editing albums

Editing an album usually consists of editing the album's information or settings. You may also want to edit specific photos within an album. For those types of edits, hop on down to the "Editing a photo" section.

Editing album name, location, description, and privacy

From the album view, look above the top row of photos for an Edit button. Click the Edit button to bring up an Edit Album screen (see Figure 11-10). It should look familiar — it's pretty much the same screen you saw when you created the album.

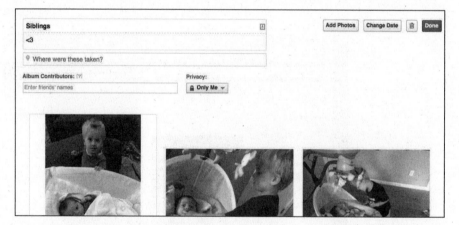

FIGURE 11-10:
Editing your album's info.

The fields at the top are the same as when you created the album: album name, description (Say Something), location (Where Were These Taken), contributors, and a Privacy menu. Remember to click Done when you finish editing this information.

Deleting an album

While you're looking at the Edit Album screen, look for a button in the upper right corner with a trash can icon on it. If you ever decide, in retrospect, that adding a particular album was a poor choice, you can click this button to remove the whole thing.

WARNING

If you delete your photo album, all the photos in it will be gone forever, so make sure you want to get rid of it completely before you delete it.

Reordering photos in the album

Chances are that if you added your photos in bulk, they don't appear exactly in the right order. And it's awkward when the photos of the sunset appear first, and the photos of your awesome day of adventure come afterward. To reorder photos from the album view, follow these steps:

1. **Hover the mouse pointer over the photo you want to move.**

2. **Click and hold the photo.**

3. **While holding the mouse button down, drag the photo thumbnail to its correct place in the album.**

   The other photos shift positions as you move your chosen photo (as shown in Figure 11-11).

FIGURE 11-11: Making your album tell a story in the right order.

4. **When the photo is in the spot you want, release the mouse button.**

5. **Repeat with the next photo until your whole album is organized correctly.**

No need to worry about saving. Facebook automatically saves the new order of your album. Click the Done button when you're done.

Adding more photos

After you create a photo album, you can add more photos later. Sometimes, depending on how organized the photos on your hard drive are, you may want to add photos in batches anyhow. To add more photos, follow these steps:

1. **From the Edit Album screen, click the Add Photos button.**

   This opens the interface for exploring your computer's hard drive.

2. **Select the photos you want to add.**

3. **Click Open or Choose.**

   The upload process begins and you go to the Create Album window. You can tag your photos, add captions, and rotate them as needed.

4. **Click the Post button after the upload is complete.**

Editing a photo

In addition to the actions you can take on an entire album, you can also take actions on individual photos within an album.

TECHNICAL STUFF

For all these possible photo edits, I assume you're already looking at the photo you want to edit in the photo viewer.

Adding a tag to an individual photo

If you skipped adding tags earlier, you can always add your tags to individual photos.

1. **Hover your mouse over a friend's face.**

   The tagging box appears, as shown in Figure 11-12.

FIGURE 11-12: Tagging a friend in a photo.

2. **Enter the name of the person you want to tag in the text box.**

   Facebook tries to auto-complete your friend's name as you type.

3. **Repeat Steps 1 and 2 until everyone in the photo is tagged.**

   Or stop after you tag a few people. You can always come back to this later.

Rotating a photo

Lots of times, photos wind up being sideways. It's a result of turning your camera to take a vertical shot as opposed to a horizontal one. You don't have to settle for this:

1. **Click Options at the bottom of the photo viewer.**

   Remember, you won't see this text until your mouse hovers over the photo. This opens a menu of options related to that photo.

2. **Click Rotate Left or Rotate Right from the menu.**

   You may have to click it more than once to actually get it properly oriented.

Adding or changing a description or date for an individual photo

Just like you can add a description to the album as a whole, you can add descriptions or captions to individual photos:

1. **Click the Edit button on the right side of the photo viewer.**

   A text box appears where you can edit the description.

2. **Enter your description in the text box.**

3. **(Optional) Add any tags you want about who was with you when the photo was taken.**

4. **(Optional) Add location information about where this photo was taken.**

   Facebook tries to autocomplete your location information as you type.

5. **Use the date selector to change the date when the photo was taken.**

6. **When you're finished, click Done Editing.**

Deleting a photo

Maybe you realized that all 20 group shots from the high school reunion don't have to go in the album, or that one photo has a whole bunch of crossed eyes. You can remove photos entirely from Facebook:

1. **Click the Options link at the bottom of the photo viewer.**

   A menu of options appears.

2. **Click Delete This Photo.**

   A pop-up window appears asking if you are sure.

3. **Click Confirm.**

   You're taken back to the album view, now with one less photo.

Automatic albums

Most of the time when you're creating a photo album, you decide what to title it and which photos go into it. There are a few exceptions to this rule. Facebook assembles certain types of photos into albums on your behalf. Most important, every time you change your profile picture or cover photo, Facebook adds it to the Profile Pictures or Cover Photos albums, respectively. Facebook creates albums of all your profile pictures and cover photos automatically.

You can access this album by clicking your current profile picture or cover photo from your Timeline. This takes you to the photo viewer, where you can click through your historical record of profile pictures. Even though Facebook created this album, you can still edit any part of it like any other album — you can caption, tag, reorder, and delete photos simply by clicking the photo you want to edit.

TIP

You can automatically turn any photo from this album back into your profile picture by clicking the Options link and selecting Make Profile Picture from the menu that appears.

Similarly, single photos that you add to your Timeline are collected into the Timeline Photos album. Photos that you add from your phone are added to a Mobile Uploads album. Videos also are collected into a Videos album.

Working with Video

Too often, videos wither away on hard drives or cameras or on mobile phones. The files are big, and they can be difficult to share or email. Facebook seeks to make sharing videos easier. So film away and then let everyone see what you've been up to.

Viewing videos

You'll mostly encounter videos in your News Feed with a big fat Play button in the center (see Figure 11-13). If you pause in your scrolling to look at the video, it will begin playing, but without sound. If you aren't interested in the video, keep scrolling. If you are, hover your mouse over the bottom of the video and click on the muted sound icon (it's a megaphone with a white X next to it). This will turn the sound on for the video.

FIGURE 11-13:
A video on
Facebook.

Videos play right inline in your News Feed. While the video is playing, you can hover your mouse over it to see the progress bar, change the volume, switch the video to HD, or expand it to full screen.

Adding a video from your computer

Uploading a video to Facebook includes going out into the world, recording something, and then moving it from your camera onto your computer. I'm going to assume you've already done that part and are now back to being sedentary in front of your computer. Now, to upload a video to Facebook, follow these steps:

1. **Choose Add Photo/Video in the Publisher at the top of your Home page or Timeline.**

    This expands a window that allows you to navigate your computer's hard drive.

2. **Select a video file from your computer.**

   This brings you back to Facebook, where your video is appended to your post. A filmstrip icon indicates that you're adding a video, not a photo.

3. **(Optional) Type any explanation or comment into the Say Something About This Video box.**

4. **(Optional) Select who can see this video using the Privacy menu.**

   As usual, your basic options are Public and Friends.

5. **(Optional) Use the icons at the bottom of the Publisher to add tags, activity or location information.**

6. **Click Post.**

   A blue progress bar appears at the bottom of the post. Uploading a video can sometimes take a while, so be patient. When it's ready, you'll be notified that your video is processing. This means that you need to wait a little while until your video is ready. You can use Facebook in the meantime; you'll receive a notification when it's ready.

Adding a video from the Facebook app

Much like photos, many of the videos you want to share most are ones you take when you're out and about: someone attempting to park a car in a spot that's too small, your kid chasing a soccer ball, the bride and groom cutting the cake. More and more often, you may find yourself using your phone to record these videos.

You could move the video from your phone to your computer and then add it to Facebook, or you could skip the middleman and share it directly from your phone using the Facebook app:

1. **Tap the Photo option at the top of your mobile News Feed.**

   Your Photo and Video roll from your phone appears.

2. **Tap the video you want to add.**

3. **Tap Done in the upper right corner.**

   A preview of your video appears in the mobile Publisher. You can play it here to make sure you want to share it.

4. **(Optional) Tap the Say Something space above the video to add a caption or description of the video.**

   The screen becomes the usual box you see when you add a status or other post, with a thumbnail icon representing the video.

5. **(Optional) Use the icons on the bottom of the Publisher to add tags, activity, or location info to your post.**

6. **Double-check your privacy by seeing who can see the video in the To: field at the top of the Publisher.**

   Remember, by default the video will be shared with the same group of people you last shared a post with.

7. **Tap Post in the upper right corner of the screen.**

   The video is then added to Facebook. Your friends will be able to see it on your Timeline and in their News Feeds (depending on your privacy settings, of course).

Discovering Privacy

While privacy is covered in detail in Chapter 6, it's worth going over a few settings again now that you really understand what it is you're choosing to show or not show to people.

Photo and video privacy

Each time you create an album, post a photo, or add a video to Facebook, you can use the Privacy menu to select who can see it. These options are as follows:

>> **Public:** This setting means that anyone can see the album. It doesn't necessarily mean that everyone *will* see the album, though. Facebook doesn't generally display your content to people who aren't your friends. But if, for example, someone you didn't know searched for you and went to your Timeline, she would be able to see that album.

>> **Friends:** Only confirmed friends can see the photos or videos when you have this setting.

>> **Only Me:** Only you will be able to see that photo or video.

>> **Custom:** Custom privacy settings can be as closed or as open as you want. You may decide that you want to share an album only with the people who were at a particular event, which you can do with a custom setting.

TIP

Another way to control who sees an album or video is to share it using Facebook Groups. So, for example, a video of your kids playing might be of interest only to people in your family. If you have a group for your family, you can share it from the Publisher in the group, and then only people in the group will be able to see it.

WARNING

If you're brand new to Facebook and have never changed a single privacy setting, by default, all posts you add — including photos and videos — are visible publicly. If you aren't comfortable with this, remember to adjust your Privacy settings accordingly when you add new photos and video.

Privacy settings for photos and videos of yourself

The beauty of creating albums on Facebook is that it builds a giant cross-listed spreadsheet of information about your photos — who is in which photos, where those photos were taken, and so on. You're cross-listed in photos that you own and in photos that you don't own. However, you may want more control over these tags and who can see them. To control this, go to the Privacy Settings page from the Privacy Shortcuts menu (which you access by clicking the lock icon in the blue bar on top of any page). From the Settings page, click the Timeline and Tagging section on the left side of the page.

The following settings can help you further control who can see photos and videos of you:

> » **Review posts friends tag you in before they appear on your Timeline?**
> Turning this option from Off to On means you get to make sure you want to be tagged in photos (and other posts) before anyone can see that you've been tagged.
>
> In other words, say that I tag my friend Eric in a photo.
>
> • If this option is *Off,* as soon as I tag him, the photo is added to his Timeline and (usually) his friends will be able to see that he's been tagged in their News Feeds.
>
> • If this setting is *On,* he has to approve the tag before it appears on his Timeline and in his friends' News Feeds. The photo itself still gets shared and is visible on my Timeline and in my friends' News Feeds.

>> **Who can see posts you've been tagged in on your Timeline?**

Regardless of whether or not you choose to review tags before they appear on your Timeline, you can control who can see posts where you've been tagged. So, for example, if you set this to "Friends" and you get tagged in a photo, even though it has been added to your Timeline, a non-friend visiting your Timeline would not see it displayed there.

>> **When you're tagged in a post, whom do you want to add to the audience if they aren't already in it?** Another way to limit who can see that you've been tagged in a post is to change this setting from Friends to Only Me or Custom.

By default, if I tag Eric in a photo, his friend Dave, whom I'm not friends with, will be able to see the photo. If Eric changes this setting to Only Me, then when I tag Eric, Dave still will not be able to see that photo.

IN THIS CHAPTER

Checking out Public events

Responding to event invitations

Creating and managing your own events

Chapter 12

Scheduling Your Life with Events

I n the real world, just because all your friends are on Facebook doesn't mean that it's the only place you interact with them. In fact, the people you interact with most on Facebook may be the same ones you see at PTA meetings or at a book club or have over for barbecues. Facebook Events can help you bridge the divide between all the things that happen online and all the things you want to have happen when you're not anywhere close to your computer.

Facebook Events work really well for the same reason lots of other Facebook features work: Your friends are here on Facebook. You can invite them to events, keep track of RSVPs, and use Facebook to send updates or coordinate participants in an event to help out. Facebook's Event Calendar also helps you keep track of upcoming events and your friends' birthdays.

You're Invited!

The first way you'll most likely find out about an event is through a notification. When a friend invites you to an event, a small red flag appears over the notifications icon in the big blue bar on top. Click the icon to open your notifications menu; then click the invitation to be taken to the event. You can also see event invites on the right side of your Home page, above trending topics.

A sample event appears in Figure 12-1. The event photo appears at the top of the page, much like the cover photo does on your Timeline. Beneath the event photo is the event's name, host (which can be a person, group, or page), and privacy info.

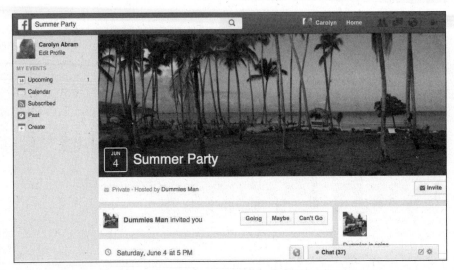

Events have two possible privacy settings:

>> **Public:** Public events are just what they sound like: open to the public. Anyone can see the event with or without an invitation, view the guest list and posts, and join the event herself.

>> **Private:** Only people who have been invited are able to see the event and join it. Depending on the event creator's settings, invitees may be able to add more friends to the event as well.

The right side of the event page shows the progress of the RSVPs. Three categories are shown (although this may depend on the settings of the event, as decided by the event admin): Going, Maybe, and Invited.

The most important info about any event is in the center of the page: where, when, and what. There's a spot here for the date and time of the event, the location, and any info the event creator wants to share with guests. If the creator put in a specific address or location, you can click to see a map of where it is and get directions.

To RSVP to an event, look below the cover photo where you can see who invited you to an event alongside three buttons: Going, Maybe, and Can't Go. Click on the appropriate button so your host can get an accurate head count.

Below the event info is the Posts section of the event (see Figure 12-2). The Posts section is where people can post messages and communicate with other guests (and potential guests) of that event. Event hosts use this section to post important updates — for example, a reminder to bring a sweater in case the weather is cold, or to let people know at which section of the park they'll be meeting. Guests' RSVPs appear here as they come in, as do posts that people actively make to communicate with other guests. Depending on the event, the posts may be from people just saying how excited they are or from people coordinating rides or the food they'll bring to a potluck.

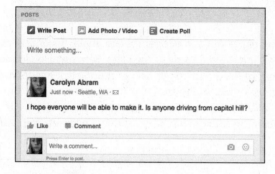

FIGURE 12-2:
Post here to communicate with other guests.

To post to an event, follow these steps:

1. **Click in the Publisher (where it reads Write Something).**

This is the same way you update your status or post to group, except in this case your post will be shared with people who can view the event.

2. **Type your message in the Publisher.**

3. **(Optional) Add photos, tags, activity, or location information by clicking their respective icons at the bottom of the Share box.**

4. **Click Post.**

Your message is posted to the Posts section of the event. Depending on settings, guests may be notified about it or see a News Feed story about it.

Public Events

Most of the time, you'll view an event because you were invited. But occasionally, especially for large-scale public events, you may see an event in your News Feed. These events look the same and have the same components as smaller, private events, but instead of the options for RSVP'ing being Going, Maybe, or Not Going, the options for public events are Interested or Going. When you are viewing the event, you can click the Going button to RSVP to the event, or the Interested button to see reminders about the event and receive updates from the event. In other words, "Interested" is the equivalent of subscribing or following someone. When you list that you are interested in or going to a public event, that may create a News Feed story that your friends could see.

Viewing Events

From your Home page, you can see reminders about upcoming events (including friends' birthdays) on the right side of the page. You can also view a complete Event Calendar by going to the Events page. To get there, click Events in the left sidebar. The Events page is shown in Figure 12-3. It lists your events (ones that you have been invited to, RSVP'd yes to, and said you are interested in). On the right side of the page are upcoming friends' birthdays and public events happening locally.

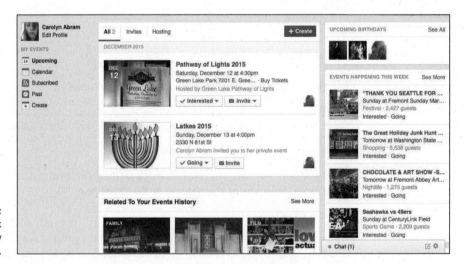

On the left side of the page is a menu of options related to Events. By default, when you come to the events page you are on the "Upcoming" tab. You can click Calendar to see a calendar of events. The calendar has events written in just as you might write in a reminder on your wall calendar at home. Click an event's name to be taken to its page. In addition to events, your friends' birthdays are marked on this calendar — look for tiny profile pictures to see whose birthday is on which day. If you forgot your reading glasses, you can always hover your mouse over the picture to see the friend's name and (if his settings allow) how old he will be.

Creating Your Own Events

Eventually, the time may come when you want to organize an event. It might be a party or a barbecue or a book club or any other gathering of your friends. No matter what the context, follow these steps to create your own event:

1. **Click Events in the left sidebar of any page on Facebook.**

2. **Click the Create Event button in the upper right side of the page.**

The Create New Event window appears, as shown in Figure 12-4.

✉ **Create Private Event** ▾   ✕

You're creating a private event. To protect the privacy of guests, you won't be able to change it to public later.

Event Name	Latkes
Location	Include a place or address
Date/Time	11/19/2015 📅 4:00 PM 🕐 PST + End Time
Description	Come celebrate Hanukkah with us!

✔ Guests can invite friends

Cancel   **Create**

FIGURE 12-4:
Create your
event here.

3. **Fill out your event's info.**

You can fill out a number of fields:

- *Event Name:* Don't fill out your name here (a common mistake); this is the name of your event. Usually events get pretty descriptive names like "Carolyn's birthday party" or "Labor Day in the park."

- *Location:* Generally speaking, events are better when people know where to go. You can type an address or a location (like a restaurant or a park). Facebook attempts to auto-complete to a specific location while you type. When you see the desired location, click it or press Enter.

- *Date/Time:* By default, Facebook assumes you're an impromptu party planner, so the date in the box is today. Click the calendar icon to change the date. Next to the date box is a box for the event's time. Type in the time your event begins. After you add a start time, a blue link appears that reads +End Time Click that link to also add an end date and time.

- *Description (optional):* This is the info guests will read about when they see the event, so provide any info that helps people understand what they're going to. For example, a bookstore event might list the readers who will be in attendance, or a party at a bar might let you know if there's going to be a cover charge to get in.

4. **Select your event's privacy from the Privacy menu at the top of the Create New Event window.**

    Remember, there are two privacy levels: Public and Private.

5. **Decide whether guests can invite friends.**

    If you'd like for friends to be able to spread the word about your event, make sure the Guests Can Invite Friends box is checked. If your event is strictly invite-only, uncheck it.

6. **Click the Create button to create your event.**

    You're taken to your event's page. Even though your event is created, you still need to make a few finishing touches, such as adding an event photo and oh, I don't know, maybe inviting some people.

Inviting guests

Trust me, your party just won't be the same unless some people show up, and the number one way to get people to show up is to invite them. Inviting people to your event isn't a one-shot deal. You can follow these steps at any time to invite people to your event:

1. **From your event's page, click the Invite button in the upper right portion of the page (right beneath the cover photo).**

    The Invite Friends window appears, as shown in Figure 12-5.

2. **Click a friend's name or face to select her.**

    Because you may have a lot of friends, you can use the search box at the top to search for people by name. You can also use the categories on the left side of the window to filter down to certain friends. For example, you may be able to look at friends who live near you, or friends who are in a particular group with you. After you've selected a friend, they appear on the right side of the window under the heading "Selected."

3. **Click Send Invites after you make all your selections.**

    At this point, your guests receive the notification of a new invitation and will probably start to RSVP.

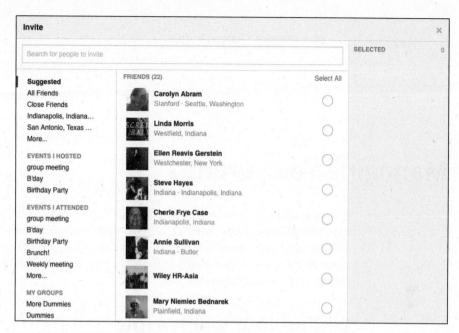

Adding an event photo

Although not required, adding an event photo to your event helps make the invitation feel a bit more official. Although it's not quite the same thing as sending out letter-pressed, hand-addressed invitations, it's the next best thing.

To add an event photo, follow these steps:

1. **From the event's page, click the Add Event Photo button in the upper right corner.**

   A menu with two options appears: You can either select from photos you have already added to Facebook or you can choose a photo from your computer's hard drive. Either option opens an interface for browsing photos.

2. **Select a photo from your hard drive or from Facebook.**

   After selecting a photo from your hard drive, you may need to click Open. After you select your photo, it should appear at the top of the event with white text that reads Drag to Reposition Event Photo.

3. **Use your mouse to drag the photo in order to position it properly on the screen.**

4. **Click the Save Changes button.**

After you add your event photo, the Add Event Photo button is replaced with a Change Event Photo button that appears when you hover your mouse over the photo. Click this button to choose a new photo, reposition the existing photo, or remove the existing photo entirely.

Managing Your Event

After you set up your event and people start RSVP'ing, you may need to manage some things. You might need to provide more info or change the location to accommodate more people. If it's a large public event, you may need to do some moderation of the people posting. Here are some common management issues you might face and how to deal with them.

Editing your event's info

Need to update the event time or add info about a dress code? You can do so at any time by clicking the Edit button at the top-right of the page, below the event photo. This opens the Edit Event Info box, which looks exactly like the Create New Event box. You can change the name of the event, the date and time, add more event details, or change the location. You can also add more hosts to the event (by default, as the creator of an event, you're already its host). Hosts have the same capabilities you have in terms of editing the event.

REMEMBER

Click Save when you're done editing.

Canceling the event

If your life has gone a bit awry and ruined your event plans, not to worry — it's easy to cancel your event:

1. **From your event's page, click the Edit button.**

The Edit Event window appears.

2. **Click Delete Event.**

A window appears asking whether you're sure you want to cancel the event.

3. **Click Confirm.**

The event is immediately canceled, and notifications will be sent to guests letting them know.

Messaging your event's guests

The most common way of communicating with your guests is simply to post something to the Posts section of the event. Much like posting something to your Timeline, you can simply click in the Write Something box and start typing.

In addition, you can start a group message thread with members of your event:

1. **Click Message Guests link underneath the RSVPs section on the right side of the page.**

A window for messaging guests appears. This window separates guests by their RSVP status. This can be useful for sending reminders to people who haven't RSVP'd or who haven't committed to attending yet.

2. **Click friends' faces to add them to the recipient list.**

When a friend has been selected, a blue check box appears to the right of their name.

3. **Type your message into the Send a Message to Guests box at the bottom of the window.**

4. **Decide whether you want to send the message as a group message.**

If you do not check the Send As Group Message box (the default), any message you send will appear as an individual message in each friend's Inbox. If you do check this box, a group message thread will be created and everyone on the list will be able to respond to each other. In other words, think of this as the difference between allowing people to reply only to you, or allowing people to reply-all on an email thread.

5. **Click Send.**

Facebook sends your message to your guest list.

Removing guests

Although removing guests isn't something that happens often, if you're hosting a large event (say, a big public fundraising effort for a charity you head), you may find that certain guests are undesirable, especially in the Posts section of the event. You can remove any posts that are inappropriate (as well as reporting spam or abuse should that happen). If there's one bad egg in particular, you can remove him from the event.

To remove a person from the event, follow these steps:

1. **On the right side of the event, click Going, which should have a number next to it representing the number of people who have RSVP'd Yes.**

   The Guest box opens.

2. **Click the X next to the name of the person you'd like to remove from the event.**

   A confirmation box appears.

3. **Click OK to confirm you really do want to remove this person from your event.**

   The person won't be told he was removed from the event; he'll just stop receiving notifications about the event. If your event also has a real-world component, you may want to compose a polite but firm message to that person letting them know they are no longer invited.

IN THIS CHAPTER

Understanding Community Pages and Official Pages

Determining whether a Facebook Page is appropriate for you

Creating and maintaining a Facebook Page

Tracking how your promotional efforts affect your business in real time

Chapter 13

Creating a Page for Promotion

icture your town or city. There's the park or school, the houses where people live, the offices where they go to work, and the stores they shop in. When you drive around town, you see all sorts of activities happening — whether people are throwing a Frisbee around, arguing politics over a cup of coffee, or working out. The world we live in is composed of people, the stuff they do, and the stuff that they need or want. People have real connections to all this stuff: the shops, the brands, the bands, the stars, the activities, the passions, and the restaurants and bars — things that are important. Facebook is all about people and their real-world connections, including the connections that aren't just friends. On Facebook, all of these non-friend entities are represented as *Pages*.

REMEMBER

"Page" is a pretty common word on the Internet, so I always capitalize the *P* in Pages when talking about Facebook Pages.

There are two main types of Pages: *Community Pages,* which are collectively updated and managed by its fans, and *Official Pages,* which are updated and managed by authorized representatives of any business entity. People who manage a Page are known as administrators, or *admins.*

This chapter is all about understanding the world of Facebook Pages. If you just want to know what these things are that you've been liking and that have been showing up in your News Feed, check out the next section, "Getting to Know Pages." If you're looking to represent your business, brand, band, or anything else on Facebook, continue on with the "Creating a Facebook Page" section.

Getting to Know Pages

You can do many of the same things with Pages that you can do with friends — write on their Timelines, tag them in status updates, and so on. The main difference is that instead of friending Pages, you like them.

When you like a Page, your information and access to your Timeline isn't shared with the Page and its admins, although any posts you make to a Page are public.

Anatomy of an Official Page

Official Pages are meant to be like Timelines, but they're intended for organizations. So if you've already read Chapter 4, most of the following will sound familiar. Figure 13-1 shows a sample Facebook Page from *For Dummies*.

FIGURE 13-1:
The *For Dummies*
Facebook Page.

Here's the anatomy of an Official Page, across the top from left to right:

>> **Profile picture and cover photo:** Just like you and your friends, Pages use one photo to represent them across the site. Usually, it's a logo or an official press photo. Pages also have a cover photo, often an image that more broadly represents the organization's brand. A blue check mark to the right of a Page name indicates that it is a *verified Page*, meaning that Facebook has confirmed this Page is actually managed by the company it represents.

>> **Like button:** The Like button is located at the right of the Page's name. To become a fan, click this button. (See the "Connecting and interacting with Pages" section for more on this topic). If you've already liked a Page, hover your mouse cursor over this button to open a menu where you can unlike the Page or adjust how you see its posts in News Feed.

>> **Message button:** Click the Message button to say something directly (and more privately) to the admins of the Page you're looking at. Not all Pages have enabled the ability to get messages, so this button may be absent from some Pages.

>> **Options (. . .):** Clicking the . . . icon opens a drop-down menu from which you can save, report, share, or block the Page. You can also use this menu to suggest edits to the Page admins or like the Page as one of your Pages (more on that in the "Using Facebook as Your Page" section).

>> **About, Photos, Likes, More:** Below the cover photo are tabs you can click to see specific content a Page has added, like photos or events.

>> **Likes and Info:** Beneath the profile photo is information about how many people have liked the Page, as well as a link to Invite friends to like this Page. Depending on the Page, there may also be additional information here about the business or person.

>> **Timeline (and Publisher):** The Timeline is the heart of a Page — it's where the admins post updates and where fans can leave posts and comments. Pages may or may not have a Publisher here, although most choose to let their fans interact as though they were friends (although the Publisher on Pages has fewer options than on your Timeline — usually just Post and Photo/Video). Scroll down to see posts the Page has added.

Community Pages

Community Pages, or Pages that don't officially represent something or someone, tend to cover a wider range of things, from basic activities to political statements. Often, the object represented by these pages is something that simply can't be owned by a corporation or individual — things like "Cheese" or "Ultimate Frisbee." You can see the Ultimate Frisbee Community Page in Figure 13-2.

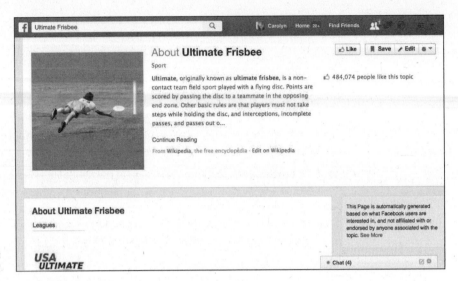

FIGURE 13-2:
Seven on the line!

Community Pages don't have a Timeline. Instead, the top portion of the Page pulls information from websites like Wikipedia. In the upper right corner of a Community Page, you can click to Like it, Save for later, or Edit the categorization of a Community Page. You can also click the gear icon to open a menu where you can share or report the Page.

The bottom portion of a Community Page is actually personalized to you. For example, if your friends have posted about Ultimate Frisbee, you might see their posts may appear here. Or you might see related Pages, or related groups. In general, Community Pages exist so that pretty much everything in the world has a way to be represented on Facebook.

Connecting and interacting with Pages

Wherever you go on Facebook, and in many places across the entire Internet, you'll see links and buttons prompting you to like something. You can like photos, statuses, comments, articles, websites, videos . . . if it's online, you can probably like it.

You can also like Pages. When you like a Page, it accomplishes a few things:

>> **Gives you a News Feed subscription.** After you like a Page, you may start seeing its posts in your News Feed. If you don't like what you see, you can remove that Page from your News Feed. To do so, go to the Page and hover over the Like button; from the drop-down menu, click Posts in News Feed. Then, in the window that opens select Unfollow to remove it from your News Feed.

>> **Provides access to the Timeline.** Just as when you add a friend, liking a Page lets you post on its Timeline, usually with the capability to add photos, links, and videos. Not all Pages allow fans to post on their Timeline, but many do.

>> **Displays the Page you liked on your own Timeline.** Keep in mind that when you like a Page, it appears in the Recent Activity section of your Timeline, and by default, this section is visible to Public/Everyone.

So what does this all mean for you? Basically, when you like something, you start a relationship with it that can be as interactive or as hands-off as you want. Frequently, people like a lot of Pages simply as a signifier or badge on their Timelines. However, just because you like *Modern Family* doesn't mean you want to read episode recaps or watch interviews with the cast. And that's fine. On the other hand, if you like seeing those sorts of things, or interacting with other fans on the show's Page, you can do that as well. It's a pretty flexible system.

Creating a Facebook Page

A Facebook Page isn't equivalent to an account. Rather, it's an entity on Facebook that can be managed by many people with their own distinct accounts. This rest of this chapter takes you through all the steps of Page creation, administration, and maintenance.

Do I need a Page?

So, you want to represent something on Facebook, but you aren't sure the best way to do so. The answer depends on what it is you want to represent and what you are trying to do on Facebook. Facebook Pages, at their most basic level, are for anything that's not an individual person and can even be useful for individuals who are celebrities or who have a public presence beyond their friends and family. That includes small businesses, big businesses, bands, pets, charities, products, and much more.

Pages are best at promotion and distribution. If what you want is discussion and collaboration, groups might be a better fit for you. For example, if you are organizing a neighborhood fun run, you might create a Page to represent the event itself, post training schedules and weather updates there, and generally let people know what's going on. At the same time, you and other organizers might choose to also create a group where you can discuss logistics. The Page is a more public presence than the group.

So whether you have a small consulting business, are fundraising for a local organization, or are a member of a performance troupe, creating a Facebook Page can work for you. You *do* need to be an authorized representative of any larger entity (for example, you shouldn't create a Page for a local congressperson unless you're working for her). But assuming that part is all squared away, you're ready to find out how to create and manage a Page.

Creating your Page

REMEMBER

Before you get started, I recommend you read the Facebook Pages Terms at www.facebook.com/terms_pages.php. The terms clarify some of the expectations for owning a Page and who can create a Page for a business. There are also a few notes about who can see your content when you create a Page and age restrictions on your Page. I cover these topics throughout this chapter, but the terms provide a nice summary. If you violate these terms, your Page may be disabled, which could negatively impact your business. On the same note, if you use a personal Timeline to do the work of a Page (as I describe here), your Facebook account will almost certainly be disabled for violating the Statement of Rights and Responsibilities (which you can read at www.facebook.com/terms.php).

If you haven't already created an account on Facebook, I highly recommend you do that first before creating a Page (although you don't have to). If you don't want to, you can still create a Facebook Page at www.facebook.com/pages/create.php. If you go this route, you'll have an additional step of entering your email address and creating a password for your Page's account.

REMEMBER

Pages can have multiple admins. If you plan to have other people managing the Page you're creating, they can do so from their own accounts. There's no reason to share the email address or password with anyone. So use your real email address and birth date; don't create a fake persona just for the Page. Your information won't be revealed to anyone else, and it makes your future interactions on Facebook much easier. To create your own Page, follow these steps:

1. **Log in to Facebook with your username and password.**

2. **Navigate to the Account menu (down arrow), located at the right corner of the blue bar, and choose Create Page from the drop-down menu.**

   The Create a Page page appears, as shown in Figure 13-3.

3. **Click the category your Page falls under.**

   You can choose from the following:

   • Local Business or Place

   • Company, Organization, or Institution

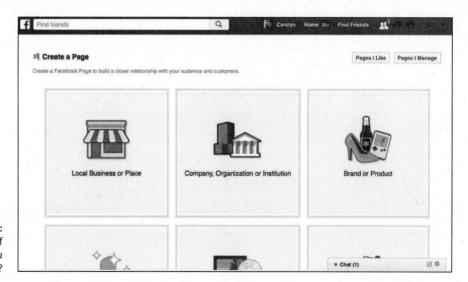

FIGURE 13-3:
What kind of
Page do you
need?

- Brand or Product

- Artist, Band, or Public Figure

- Entertainment

- Cause or Community

When you choose your category, a registry field appears.

4. **Choose your subcategory from the Choose a category menu.**

   Depending on the category you choose, there may not be sub-categories. For the purposes of these steps, I chose Artist, Band, or Public Figure.

5. **Enter the name of your Page into the Name text box.**

REMEMBER

   Use the exact name of your business, just as you need to use your real name on your Facebook account. For example, if you are creating a Page to represent Anthony's Pizza, that should be the name of your Page, not *Anthony's Pizza Official Facebook Page.*

6. **Click Get Started.**

   Remember, when you click Get Started you are agreeing to the Terms of Service.

Getting started

In this section, I go through the some of the steps Facebook takes you through to get your Page set up, as shown in Figure 13-4. Remember, this example is categorized as an Artist, Band, or Public Figure, so the fields you see on your own Page may be somewhat different.

TIP

FIGURE 13-4:
Begin setting up
your Page.

The first step is required to begin using your Page. You can skip the other steps and return to them at any time from your Page.

Step 1: Tell everyone about yourself

First, you're prompted to add a short description of yourself or your business, organization, band, or whatever your Page is about, and a link to any other web-sites that represent you. This can be anything from a Twitter feed to your personal website. You also create a unique Facebook web address to make it easier for peo-ple to get to your Page. It's much easier to tell people to like you at www.facebook.com/myname than it is to tell them to go to www.facebook.com/8u53285y2lefsjlf 0?fjdklfs.

WARNING

You can change this address only once after your initial pick, so take your time thinking about it before committing.

Step 2: Add an image

The second step is to get your Page's profile picture in place. You have two options for selecting an image:

>> Click Upload from Computer to select an image from your computer's hard drive.

>> Click Import from Website to choose from the images Facebook finds on your website.

When the photo is successfully uploaded, it replaces the default profile picture on the left side of the Page.

TIP

Profile pictures must be at least 180 x 180 pixels, and it will be cropped to fit in a square. You want your picture to be as close to square as possible to prevent it getting cropped oddly.

Step 3: Add your Page to Favorites

To make is easier for you to get to your Page when you use Facebook, click the green Add to Favorites button. It will then appear in the Favorites section of the left sidebar whenever you use Facebook.

Step 4: Pick your audience

Most of the time when you are creating a Page, it's because you are trying to reach people. Those people may be your customers or your fans. But chances are you know at least a little bit about them. Where they live, for example. If you're a coffee shop in downtown Seattle, you might not want people in Portland to find your shop when they search for coffee, but you may want them to find it if they live in Seattle or travel to Seattle. You can specify a preferred audience by Location, Age, Gender, and Interests. When you're done, click Save to be taken to your Page.

Step 5: Like yourself

Now that your Page is live, you can be the first person to like it! Just click the Like button when prompted to become your first fan.

Step 6: Invite your friends

One of the first steps in starting your Facebook account was to get some friends. This is even more important for Pages: Without likes, your updates and information won't reach anyone. A good way to start getting likes is to suggest your Page to your own friends. You may be prompted to suggest your Page to your email contact list (though this might not happen until after Step 7). Your friends receive a notification that you invited them to like this Page. If you don't get prompted to share your Page, look for the Invite Friend to Like This Page link on the right side of your Page.

Step 7: Add a cover photo

You want to make a good first impression with your Page, and one of the easiest ways to do that is to choose a beautiful cover photo. To add it, click the Add a Cover button (above the profile picture on your Page). You can select to Choose from Photos or Upload Photos. Keep in mind that "Choose from Photos" means choose from the Page's photos, so if you haven't added any photos yet, you'll want to upload something. When you're sure the photo is positioned properly, click the blue Save Changes button.

Sharing as a Page

After completing the previously described steps, you'll be looking at a fairly empty Page Timeline. You can add a bunch of content right away, or, like your personal Timeline, choose to fill it up over time. Your Page will be visible on Facebook right away, so if you are going to create it, be ready to start using it on a regular basis so that it remains active and interesting to people.

TIP

There are a few ways to quickly get to your Page when you log in to Facebook. You can click its name in the Favorites section of your left-hand menu, or search for it by name and click on it when it appears in your search results.

The Publisher

If you have a personal Timeline, your Page's Timeline will feel very familiar; it's the virtual scrapbook of posts you've added to Facebook. Your Page also needs a virtual scrapbook.

If you're a Page, the same things are true: People are going to want to hear from you and learn about you, and the place they go to do so is your Timeline. Any content you post to your Timeline also shows up in your fans' News Feeds. In other words, it's a very important place to represent yourself honestly and engagingly through continual updates.

REMEMBER

When I talk about "you" in this context, I mean your Page. So if you're a coffee shop, people want to know about your holiday drinks. If you're a band, people want to know about your shows. If you're a dog, people want to know what sort of trouble you've gotten into recently.

As a Page admin, the most important part of the Timeline for you to understand is the *Publisher.* The Publisher, as shown in Figure 13-5, is where you and your fans create the posts that populate your Page.

FIGURE 13-5: Use the Publisher to send posts out to fans.

The most basic post you can make is a *status update,* a short message letting people know what's going on, what you're up to, thinking about, and so on. Just like status updates from your personal Timeline, updates from your Page can be done quickly and easily, or with more options.

The basic steps:

1. **Click in the Publisher (where it reads Write Something at the top of the Timeline).**

2. **Type your update.**

3. **Click the blue Publish button.**

   The post now appears in your Timeline and will potentially appear in the News Feeds of people who have liked your Page.

ADD PHOTOS TO YOUR POST

Facebook actually offers some cool options to add albums or scrolling photo displays to your Page (covered in the later "Photos and videos" section). However, if you simply want to post a quick photo — for example, a company posting a photo from its holiday party, you can do so in Step 2 by clicking the camera icon at the bottom of the Publisher.

This opens an interface for exploring your computer's hard drive. Click on the photo (or photos) you want to add and click Select, Choose, or Open. Once you do so, you return to the Publisher, and the photo you selected appears as a thumbnail at the bottom of the post.

WARNING

The Publisher on a Page, though very similar to the Publisher on your Timeline, doesn't have all the same photo-editing options that your personal Timeline does. Make any edits such as rotation or adding filters before you add the photo here.

Click the X in the upper right corner of the thumbnail to remove a photo from a post, or click Publish when you're ready to share.

ADD FEELING OR ACTIVITY INFO TO YOUR POST

You can add information about what you (not you personally, but you the Page) are doing by clicking the smiley face icon at the bottom of the Publisher. Doing so opens a menu of various activities, and you can choose from any number of emotions your Page might be feeling or activities your Page might be doing. When you choose to add activity info, that info gets appended to the beginning of your post along with an emoji (or icon) representing that activity or feeling. You can see what this looks like in Figure 13-6.

FIGURE 13-6:
A day in a
dog's life.

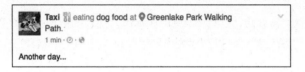

Taxi 🐾 eating dog food at 📍Greenlake Park Walking Path.
1 min · ⊘ · 🐾

Another day...

ADD LOCATION INFO TO YOUR POST

You can add information about where you are when you post something by clicking the location pin icon at the bottom of the Publisher. This opens a text box where you can type in where you are (or where you were). Facebook attempts to auto-complete as you type; when you see the place you are looking for, click on it.

Location info gets appended to the beginning of your post. You can see an example of this in Figure 13-6.

ADD TIME INFO TO YOUR POST

You can set a specific date and time when your post happened by clicking the clock icon at the bottom of the Publisher. This opens up a drop-down menu labeled "Year." You can then select a year, and once you do that you can select a month, then a day, then even a time when whatever you are posting about happened. Posts appear on the Timeline according to when they happened, so this is one way to create backdated posts that appear further back on your Timeline.

By default, if you don't change the date or time info, posts are time-stamped with the date and time on which you clicked Publish.

SCHEDULE OR BACKDATE YOUR POST

Many Pages find that it's useful to coordinate their posts with events or real-world happenings. You might not want to promote your holiday sale until a certain time or date, or you might want a specific post to appear on Thanksgiving, but not want to be sitting at your computer at either of these times. You can schedule posts to appear in the future by clicking the tiny down arrow to the right of the Publish button in the Publisher. Doing so opens a drop-down menu with three options: Schedule, Backdate, and Save Draft.

When you select Schedule, a window opens that allows you to choose when your post will appear. You can also choose to schedule an "End Date" for your post. An End Date doesn't mean your post will be deleted, but it does mean it will stop appearing in people's News Feeds. This can be really useful if you are promoting a limited-time offer or if you just want to make sure that your Page doesn't ever seem "stale" in News Feed.

When you select Backdate, a window opens that allows you to choose a date for your post. Posts that you backdate will appear further back on your Timeline, but could still appear in News Feed as a new post unless you check the Hide from News Feed box.

SAVE YOUR POST AS A DRAFT

You can save a post you are working on as a draft and return to it later. At any point while you are working on a post, click the down arrow next to the Publish button to open an options menu. Select Save Draft.

Drafts appear in a small box below the Publisher (only you and other admins can see this box). Click on the link to See Draft. This brings you to the Publishing Tools tab of your Page (more on that in the "Managing a Page" section). From there, you can click on the draft you want to work on, which opens up the post in a new window. You can click on the Edit button to change the content of the post and save the new draft. When you decide it's ready for publication, click the down arrow on the right side of the Edit button and choose Publish. You will be asked to confirm that you want to publish the post.

BOOST YOUR POST

Boosting your post is a form of paid promotion. In other words, it's a Facebook specific form of advertising.

Photos and videos

In addition to adding photos or videos to your posts by clicking the camera icon in the Publisher, Facebook offers a few options for displaying photos. You can see these options by clicking the Photo/Video tab at the top of the Publisher.

UPLOAD PHOTOS/VIDEO

Choosing to Upload Photos or Video basically functions exactly the same as clicking the camera icon in the Publisher. This opens an interface for navigating your computer's hard drive. Select the photos or video you want to post and click Select or Open. That brings you back to the Publisher where you can preview your photos or videos and write a little something to go with the post.

CREATE PHOTO ALBUM

Creating a photo album is a way to organize lots of photos. So a band might create an album of photos from shows, or an album of photos of merchandise, or an album of photos of the band on the road. Or all three. Selecting Create Photo Album opens an interface for choosing photos from your computer. Choose as many photos as you want and then click Select or Open. This brings you to the Create Album window, shown in Figure 13-7.

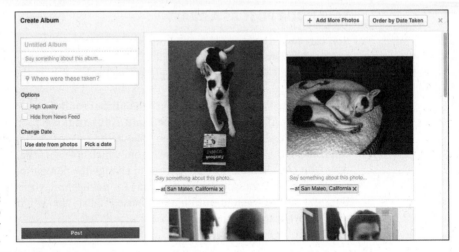

FIGURE 13-7:
Create a photo
album for
your Page.

Creating photo albums is covered in detail in Chapter 11. So if this is looking overwhelming to you, hop on over there for a tutorial. As a brief refresher, from here you can:

>> Create an Album Title and Description

>> Add location info about where photos were taken

>> Decide whether the photos should appear in High Quality

>> Decide if the Album should appear in News Feed or not

>> Pick a date for the album (or use the date information from the photos)

>> Tag people in the photos

>> Add captions to photos

>> Rotate individual photos

>> Add more photos

After you edit your album to your heart's content, click the blue Post button to post it to your Page.

CREATE A PHOTO CAROUSEL

Photo carousels are built using photos from external website. So if you already have a band web page, you can reuse the photos that live there by simply entering your web address into the Destination URL box that appears when you click to Create a Photo Carousel. Doing so imports a selection of three photos from your site. When you click Publish, the post appears as photos people can rotate through. They can then click on any of them to be taken to your website.

CREATE SLIDESHOW

Slide show are created by allowing you to choose 3-7 photos from your computer's hard drive. After you select these photos (the same way you would choose photos for a post or an album), Facebook automatically generates a slide show that plays as a video from your Page's Timeline.

Events

If you ever host an event for your business, you'll get a ton of value from using Facebook Events. Stores create events for their big sales, comedians create events for their shows, and clubs create events for their special-party nights. To create an event, click Event, Milestone + in the Publisher, then click Event. The Create New Event window appears. Fill in the Event info and click Create. Head on over to the event's page to invite your friends and add an event photo. Events you create for your Page are Public by default, meaning anyone can see and join the event.

If you haven't used Facebook Events before, see Chapter 12 to learn more about creating and managing your own events.

Milestones

Much like on your personal Timeline, adding milestones is something you can do for your Page to acknowledge big moments in your history. If you're a charity you might want to create milestones for the date you were founded, or the day you reached a certain fundraising goal. You can add milestones on an ongoing basis as well as create as many milestones as you want to go in the past. Clicking on Milestone in the Publisher opens the Create Milestone window, shown in Figure 13-8.

When you add milestones to your personal Timeline, Facebook asks you to choose the type of milestone so it can assign a particular icon to it and provide specific fields (for example, birth dates for the milestone of having a baby). On Pages,

Facebook simply shows a generic milestone template and lets you edit it as you will. You can create a title (for example: opened new offices downtown), then add photos, information about locations and dates, and provide an additional "story." When you're done, click the blue Save button and the milestone will be added to the proper place on your Page's Timeline.

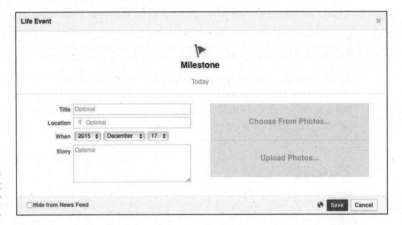

Life Event ✕

Milestone

Today

Title | Optional
Location | ⦿ Optional
When | 2015 ⬍ | December ⬍ | 17 ⬍
Story | Optional

Choose From Photos...

Upload Photos...

☐ Hide from News Feed   ↻ **Save** Cancel

FIGURE 13-8:
Add an important event to your Page's Timeline.

TIP

If you are creating a lot of milestones as you set up a Page, make sure to check the Hide from News Feed button, which prevents those items from appearing as News Feed stories for people who have liked your Page.

Notes

Notes is Facebook's blogging service. Notes look similar to the posts you might see on the blogging platform Medium.com — in other words, a big pretty photo on top and big centered text beneath. Previews of your notes appear as posts on your Page's Timeline. To create a note, click the "Event, Milestone +" tab in the Publisher, and then click Note. This opens the Create Note window. Click on the top grey section to add a photo to the top of the Note. Click on the Title to add a title to the note, and click where it says "Write Something. . ." to write up your note or blog post.

While you are writing, you can click on the grey photo icon on the left side of the Create Note window to add a photo to the text. You can click on the formatting icon (a series of parallel lines) to add formatting such as headers or bullet points to your text. When you're done, click the blue Publish button to publish your note. If you want to save and come back later to keep working on your note, click the grey Save button.

Using Facebook as Your Page

Part of using Facebook as a Page is being interactive. Pages aren't just ways for you to distribute information to people who like your business or band or book. Pages are a way for you to engage in conversation and be human (or as human as a Page can be) with people. Part of that is liking and commenting on behalf of your Page.

Liking, commenting on, and sharing posts

As a Page admin, when you are looking at posts on Facebook, you have the opportunity to like and comment on many of them *as* your Page. When you are looking at a public post from another Page, look in the lower right corner of the post, where a tiny thumbnail of your (personal) profile picture appears next to a down arrow. Clicking that arrow opens a window for selecting who you want to comment as, shown in Figure 13-9.

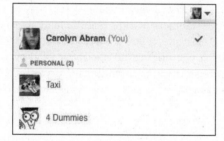

FIGURE 13-9:
Like or comment as your Page.

Select the Page you would like to use to comment or like, and then click on any of the links at the bottom of the post to like, comment, or share that link on your Page.

When you like, comment, or share as a Page, changing who is commenting only works for that particular post. In other words, if there are ten articles you want to comment on as your Page, you will need to switch from your personal account to your Page as described above each of those ten times.

Liking other Pages

You can like other Pages as your Page. To do so, follow these steps. For clarity's sake, I reference your Page as LocalCoffeehouse and the Page you want to like as MajorCoffeeBrand.

1. **Go to the Page you want to like (MajorCoffeeBrand).**

2. **Click the More [. . .] button in the lower right corner of the cover photo.**

   A menu of options opens.

3. **Click Like As Your Page.**

   A confirmation window appears where you can choose the Page you want to use to like MajorCoffeeBrand.

4. **Use the drop-down menu to choose LocalCoffeehouse.**

5. **Click Save.**

When you like other Pages, those Pages appear in your Pages Feed, which you can get to from your Page. Liking other Pages can be a great way to be involved with the other entities your Page interacts with in real life, and also a way to get ideas for what to post about. For example, if you are a restaurant and you like the Pages of other restaurants nearby, you might find out about local events that you also want to promote. There are so many possibilities for using your Page over time; this chapter really just gives you the basics. Other Pages can teach you a lot.

Managing a Page

The basics of using a Page are fairly simple: Pages are timelines for non-people (or famous people); use them to share and interact with your customers and fans. Up to this point, this chapter has focused on those basics.

Once you have the basics down, however, it's worth noting that Pages is an incredibly powerful and diverse product. Pages can be created to represent the family dog or to represent the next President of the United States. The needs for those two entities are pretty different, and yet Pages accommodates them both. In this section, I'm going to go over many of the settings and tools that Pages offers you beyond simple sharing. Some of these tools might seem superfluous to you. Some of the settings might not apply to you. I might miss certain settings that only apply to certain Page types (since my test Pages might be from different Page types). If you find yourself with a question I don't answer here, Facebook itself provides a lot of material for Page owners to explore and learn from. A good place to start is www.facebook.com/business/products/pages/.

You may notice that when you look at your Page, there is an additional menu bar across the page, right below the blue bar on top. Pictured in Figure 13-10, these tabs are only visible to you as the Page's admin. People who like the Page don't see this.

FIGURE 13-10:
Page
management
tabs.

The first tab, Page, simply brings you back to your Page's Timeline. The other tabs are where you get into some other options that help you get the most from your Page.

Messages

Much like your personal Facebook account, Pages have an Inbox where you (and other admins) can respond to messages from people who encounter your Page. People don't have to like your Page to message it, and the sorts of messages you receive may vary. Figure 13-11 shows a sample Inbox, with an open message.

At first glance, this Inbox looks very similar to your personal message center, and it does have some similarities. Your message list is displayed on the left side of the page, with the newest messages appearing at the top of the list. Unread messages are in **bold.** The message you have open is displayed in the center of the page. You read a message thread from top to bottom (scroll up to see the oldest messages) and you can type your reply at the bottom of the thread.

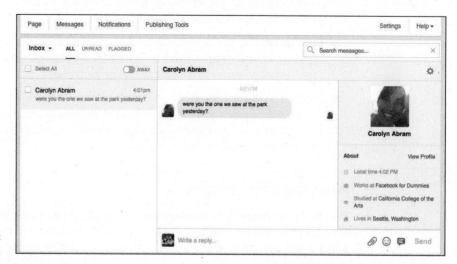

FIGURE 13-11:
A Page Inbox.

Unlike your personal Inbox, the right side of the page displays any publicly available info about the person you are messaging with. This gives you a sense of whom you are talking to — where they are from, where they work, all the sorts of things that might be important to learn if someone is trying to contact you to make a professional connection.

Depending on what your Page represents, you might also get a lot of "customer support" type questions in your messages as well. In those cases, it might be less important to know these biographical details about your customer, but it never hurts to put a name with a face when you are talking to your customers.

You can use the search box on the top right side of the page to search through your Page's messages by keyword.

Message options

When you are looking at the list of messages down the left side of the page, you have a few options for keeping track of messages. Hover over any individual thread and click the gear icon that appears to access these options:

>> **Flag:** Flagging a message thread ads a tiny orange corner to that thread in the Inbox. You can flag a message for any reason and it's up to you and your fellow Page admins to decide what types of messages get flagged. You might choose to flag any message that requires a reply, or to flag messages that require urgent action. It's up to you.

>> **Report as Spam:** If you receive messages that are spam, click this option to remove them from the Inbox. Messages you mark as spam get moved to your Spam folder, which you can access by clicking the down arrow next to the word Inbox at the upper left corner of the Inbox.

>> **Mark as Unread:** You can choose to mark messages as read or unread, again, signifying whatever you and your fellow admins agree upon. I usually mark messages as unread when I intend to reread them later.

>> **Archive:** Archiving a message moves it to the Archived folder, which you can access by clicking the down arrow next to the word Inbox at the upper right corner of the page. Archived messages reappear in the Inbox if either you or the other person adds another message to the thread.

Replying to messages

The basics for replying to messages as a Page are pretty much the same as any email, text, or instant message service. Type your response and click Send. Additionally, you can add attachments or emoticons by clicking the paperclip or smiley icon, respectively.

Facebook also provides the ability to send what it calls *saved replies*. Saved replies are just what they sound like, common replies that you can save to more quickly send to people. Are people always writing in to ask what the delivery window is for your pizza shop? Create a saved reply explaining your policies. Then, anytime someone writes in asking that question, you can respond in just a few clicks; no typing necessary. Click the speech bubble icon to open the Saved Replies window, shown in Figure 13-12.

FIGURE 13-12:
Create Saved
replies here.

Saved replies are designated by titles (which the person you are messaging doesn't see). If you have a lot of saved replies, you can search through the options using the search box at the top of the Saved Replies window. To select one of the saved replies, simply click on the reply you want to send. This fills the reply box with the text from the saved reply. Then click Send.

You can click the blue link to Create New Reply. This opens a window for entering the title and text of the saved reply. You can click to personalize the saved reply with things like the name of the admin who is replying, or the name of the person who originally sent the message. You can also add images from your computer's hard drive. Click Save Reply when you're done creating the reply.

Notifications

Whenever anything happens to your Page such as someone liking it, liking a post your Page made, commenting on a post, sharing a post, and more, it creates a notification. All the notifications about your Page are collected on the Notifications tab, shown in Figure 13-13.

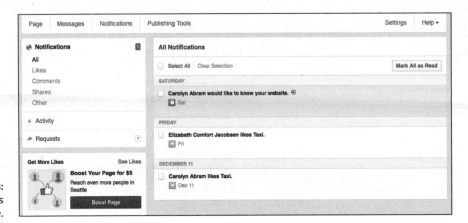

FIGURE 13-13:
Notifications
go here.

Notifications may or may not be something that winds up mattering to you as a Page owner. In general, evidence of people interacting with your Page and the content you post is considered to be a good sign of engagement, so if suddenly the amount of notifications change a lot or a little, that can be important to note. You can mark notifications as read or unread by selecting individual notifications (via the check box to each one's left), and then clicking the Mark as Read or Mark as Unread buttons.

In addition to notifications of actions, the Notifications tab shows you a record of *activity* and *information requests.* Activity includes things like people mentioning (or tagging) your Page in a post. Information Requests show up when someone comes to your Page and wants to find out something that isn't there. For example, if you didn't add a website to your Page when you set it up, people can click a link to ask for your website. Those requests come to this portion of your Page's Notifications tab.

You can control how you receive notifications from the Settings tab. I go over that a little later on in this chapter, in the section, "Settings."

Publishing Tools

The Publishing Tools tab gives you the ability to quickly review your posts — ones you have already made, ones you have drafted, and ones you have scheduled. As shown in Figure 13-14, the Publishing Tools tab shows a list of your posts, along with some data about those posts.

The left side of the Publishing Tools tab categorizes your posts so you can quickly get to the type of post you want to review. For example, if you are logging in to see what posts other admins have scheduled for the upcoming week, you can click on Scheduled Posts to view only those posts. You can also use this menu on the left side to jump to your video library and to any forms you have created for Lead Ads.

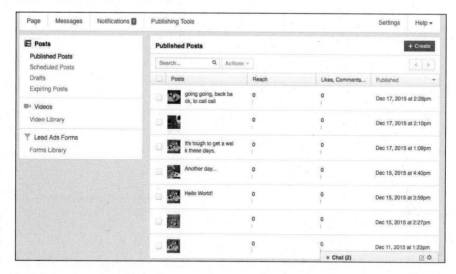

FIGURE 13-14: Review your posts and their impact.

When you are looking at Published Posts, you can see a thumbnail of whatever image accompanied the post and the title of it (if it had one). You can then view your *reach* for that post. Reach means the number of people who saw the post. Remember, News Feed (the main way your posts get distributed) works on an algorithm so that each person using Facebook sees what is most likely to be interesting to that person, so not all the people who have liked your Page will see your post. You can also see how many people liked or commented on your post. Finally, you can see when your post was published on the right side of the screen.

Settings

As I mentioned previously, Pages is a powerful and in many ways very flexible system that accommodates virtually every type of entity that isn't a person. In order for a system to be that flexible, it needs to have a lot of options. And nowhere is the number of options available more apparent than on the Settings tab (see Figure 13-15). Here, I go through each setting. I try to include examples of how some of the more obscure settings might be used. Remember, depending on your Page and how you use it, many of these might not be very relevant to you. Many settings will seem especially irrelevant if you're just starting out with your Page and don't have a lot of people who have liked it. If your Page has recently picked up in popularity and you are feeling overwhelmed by managing it, you may want to revisit some of the settings you had previously ignored.

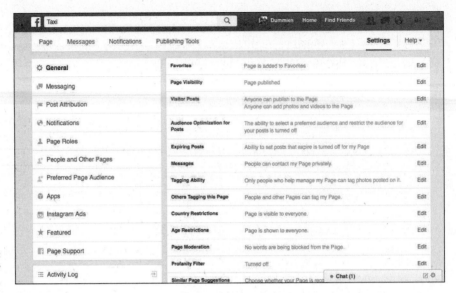

FIGURE 13-15:
Settings, so many
settings.

General

General settings include a variety of settings about how your Page posts and interacts with other people and Pages on Facebook. To open the settings related to these categories, click Edit to the right of each setting. When you adjust a setting, remember to click Save Changes.

>> **Favorites:** This adds your Page to the Favorites section of your left sidebar.

>> **Page Visibility:** This controls whether or not your page is Published (publically visible) or not. If you want to make a lot of edits to your Page without people seeing those edits, you may want to opt to Unpublish the Page for a period of time while you make your changes.

>> **Visitor Posts:** By default, people can post to your Page as they would post on a friend's Timeline. You can disable this, or choose for people to be able to post text, but not photos and videos, or choose to review posts before they appear on your Page.

>> **News Feed Audience and Visibility for Posts:** If you want the ability to "target" your post to certain demographics (for example, a post about your band's upcoming show in New York only being shown to people who live in New York), you can turn this setting on. Once it's turned on, you'll be able to access the Audience Selector by clicking the globe icon that appears in the Publisher.

>> **Expiring Posts:** You can choose whether or not admins and editors can create posts that expire.

>> **Messages:** If you don't want people to be able to message your Page, you can turn off that ability here. There are any number of reasons you might not want to use the message features — you don't think you'll have the time to respond to messages, or you would rather people contact you elsewhere, or you just don't think it makes sense for you.

>> **Tagging Ability:** You can choose to allow everyone to tag photos and videos you post, or you can choose to only let you and other admins tag photos and videos posted by your Page.

>> **Country Restrictions:** By default, everyone the world over can find and view your Page. You can choose to hide it from certain countries, or only allow certain countries to see it.

>> **Age Restrictions:** By default, anyone of any age (well, older than 13, which is the youngest age at which you can use Facebook) can see your Page. You can choose to restrict this so that people under 17, 18, or 21 can't see your Page. This is most relevant to you if you are creating a Page to represent a brand of alcohol or tobacco (and there is, in fact an "Alcohol-related" setting that automatically adjusts the age restrictions for your Page.

>> **Page Moderation:** You can create a list of words that, if they are detected in a post, cause that post to be immediately reported as spam and taken down.

>> **Profanity Filter:** You can choose to turn on Facebook's profanity filter, which has two settings: Medium or Strong. If someone tries to enter a post with a profanity, that person will be unable to add it to your Page.

>> **Similar Page Suggestions:** This controls whether or not your Page will appear in Facebook's automatically generated "Page Suggestions." By default your Page appears in Page suggestions.

>> **Comment Ranking:** If you are a very popular Page that gets lots of comments and replies to every post you make, you may want to turn on comment ranking. This basically tries to determine the most relevant comments (as determined by people liking and replying to that comment) at the top of the comments section. If you don't turn this on, the most recent comments are displayed first.

>> **Merge Pages:** If you wound up with more than one Page for the same thing (it happens), you can merge the two so that it's easier to reach everyone who has liked either Page.

>> **Remove Page:** If you want to delete your Page entirely from Facebook, follow the prompts in this setting.

Messaging

The Messaging section of your Page is where you'll go to communicate directly with customers and fans. Assuming you have kept your Page's ability to receive messages, you can adjust a few settings here:

>> **Response Time Display:** If you visit your Page at least once a week and typically respond to 90% of your messages, Facebook automatically displays your average response time to people who visit your Page. If you don't meet these two criteria, then no information is provided related to response time. You can choose to show either your average response time, or what you want people to expect as a response time (an hour, a few hours, a day).

>> **Instant Replies:** Even if you don't intend to respond to messages instantly, you can enable an *Instant Reply*, or auto-reply that gets sent to people whenever they write to you. Instant replies can include any information you think is relevant to messaging with your Page. Remember to click Save Reply when you're done writing your instant reply.

Page Info

Clicking the Page Info section of the Settings tab brings you to the About section of your Page. Here, you can see all the possible fields you can fill out, and then click to edit or add the information there. Remember to save any info you change.

Post Attribution

Post Attribution settings dictate whether, by default, your posts to your Page will be attributed to you personally or to the persona of your Page. In other words, if I create a Page for my dog, Taxi, I can decide whether posts to Taxi's Page come from me, Carolyn, or from Taxi.

Notifications

Notifications always appear in your Notifications tab for your Page, but you can also choose if they go into your Facebook notifications (where your notifications for your personal account also appear), your email, or via text message on your phone.

If you do want to see Notifications on Facebook but are feeling a bit overwhelmed by receiving too many, you can also choose to receive a summary of notifications every 12–24 hours. You can also choose to turn off specific types of notifications (for example, you might want to be notified about new comments, so you can reply right away, but you might not want to be notified whenever someone likes a post).

You can also turn off notifications about messages your Page receives. This can be helpful if most of the time you are using Facebook as yourself, and not your Page. Your Page's messages will always be available in the Messages tab.

Page Roles

Page Roles represent the different responsibilities that people who manage Pages may have. Often, you aren't the only person who represents your Page. You might have a small business and you may want all your employees to be able to post photos and announcements on behalf of your Page. Or you might need moderators to respond to people's comments and messages that you cannot respond to yourself. There are five different types of page roles, outlined below:

» **Admin:** If you created a Page, you are automatically its admin, and you can control all aspects of your Page. That includes: adding other people as admins or other roles, editing your Page's settings, editing the Page and adding apps, posting from the Page, sending messages as the Page, responding to and deleting comments and post as the Page, removing and banning people from the Page, creating ads, viewing insights, and seeing who published as the Page.

» **Editor:** Editors have all the same abilities as admins, but they *do not* have the ability to edit all of the Page's settings or assign Page roles to other people.

» **Moderator:** Moderators have many of the same abilities as admins and editors, but they can't edit the Page or create posts as the Page.

» **Advertiser:** Advertisers only have the ability to create ads, view insights, and see who published as the Page. Lots of companies specialize in helping people manage their online advertising presence, which is why this is a unique position you can assign out.

» **Analysts:** Analysts can see your Page's insights and see who published as the Page.

As the admin, you can add someone as any of these roles from the Page Roles section of the Settings tab. When viewing this page, you can see yourself listed as the admin. Click the link beneath your name to Add Another Person. Type a name or email address into the text field that opens, then decide what type of role you would like that person to have in managing your Page. Click Save when you are done.

People and Other Pages

The People and Other Pages section of the Settings tab displays all the people and Pages who have liked your Page. Hover over any name and click on the gear icon that appears to take any of the following actions:

>> **Assign Page Role:** You can choose a Page Role (as described a few paragraphs ago) from among the people who have liked your Page.

>> **Remove from Page Likes:** Removing people from Page likes means that person will no longer be shown as someone who likes your Page. It's basically a way to force someone to unlike your Page.

>> **Ban from Page:** If someone is being abusive or inappropriate on your Page, you can ban that person from ever interacting with your Page again.

Preferred Page Audience

When you set up your Page, you were asked to describe your preferred audience. You can come to the Preferred Page Audience section to edit or refine the information about your preferred audience. You can add preferred categories by location, age, gender, and interests. After you add an interest or two that your preferred audience might have, you can click the Suggestions button to get suggestions from Facebook about other interests that might indicate an interest in your Page. For example, when I put in that people who were interested in dogs were my preferred audience for my Page, Facebook suggested that I might also be of interest to people who were interested in Cats or Horses. Remember to click Save when you're done editing your preferred audience.

Apps

Apps are a way for companies that are not Facebook to build functionality that works on Facebook. Apps for Pages often add specific tabs to your Page for things like creating an online shop or displaying content from another website. One way to get ideas for apps that might be useful to your Page is to look at similar Pages and see what apps they use.

The Apps section shows you all the applications your Page is using. If you no longer use some of these applications, click the x to remove them.

Instagram Ads

From the Instagram Ads section, you can link your business's Instagram account to its Facebook Page. After you link these accounts, you can create ads on Facebook and show those same ads on Instagram.

Featured

The Featured section is where you can choose to feature certain Pages your Page has liked or to feature Page Owners. A selection of Pages your Page has liked always appears on your Page, so choosing to feature some merely allows you to specify which ones you'd most like people to know you like.

If you choose to feature Page Owners (and, in most cases, that would probably include you), those people's personal profiles (meaning their profile picture, name, and other publicly available info) gets displayed in the About section of your Page. Additionally, the Page will be listed on their personal profiles as one they own.

Page Support

Page Support is a special Inbox for communicating with Facebook's support team about your Page. If you ever wind up needing help from Facebook with your Page (for things like resetting your password or following up on reported material), those messages can be found in the Page Support section of your Page.

Activity Log

The Activity Log is a chronologically ordered list of every action your Page has taken (such as posting a photo) as well as every action involving your Page (such as being tagged in a status update).

Insights: Finding Out Who Is Using Your Page

After you create your Page and enough people like it, you might notice an additional tab at the top of your Page: Insights. The Insights tab contains all the data that Facebook can give you about who is looking at your Page, what they liked or didn't like, how they've been interacting with your Page, and how that all has been changing over time. You can see a sample Insights Overview in Figure 13-16.

Much like many of your Page's management tabs, a menu down the left side of the page lets you dig into different statistics: Likes, Reach, Page Views, Posts, Videos, and People. By default, you land on the Overview section, which gives you, well, an overview of all those different stats.

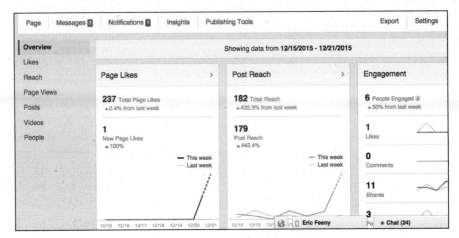

FIGURE 13-16:
View your Page
Insights here.

At the top of the Overview section the date range of the data is noted. Underneath are three boxes, each with some numbers and graphs.

>> **Page Likes:** Likes are the most basic metric for measuring how your Page is doing. Likes aren't everything; if you're trying to draw attention to your Page, someone clicking Like and then never visiting your Page again or reading anything you post isn't actually so useful. But your "Likes count" is a good baseline number to pay attention to. The Page Likes box shows you how many likes you have, and how much it's changed in the last week. If you notice a sudden uptick or downtick in likes, you might want to think about anything your Page has done or posted in the last week that might have mattered to people.

>> **Post Reach:** Post Reach shows you how many people have seen posts you've made in the last week, and how much that's changed from the previous week.

>> **Engagement:** Engagement keeps track of how many people have liked, commented, shared, or clicked on one of your posts in the last week, and how that's changed from the previous week.

None of these numbers, alone, really matter. But together, they paint a picture of what your customers and fans are doing, and if you are truly interacting with them, or simply shouting into the void. And, the way these numbers trend over time helps you learn more about your customers and fans and how they want you to interact with them.

Below the Page Likes, Post Reach, and Engagement boxes are insights about your five most recent posts. You can see each post gets a row with a link to the post if you want to view it. You can see what type of post it is (link, picture, video, and so on), how it was targeted (everyone or a specific demographic), the reach of that post, and the engagement with that post. Again, you're not looking to achieve any one particular goal here, but you can learn a great deal. You might see that you have more engagement with photo posts, or greater reach when you target a post by demographic. Because managing a Page is an ongoing thing, these types of insights let you make small adjustments to how you manage your Page and share with people who like your Page.

You can also click to boost any of your recent posts.

Chapter 14

Using Facebook with Games, Websites, and Apps

This book spends a lot of time defining what Facebook is — it's a way to keep up with friends, it's a constantly updating newsletter about your friends, it's a way to share photos and posts. There's one more definition to add to the list: Facebook is a collection of information about you. It's not the cuddliest definition, but it's an important one to understand as you learn about *Facebook Platform*.

Facebook Platform is the means by which Facebook takes your collection of information and (with your consent) makes it available to other websites, game manufacturers, and app developers. What this means in practical, concrete terms is that you can choose to use your Facebook information to, for example, log in to a website like Pinterest and share your pins with Facebook friends. You can also use your Facebook information to start playing games like Candy Crush or Bejeweled Blitz with your friends, both on Facebook, and on your mobile phone.

The ways you'll see Facebook Platform integrating into your experience on Facebook may change over time. Right now, you'll likely see it mostly as games and as ways to log in to other websites, and then post stories back to Facebook. No matter what forms it may take in the future, it's important to understand what you share with apps. After that, I go into the more common examples of how you'll wind up using apps, and then I go into managing your apps and your information over time.

What Apps Need

For the purposes of this chapter, when I talk about apps, I'm talking about games and websites that were built by companies other than Facebook. But for the purposes of the next few sentences, I want to talk about an app that Facebook did build: Photos. As I cover in the Chapter 11, Facebook Photos is an incredibly useful tool because it's easy for people to see your photos, as well as photos of you.

Photos works well because Facebook knows some really important information about who you are (your name and face) and who your friends are (people who would likely want to see your photos). Facebook also knows that you are okay sharing your photos through News Feed, because, hey, you're using Facebook to share your photos. In other words, Facebook uses your information — who you are, who your friends are — to create a useful experience — sharing photos.

Other apps, ones not built by Facebook, require the same things to work. They need to know who you are and who your friends are. Some of them may need to know when your birthday is or the type of music you like. Unlike an app like Photos that has your permission as soon as you start using Facebook, websites, games, and apps need to obtain your permission before they can get this information. Here's how to think about the information apps need and get when you use a game or outside website.

The basics

All apps need your basic information and your email address if you want to use them. In other words, if you're not comfortable sharing this information with an app, you can't use it. Your *basic information* refers, in this case, to any information about you that is set to Public. For everyone on Facebook, this includes

>> Your name

>> Your profile picture

>> Your gender

>> Your user ID (This is the number associated with your Facebook account; everyone has a unique ID.)

>> Any other information you have shared publicly

In addition to this, when you start using a game or app, most apps will request that you share your contact email address with them. It will be allowed to store that email address in order to contact you in the future. This allows you to establish a direct relationship with the app so that the developers can always get in touch with you, without Facebook acting as an intermediary.

Giving your email to an application means you can get email newsletters and other updates direct from the source without logging in to Facebook. If at any time you don't want to share your email address with a certain application anymore, you need to unsubscribe from its email list through *the app developer* (in other words, through whatever company makes the app) as opposed to through Facebook.

The slightly less basic

In addition to basic information, apps might require specific types of information that is not publicly available. What information this includes depends entirely on the app and what it does. Here are some examples of information an app might want to use:

>> Your list of friends

>> Things you like (books, music, movies, Pages, and so on)

>> Things your friends like (books, music, movies, Pages, and so on)

>> Location information (Hometown, Current City)

>> Your birthday

>> Your photos

>> Your posts

>> Posts that have been shared with you

>> Other profile info, such as your education, work history, and relationship information

Permission to act

In addition to all the types of information apps need from you, apps also need permission to take certain actions, including things such as the following:

>> **Posting to your Timeline on your behalf** (for example, creating a post when you win a game). You can choose who can see these posts using the regular Privacy menu, which I discuss at length in Chapter 6.

>> **Sending you notifications.** Notifications are similar to the notifications you receive from Facebook about being tagged in a photo or invited to an event. Games or apps may send you notifications about it being your turn in a game, or receiving an item or challenge from another player.

Games on Facebook

The most common type of app on Facebook at the moment is a game. Games can range from matching games like Bejeweled Blitz or Candy Crush to casino games like Texas HoldEm or Bingo Blitz. Whenever you click to play a game on Facebook, you see the Continue to Game window, shown in Figure 14-1.

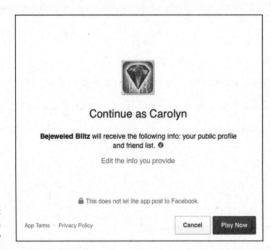

FIGURE 14-1:
Continue on to
play your game?

The moment that you see this window is the moment of truth in terms of deciding whether or not you want to share your information with the game in order to play it. The window provides a few pieces of information to pay attention to:

>> **Your Name:** If you share your computer with other people, when you see this window you want to make sure that your name is the one you are looking at.

>> **What the app receives:** Facebook provides a list of the information the app will receive when you click Play Now. Often that is just the basics I list earlier (also known as your public profile). Sometimes it will include other pieces of information such as your email address, birthday, or Friend List. You can choose to edit what you provide to an app by clicking the Edit the Info You Provide link. Clicking this link opens a list of the information that the app has requested (shown in Figure 14-2). Uncheck the circle to the right of any piece of information to prevent that info being shared with the game.

REMEMBER

You can't uncheck sharing your Public Profile with a game. If you don't want to share your basic information with a game, you don't get to play it.

>> **Permission to Act information:** Most games have a notice at the bottom of the Continue to Game window that says "This does not let the app post to Facebook." Most games will ask for permission to post later on, once you've already started playing. If this notice does ever say that it will allow the game to post to Facebook, make sure you are comfortable with that happening before you click Play Now.

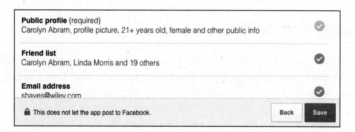

When you have reviewed this information and are comfortable with what you are about to share with the game, click the blue Play Now button to go to the game's Home page.

Game Home pages on Facebook

You can see a sample Home page (for *Candy Crush Saga*) in Figure 14-3. Its Home page basically prompts you to start playing the game. Notice that the blue bar is still at the top of the screen, which means that if you get bored playing this game, you can easily go back to your Facebook Home page or Timeline.

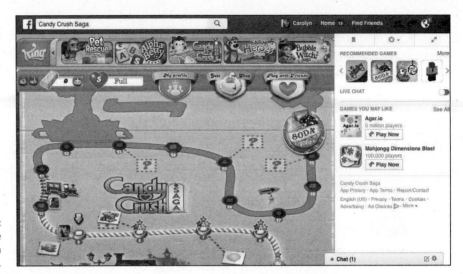

FIGURE 14-3:
The Home page
for Candy Crush
Saga.

Some games don't have Home pages within Facebook; instead when you click on them you get taken to a new browser window or tab to play your game on the game's website. Depending on what game you're playing, you can follow that game's prompts to learn how to make matches, find the bad guy, or win the poker pot!

Sidebar links

The left sidebar on your Home page is where you go to get to different parts of Facebook: your groups, News Feed, events, and so on. Links to the games you play most often will also appear in the Apps section of the sidebar.

You can add the games you play most often to the Favorites section of your sidebar. Mouse over the game you want to add and click the gear icon that appears next to it. You can then select "Add to Favorites" from the menu that appears.

TIP

If you've used lots of games and apps over time, you might not see all of them listed in the sidebar. If this is the case, hover your mouse cursor over the word "Apps" and click to More link that appears to be taken to a full list of your apps.

Invitations and notifications

Just like you can invite friends to events, you can also invite friends to play games with you. After your friends are playing the same game as you or using the same application, you can send them requests for specific actions. Both of these appear in your friend's notifications on the friend's Home page.

When you send a notification or invitation through a game, a preview window appears, as shown in Figure 14-4. This shows you what your friend will see in his notifications and asks you to confirm that you want to send the invitation or notification.

FIGURE 14-4:
Sending requests.

WARNING

In Figure 14-4, note the Don't Ask Again Before Sending Requests To <*friend*> From This App check box below the preview. If you leave this check box selected, the app will be able to send that friend requests on your behalf as often as it wants. Clear this check box so that you always know when an app is sending your friend a request.

Posts

As you play games, you may also be prompted to post things to your Timeline. Figure 14-5 shows what one such prompt might look like. In this case, it's a game prompting you to share that you completed another level. If you want to share these achievements with friends, that's great; click the Share button and feel free to add your own comments to the text field.

FIGURE 14-5:
Posting to your Timeline.

If you'd rather not post to your Timeline about something like this, just click Cancel and continue on with whatever it was you were doing.

The Game Center

If you find yourself really into playing games on Facebook, the Game Center can be a great place to find out about the new games. To get there, click on the Games link in the left sidebar (under the Apps heading). Figure 14-6 shows the Game Center.

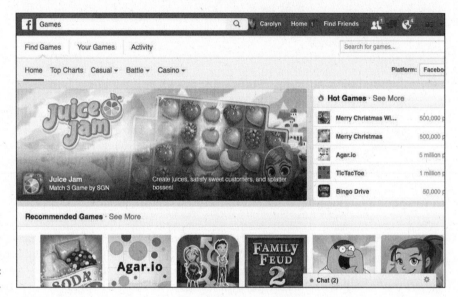

FIGURE 14-6:
The Game Center.

The top portion of the Game Center showcases a rotating number of "Featured" games. You can also see "Hot Games" listed on the right side of the page. You can click to look at games by category (Casual, Battle, or Casino), or scroll down to see recommended games. You can search for games in the top right corner of the page.

At the very top of the page, right below the blue bar, are three tabs. By default, whenever you click to go to the Game Center you arrive on the Find Games tab. You can click to go to the Your Games tab or the Activity tab. The Your Games tab allows you to see all the games you play. You can click to begin playing any of those games, or click on the gear icon to edit how that game interacts with your Facebook information (more on this in the "Managing Your Games, Apps, and Websites" section).

Whenever you click on a game in the Game Center, a Continue to Game window opens. If you want to learn more about the game, click on the arrows in the upper portion of the window to page through a slide show with screen shots and information about how to play the game. You can use the buttons at the top of the window to like or share the game, or to visit the game's Page on Facebook. If you decide you don't want to play the game after all, click on the X in the upper right corner to close the window and return to the Game Center.

Using Facebook Outside of Facebook

Believe it or not, there are websites out there that aren't Facebook. Websites like Yelp can help you find a place to eat. Or you might watch television at www.hulu.com. Or you might create pin boards of interests on www.pinterest.com. Many of the most popular websites out there allow you to use your Facebook credentials to speed up the process of getting started on a new site, as well as to share activity more widely with your friends on Facebook.

Log in with Facebook

Figure 14-7 shows the landing page for www.pinterest.com. Pinterest is a website that allows you to create collections (called boards) of interesting links or images you find on the web. For example, if you're planning on getting a haircut, you could create a board where you "pin" images of hairstyles you like. What's important in Figure 14-7 is that there are two ways to get started on Pinterest — you can enter your email and create a password or you can click the big blue Continue with Facebook button. On some websites, this might say Log In with Facebook, but the effect is the same; clicking it brings up the Log In with Facebook window, shown in Figure 14-8.

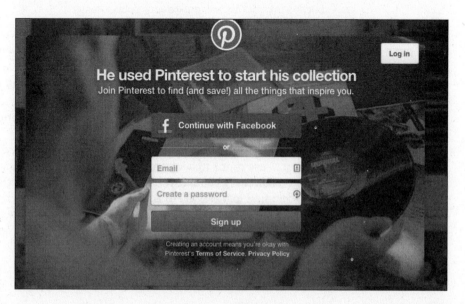

FIGURE 14-7:
Two ways to join.

FIGURE 14-8:
Log in with
Facebook.

If this looks familiar, that's because it's more or less exactly the same as the Continue to Game window shown in Figure 14-1. That's because the same thing is happening here: You are deciding if you want to share your Facebook information with a company that is not Facebook. Just like the Continue to Game window, the Log in with Facebook window tells you the following information:

>> **Your name:** *Your name* is your first name that you use on Facebook.

>> **The name of the website you are about to log in to:** In this example, Pinterest is the website you are about to log in to.

>> **The information that website will receive:** You can click the Edit the Info You Provide link to change the information that you allow the website to get, but at a minimum it will require your public profile.

>> **Information about permission to act:** In other words, it tells you whether or not clicking Okay will allow the website to post information back to Facebook.

If you're okay sharing this information, click Okay to continue on to using the website. Some websites may ask you to enter your email address after this step, in order for them to be able to contact you directly, instead of through Facebook.

I chose Pinterest as an example because it shows some of the ways you might find it convenient to use your Facebook account to log in. At its most simple, signing up through Facebook saves you the time it takes to create a new account. Most websites when you first join ask you to enter your name, birthday, create a password, add a profile picture, and so on and so on. Signing up through Facebook takes care of that for you (in fact, you can see your Facebook profile picture appear on the site you are using).

SHARING ON FACEBOOK FROM OFF FACEBOOK

One way in which you can use Facebook when you're actually using other websites is to share articles, links, images, videos, and websites back to Facebook as a post. Most major news sites or blogs include links to share articles, and usually sharing on Facebook is one of the options. When you click to share content back to Facebook, a window opens that looks similar to the Publisher you know and love at the top of your News Feed. You can write a post from there and it will be shared with your friends on your Timeline and via News Feed.

Behind the scenes, clicking a Share button off of Facebook works a bit differently than clicking to log in with Facebook or continue with Facebook. When you click a Share button, you are not giving the website access to your information. The same is true if you see a Like button or Send button with a Facebook logo. Those buttons do help you share content back to Facebook, but it's not the same thing as linking your account to a particular website, app, or game.

Perhaps more important, sites like Pinterest have a social element to them: You likely care about the things your friends have pinned, reviewed, watched, and so on. By logging in with Facebook and giving it access to information like your Friend List, Pinterest can quickly help you find people you want to follow or invite to join Pinterest, by matching your Friend List to their own lists of users.

You can also choose to share your boards on Facebook, which means even if your Facebook friends don't use Pinterest themselves, they'll be able to see when you've created a new collection you want them to know about.

Mobile Apps and Facebook

If you have an iPhone or other smartphone that uses apps, you can connect your Facebook account with mobile apps. This is very similar to the way you connect your account with websites. In fact, because many websites, like Pinterest, also have mobile apps, you may wind up signing up with Facebook on the web, only to use an app on your phone, or vice versa. Similarly, many games you play on Facebook have mobile app counterparts, so you can continue a game on your phone whenever you are forced to step away from your computer.

Figure 14-9 shows an example of the mobile Log In with Facebook screen. Like the Log in with Facebook screens you would see when using Facebook on the web, the moment you tap OK on this screen on your mobile device is the moment you share your information with the app and link your Facebook account to the app.

FIGURE 14-9:
Logging in to an app with Facebook from your smartphone.

And like the permission windows you see on your computer screen, this screen on your mobile shows the following information (refer to Figure 14-9):

>> The app's name

>> Your name

>> The information the app will receive

>> Information about whether the app can post to Facebook

When you use Facebook to log in to an app on your phone, you reap the same benefits as using it to log in to a website:

>> Automatic creation of your account and profile without having to enter in your details

>> Use your Facebook Friend List to find friends within the app

>> Share content from the app back to Facebook quickly and easily when you want to

Managing Your Games, Websites, and Apps

There are so many apps and games out there that I couldn't even begin to write Apps and Games For Dummies. You'll need to learn about the games you choose to use by playing them, and the websites you log in to by using them. At the same time, because you are using Facebook with these games, websites, and apps, you still control your Facebook information and how it gets used.

For the purposes of talking about how you can change settings related to games, websites, and mobile apps, I will be referring to all these incarnations as *apps*. You can view your current settings for any particular app by following the steps below:

1. **From any page on Facebook, click the Privacy icon in the big blue bar on top.**

   This opens up the Privacy Shortcuts menu.

2. **Click on See More Settings at the bottom of the menu.**

   This brings you to the Privacy Settings pages.

3. **On the left side of the page, click on the Apps tab.**

   This opens the App Settings page. The top portion of the page displays the games you've used, websites you have connected to your account, and mobile apps you have logged in to with your account.

4. **Hover your mouse cursor over the app you wish to review and click the pencil icon that appears.**

   This opens a window, shown in Figure 14-10, that displays information about that app and your information.

App visibility

The top portion of the App Settings window displays the current *visibility* of the app. In this case, visibility refers to who can see that you use the app in question.

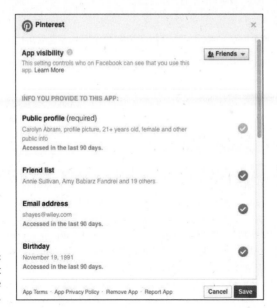

FIGURE 14-10:
Edit what
permissions the
app has here.

The visibility is controlled by the same privacy menu that you use to choose who can see posts you make. Click on the drop-down menu to choose whether this information is visible publicly, to just friends, or to a custom set of people.

Info you provide

The bulk of the App Settings window reviews the information that you shared with the app when you started using it. Each type of information is listed here, and a blue check mark signifies that it is currently being shared. Beneath the information type, you can see more specifically what is shared, and when it was last accessed by the app. For example, you might see that you share your Likes with an app, and those likes include MTV, Barack Obama, and 21 other pages, and that information has been accessed in the last 90 days.

You can click to uncheck any type of information from the list except your Public Profile (which, remember, includes your name, profile picture, age, gender, and other information you share publicly).

This app can

The This App Can section reviews what permissions the app has, usually just whether or not it can post to your Timeline on your behalf, and if it can send you notifications. Use the drop-down menus to change these permissions.

Learn more

The Learn More section provides links to the Help center where you can learn about many of the topics covered in this chapter, including how to get in touch with the developers of the app.

REMEMBER

If you change any of the settings in the Edit App Settings window, click the blue Save button at the bottom of the window to make sure the new settings are saved.

Removing apps

The simplest way to adjust how an app interacts with your information is simply to revoke its ability to interact with your information. This option makes sense only if you are 100 percent done with an app — that is, you don't plan to use it again in the future.

To remove an app, go to the App Privacy page (Steps 1–3, earlier) and hover your mouse cursor over the app you want to remove. Click the X that appears when you mouse over it. A window pops up explaining that doing so removes it from your Facebook account, but that the app may still have some of the data you shared with it (it just won't get any new data going forward). You can then choose to delete all the app's activity on Facebook by selecting the Delete All Your <app> Activity On Facebook check box. Clicking the Remove button finishes the process.

When you remove an app, you will no longer be able to use the app, and it won't be able to send any information or posts to your Timeline or invitations to your friends. At the same time, because so many apps exist outside of Facebook, you have to keep in mind that it will still be able to contact you via your email address, and it may still have an account for you created via Facebook. If you want to cut off an app completely, you may have to delete your information and close your account on another website entirely.

Apps others use

When your friends use other websites and apps in conjunction with Facebook, they may find it useful to see their friends' (in this case, your) information — for example, a game might want to know if your friend's friends (for example, you) are online so they can challenge someone to a new round of the game. This information can be made available through your friend even if you are not a user of that game, app, or website.

To control what information apps can see about you through your friends, click Edit in the Apps Others Use section of the Apps Settings tab. In the window that opens, use check boxes to select (or deselect) what information can be made available to apps through your friends.

Opting out

If you've been reading this chapter and you're getting more and more queasy about the idea of using games and apps, you can consider opting out of using apps entirely. This isn't a step I personally recommend because applications can be a lot of fun and very useful. But if you're very protective of your information, you can effectively turn off apps.

From the App Settings page, click Edit in the Apps, Websites, and Plugins section of the page. The window that opens explains what Platform is and how you can use it, as well as what you will and won't be able to do if you turn it off. If you are confident in your decision, click the blue Disable Platform link.

Clicking this button effectively removes all the apps you have used and prevents your account information from being used by any application ever again. If, at some point in the future, you find an app you do want to use and you click any of the App Install Screen buttons, this setting will automatically turn back on.

Controlling what you see from friends

News Feed can be a great way to discover what apps your friends use, but it also can be overrun with app stories, blocking out the interesting content that's not related to those games and apps. Here are a few tips to keep your News Feed (and the rest of your Facebook) from being cluttered by apps:

>> **Hide from News Feed.** If your News Feed is inundated with posts from apps, click the small gray arrow that appears when you hover over that post. A menu of options appears, including Hide All From *<app>*. When you click Hide, the post disappears from News Feed and is replaced by text confirming that it has been hidden.

>> **Block an app.** If you find an app offensive or it keeps sending you invites or requests, you can block it. From the Settings page, navigate to the Blocking tab using the left menu and enter the app's name in the text field in the Block Apps section. The app will no longer be able to contact you via Facebook or see any of your info.

» **Block a friend's invites.** Sometimes just one person is the problem. The person may be sending you invites or requests from multiple apps, and it's driving you nuts. Navigate to the Blocking section of the Settings page, and enter your friend's name into the text field in the Block App Invites section. Then, any invites or requests she sends you will automatically be ignored and won't generate any notifications on your Home page or in your email. You'll still be friends with her, and you'll still see posts from her such as status updates and photos; you just won't get the app stuff anymore.

Reporting offensive apps

If you are using an app and you think it is offensive, using your information inappropriately, spammy, experiencing bugs, or not working properly, you can report that to either Facebook or the app developer. Follow the steps at the beginning of this section to open that app's App Settings window. At the very bottom of the window are links, including one to Report App.

Once you click that link, a window opens with possible reasons that you are reporting the app. Depending on what you choose, you will be prompted to send the report either to Facebook or to the app developers.

5

The Part of Tens

IN THIS PART . . .

Some new — and tried and true — ways to get the most out of Facebook

Benefits that Facebook can bring to real life

Answers to common questions

Guidance for parents of teens on Facebook

Chapter 15

Ten Ways to Make the Most of Your Facebook Content

I spend a lot of time in this book emphasizing how easy things are to do, or reminding you of the simplest way to do things. Want to update your status? Click, type, post. Want to post a picture from your phone? Tap, select, post. Using Facebook is meant to be easy and seamless when you want. This chapter, however, is about some of the ways you can go beyond the basics. Some of these things are ways to make your content a little more special, a little less rushed. Others are ways to take stock of your history on Facebook, organize it, and get nostalgic for it. These are the kinds of things that when I've seen them on Facebook, I think to myself: How do I do that? Well, here's how.

Remember the Past

Quick, what were you doing a year ago? Not, like, in general. But exactly 365 days ago. Were you having a good day or a bad one? Did you go to the grocery or to a party or just to work like normal? If you've been using Facebook for over a year, and like most people, use it every day, you can find out using the On This Day app. On This Day is an app created by Facebook and is available to you as soon as you create your Facebook account. You can find it by looking in the Apps section of the left sidebar and clicking On This Day.

On This Day is pretty simple: It resurfaces posts you made on this day in the past. Depending on how long you've been on Facebook, it could be from several years ago or from just last year. Your memory might be a photo you shared or a status post or a wall post someone left for you. Sometimes it might be a bit boring, but at the same time it's fascinating to see how things have or haven't changed. And sometimes it brings up something so delightful you can't believe you've forgotten it — a funny photo you took or the sweet words of a friend. You can repost or comment on these types of discoveries and share the memory that way. You can also choose to be notified about your On This Day memories or you can just check out the app whenever you're in need of a bit of nostalgia. Facebook will also occasionally post a memory to the top of your News Feed (it won't be shared with your friends unless you choose to share it with them).

Scrapbook Your Baby Photos

If you're the parent of young kids and you choose to share photos of them on Facebook, you might run into a problem where you and your spouse or partner are constantly adding one-off photos of the cuteness, but then it's hard to find a particular photo on Facebook when you want to. Facebook created a special way to compile photos of your kids called Scrapbook. Scrapbook lets you create a tag for your child without creating a profile for them. You can then tag your kid in photos. Only you and your partner are allowed to tag your child, so you don't have to worry about them being tagged in photos without your permission.

To create a scrapbook, navigate to the About section of your Timeline and click to add a family member in the Family and Relationships section. When you add your son or daughter, you can click a box to "Add Scrapbook." Once you've saved the relationship, the scrapbook is created and you will be prompted to tag photos you've already added to Facebook. After you've created your scrapbook you can keep adding to it by continuing to tag your child in posts about her.

Say Thanks

Facebook's Say Thanks feature allows you to create a quick little video to thank a friend for being, well, your friend. Videos scan through a few photos with text interwoven to tell your friend thanks for just being them. You can choose from three basic scripts: Old Friend, Friend, or Family.

To create your Say Thanks video, go to www.facebook.com/thanks. There, you can choose the friend you'd like to say thanks to. Once you've chosen the friend, Facebook displays a collection of photos you've both been tagged in. You can choose the photos you want in your video by clicking on them. Preview your video and then click the green Share Video button at the top of the page to add it to Facebook. All your friends will be able to see the video. If you're someone who is prone to crying, don't forget the tissues.

Give Your Photos Some Flair

Whenever you add a photo from the Publisher, you can add some creative touches to the photo by clicking the "Edit Photo" paintbrush icon. These editing options are just that — options. They aren't required and no one will mind if you just post your photo as a photo. At the same time, these options can just make your photo a little more . . . exceptional.

Options include adding filters; cropping and rotating your photo; adding text to your photo; and adding stickers to your photo. If you want more specifics on how, exactly, to add these pieces of flair to your photos, check out Chapter 11.

Review the Last Year (or Years)

Every winter Facebook offers the ability to look back on everything that's happened to you in the last year. Often played as a slide show, Year in Review videos highlight the most important parts of your year — the milestones compiled into a digital album, no trip to the scrapbook store required.

Facebook periodically makes other sorts of review videos for various occasions. On its birthday (February 4) it often offers the ability to "Look Back" through everything that you've ever done since you joined Facebook. Keep your eyes peeled for Facebook promoting these sorts of videos at the top of your News Feed. You aren't required to make one, but they can be pretty fun.

Track Your Feelings

One way to enhance your status updates is to include extra information about what you're feeling. To do this, you just need to click the smiley face icon in the bottom of the Publisher. This opens a menu for adding details about what you're doing or feeling. Choosing to add what you're feeling lets you choose from a host of different emotions (and accompanying emoji). When your friends see your post, they'll also see what you were feeling. Adding your emotional state to a post isn't required, but it is a neat way to provide commentary on whatever it is you are posting about. You could post a photo of a beautiful sunset, but you might be feeling blessed or lonely or bored or impatient. Sharing what you're feeling helps your friends feel closer to you.

Add Tags

In addition to tagging friends in photos and posts, you can tag almost any *thing* in your posts. You can tag famous people, television shows, movies, bands, companies. Honestly, almost anything. To start tagging, simply type the @ symbol and begin typing the name of the person, place, or thing you want to tag. As you type, Facebook will auto-complete with suggestions. When you see the one you want, click on it. So if you're excited for the new *Star Wars*, you can tag it, and when friends mouse over the tag, they will see a preview of its Page. They can then click on the tag to view the *Star Wars* Page and check out all the cool movie posters. You don't have to have previously liked a Page to tag it; just type @ and go.

Riff with Friends

If you're someone who likes to create videos with friends, Riff is the app for you. Riff is an app built by Facebook for your smartphone. You can use it to quickly create a topic and then film a clip about that topic. You can share it with friends and they can add their own video clips to the topic. Whenever you get the video to a point that you like, you can choose to share it on Facebook (or just enjoy it from the Riff app).

Use Stickers or GIFs in Your Messages

In conversations, there's so much more going on than what's said. There are gestures, expressions, emphasis. No matter how fast we get at communicating via text, there's always something that gets left behind. While that gap can't quite be fixed by using stickers and GIFs, it can be made a little less wide by doing so. Stickers and GIFs are visual ways to represent sentiments, and using them can function as a sort of punctuation to the messages you send to friends. Click on the Sticker or GIF buttons at the bottom of a chat window to browse the hundreds upon hundreds of options Facebook offers you. Stickers and GIFs can represent emotions, activities, people, places . . . anything really. You can also choose from sticker packs or GIF libraries that have been created by companies other than Facebook.

Friend-a-versaries

One of the On This Day memories you may occasionally see is the memory of the day you first became friends with someone important in your life. Congratulations, you can celebrate your friend-a-versary on Facebook! The easiest way to celebrate is to share the post about your friendship's ripe old age and include a little note about why that friend is important to you, or what you think about the fact that you guys have been friends for so many years.

It's important to note that Facebook only marks the anniversary of the day you became friends on Facebook. If you were actually friends long before that, your friend-a-versary might seem a bit inaccurate. Still, it never hurts to tell a friend how happy you are to be friends with them.

Chapter 16

Ten Ways Facebook Uniquely Impacts Lives

Sometimes people are dismissive of Facebook, saying, "I keep up with my friends by calling them and visiting them. I don't need a website to do that for me." And you don't *need* a website to do that for you. At the same time, though, Facebook can supplement your existing relationships in very real ways. Here are some ways that maintaining a friendship on Facebook can have big impacts in the real world.

Keeping in Touch with Summer Friends

I once spent a summer leading a troop of sixth graders into the wild. After two weeks of backpacking, kayaking, climbing, and bonding, the kids were given a big list of email addresses and phone numbers, said their goodbyes, and were packed off to their respective homes. I, about to head out west to work at Facebook, lamented the fact that the kids were too young to be on Facebook because they almost assuredly would lose that sheet of paper. I quickly friended my co-counselors (who were all old enough to be on Facebook) and kept up with them through photo albums, messages, and posts. As an added bonus, years later, when one of my co-counselors needed a reference, he knew exactly where to find me.

Not just for me, but for thousands of high school students, the best-friends-for-the-summer — who had a tendency to fade away as school and life took over — are now a thing of the past. Camp friends immediately become Facebook friends, and on Facebook, no one gets lost. Plus, it's easy to share the memories of a fun summer via Facebook Photos.

Preparing to Head Off to School

Everyone has a story about leaving for college. Whether they're dropping off a child or an older sister or heading off themselves, people remember some form of anxiety, nervousness, or blinding fear of the unknown. Who were these people in the hallway or sharing the bathroom? Who was this so-called roommate?

In fact, there are special groups on Facebook for colleges and universities that only students and faculty can join. As soon as incoming freshmen receive their .edu email addresses, they can join this group and start connecting with other students. As they get to know the people in the group, they may find that by the time they arrive on campus, they already know some people. Instead of wandering into the great unknown, college students go off to school having been introduced to their future roommates, classmates, and friends.

Going on Not-So-Blind Dates

Ever been a matchmaker? Ever had a particularly difficult "client" — a friend who has a million requirements for "the one"? Ever been embarrassed because you didn't realize just how picky your friend was until after the date? Enter Facebook. Now, "He's smart, funny, has a great job, lots of cool hobbies, a nice family, and nice friends" can be condensed into a Facebook message with a shared Timeline. From there, both parties can decide based on the Timelines — looks, interests, or the combination of all the information — whether they want to go on a date.

TIP

While showing a friend someone else's Timeline can be the right way to prevent a complete disaster, don't let your friend get too picky with the information there ("I could never date someone who didn't listen to Bowie!"). Encourage her to take a glance at a few photos, point out some of the things the two have in common, and then point them to a coffee shop or bar where they can meet in person.

Meeting People in Your New City or Town

Heading off to college isn't the only time in people's lives that they find themselves someplace new without a lot of friends. But active Facebook users often find that there are many ways Facebook can help alleviate the confusion. I got the following message from my friend Shelby, who was living in Abuja, Nigeria, at the time:

So I was friends with this Marine in Liberia. We lost touch when I left Liberia. He joined Facebook two weeks ago, and requested me as a friend. We started talking again. He put me in touch with a friend who works for the U.S. Consulate in Lagos, Nigeria. I Facebooked her. She found my blog address on my Facebook profile, and forwarded it to her friend who works for the U.S. Embassy in Abuja.

Tonight, I went out with this girl from the Embassy and a bunch of other Embassy people. And I have plans (finally!!) for a couple of days next week with these people.

And all of this is because of Facebook.

Shelby's story is just one example of how Facebook makes moving less of an ordeal — a neighborhood is waiting for you when you arrive. When I moved from California, I used Facebook Search to look for friends of mine who lived in Seattle. To my surprise, more than a few friends from college and people I used to work with had settled there as well. It was wonderful to feel like I wasn't surrounded by strangers, but by friends.

Reconnecting with Old Friends

Long-lost friends. The one who got away. I wonder whatever happened to her. Have you heard about him? These are just some of the ways people talk about the people they somehow lost track of along the way. Whatever the reason for the loss, this sort of regret can be undone on Facebook. Finding people is easy, and getting in touch is, too.

Many recent graduates exclaim that going to a reunion is unnecessary — you already know what everyone is doing five years later; you found out from Facebook. But even for the not-so-young alums, the Find Classmates and Find Coworkers features provide a direct line to search anyone who's on Facebook that you remember from way back (or not so way back) when.

Facebook gets emails every so often about people who find birth parents or biological siblings on Facebook. However, the majority of the time, people are looking for and finding their old classmates and reminiscing about the good old days. Better yet, they are re-igniting a spark in a friendship that can last far into the future.

Keeping Up with the 'Rents . . . or the Kids

Face it: Keeping your parents in touch with everything that's going on is difficult. However often you speak, it sometimes feels as though you're forgetting something. And visits often feel rushed, as though you don't have enough time to truly catch up.

I've found that Facebook Photos is one of the best ways to easily and quickly share my life with my parents. Because I can upload photos so quickly — both from my mobile phone and from my computer — they can feel as though they were present at the *<insert activity here>*. Whether that's the walk I took around the lake, the concert I attended, or the really tasty pie I made, it's as though I called to tell them about it right after it happened. And of course this can happen in the other direction as well: I can see when my parents post photos of their own adventures in the world.

For new parents, Facebook is invaluable for connecting kids with their grandparents. There are few things grandparents like more than photos of their grandkids being brilliant, and you can have those in spades on Facebook. The more generations you have on Facebook, the more fun it can be for all.

Facebook Networking

If you've ever found yourself job hunting, you probably are acquainted with the real-world version of *networking*. You ask friends for their friends' numbers and job titles; you take people out to coffee; you go on interviews; you decide whether the company is right for you; you repeat the whole process.

Although finding the right job hasn't gotten any easier with Facebook, a lot of the intermediate steps have. Asking your friends for their friends' info is as easy as posting a status. You can also search for people who work at companies that interest you, and see if you have any mutual friends who can introduce you. After you receive some names, send them a Facebook message (or an email, whichever is more appropriate) to set up the requisite "informational coffee date."

After interviewing, a great way to get information about a company is to talk to people who work there. Use Find Coworkers to search for friends who've listed that company in their Timelines.

WARNING

The only caveat to this approach is that you're now using Facebook to represent a professional portion of your life. If you contact people via Facebook and they feel a little uncomfortable with the content in your Timeline, whether that's your profile picture, a recent status that can be easily misinterpreted, or a post from a friend that reveals just a little too much information, it could make a bad first impression — just as if you'd shown up to the interview in torn jeans and the shirt you slept in. As a well-educated user of Facebook (because you *have* read all previous 15 chapters without just skipping directly to this one, right?), you're well aware of the myriad privacy settings that enable you to tailor what different parties see and don't see. However, if anything on your Timeline might be particularly misunderstood, simply hide it until you sign your offer letter.

Facebook for Good

If you were on Facebook in the summer of 2014, one thing you probably couldn't avoid were videos of people dumping buckets of ice water over their heads. As part of an awareness raising campaign for ALS (Lou Gehrig's disease), people would film themselves dumping a bucket of water over themselves, post the video to Facebook, and tag six friends, who would then be tasked with the same action. Then they would tag six friends. And so on. The charity referenced in the ice bucket videos reported raising double the amount of funds compared to the previous year.

Facebook has always been impressive at gaining support for important causes. Whether it's a monk-led protest in Myanmar, raising money to support Haiti after the devastating earthquake, creating a massive rally in Colombia denouncing a terrorist organization, or raising Autism Awareness in the United States, Facebook lets ideas spread from friend to friend to friend. Sometimes groups are the tools used, sometimes it's encouraging people to change their profile pictures to a specific image in support of their cause. There's no perfect formula for creating a Facebook revolution, but don't hesitate to share your beliefs on your Timeline or express support for causes around the world.

Goin' to the Chapel

A small bit of Facebook trivia: There has, in many circles, arisen the idea of *Facebook Official (FBO)* — the act of moving from *single* to *in a relationship* and listing the person that you're in a relationship with on your Timeline. For any fledgling couple, this is a big deal for their personal lives; however, becoming Facebook Official also serves notice to friends and anyone who happens upon one's Timeline: I'm taken.

Because of this relationship function, Facebook has become the fastest way to spread a wedding announcement to extended friend groups. Of course, people still call their parents and their closest friends, but *everyone* can find out and share in the happiness via News Feed. Congratulatory Timeline posts ensue, as do copious numbers of photos with *the ring* tagged front and center.

After the wedding has taken place, Facebook becomes a wonderland of virtual congratulations as well as photos of the big day. And in case anyone missed it, he can share in the after-party online.

Hey, Facebook Me!

Before Facebook, in both romantic and platonic contexts, it was hard to get from "Nice to meet you" to "Will you be my friend?" Now, the simple phrase, "Facebook me!" expresses this sentiment and so much more. "Facebook me!" can mean *get in touch, look me up,* or *I want you to know more about me* but in a pressure-free way. It doesn't mean *take me to dinner,* or *let's be best friends forever and ever.* It's simply a way to acknowledge a budding friendship.

"Facebook me!" can also be how good friends say, "Keep up with my life; I want you to know about it," which acknowledges that people are busy and that it's difficult to find time to see each other or talk on the phone. However, even when you're incredibly busy, a quick check on Facebook can make you feel connected again.

IN THIS CHAPTER

Bringing back the old Facebook

Convincing your friends to join Facebook

Setting up Facebook to ensure your privacy

Chapter 17

Ten Frequently Asked Questions

Having worked for Facebook and on this book for several years, I know a lot about the specific complications, confusions, and pain-points people come across while using Facebook. At dinner parties, group functions, family events, or even walking across the street wearing a Facebook hoodie, someone always has a suggestion or a question about how to use the site. It's understandable. Facebook is a complex and powerful tool with a ton of social nuances, many of which have yet to be standardized. There are a lot of different features, and Facebook changes a lot. Each year, Facebook modifies parts of the site, redesigns how certain pages look and feel, and adds features. To keep up on what's happening with Facebook, you can like the official Facebook Page, found at www.facebook.com/facebook, and you'll get updates straight from the horse's mouth.

What follows are the questions I hear most often from friends and family (and the occasional message from a stranger who really needs help), often with strain in their voices or pain in their eyes. The goal of highlighting the more complicated questions is to save you the stress of encountering these issues and wondering whether you're the only one who just doesn't get it.

Do People Know When I Look at Their Timelines?

No. No. No. When people see stories about their friends pop up on their Home page, they sometimes get a little anxious that this means Facebook is tracking everything everyone does and publishing it to everyone else. That's not true. Consider two types of actions on Facebook: creating content and viewing it. Creating content means you've intentionally added something to Facebook for others to look at or read, such as uploading a photo or a video, commenting or liking something, or posting a status. These types of actions are all publishable posts — that is, stories about them may end up on your Timeline or in your friends' News Feeds — although you have direct control over exactly who gets to see these posts.

The other type of action on Facebook is viewing content such as flipping through photos, watching a video, clicking a link your friend has liked, or viewing someone's Timeline. Unless someone is looking over your shoulder as you browse, these types of actions are strictly private. No one is ever directly notified about them, and no trace of the fact that you took that action is left on your Timeline or in your friends' News Feeds. So now you can check people out to your heart's content.

I Friended Too Many People and Now I Don't Like Sharing Stuff — What Can I Do?

The good news is, you can fix this problem by using Friend Lists. The less good news is, it's going to be a little time-consuming to set up the correct Friend Lists. Chapter 8 deals with finding friends and creating Friend Lists in great detail, but here's what you can do to deal with this exact problem:

1. **Click the lock icon in the big blue bar on top of the Facebook window.**

   This opens the Privacy Shortcuts menu.

2. **Click See More Settings at the bottom of the menu.**

   This brings you to the Privacy Settings and Tools page.

3. **On the left side of the Privacy Settings and Tools page, click Blocking.**

   This brings you to all the blocklists you maintain on Facebook. The first item at the top of the page is the Restricted List. When people are on your Restricted

List, they are still listed as your friends, but they see only those posts that you share publicly.

4. **Click Edit List across from the Restricted List.**

   A pop-up window displaying the people currently on the Restricted List opens.

5. **In the upper left corner of the pop-up window, click to change the display from On This list to Friends.**

6. **Go through your friends and click the faces of people you don't want to see your posts.**

   This is the time-consuming part. If you have a lot of friends, this can take a while.

TIP

   You can always add more people to the list later if you want to stop for a break. Just click Finish to save your work so far.

7. **When you're done, click Finish.**

Alternatively, you can create a Friend List of best friends and share exclusively with them. You can also unfriend lots of people. Either way, you have to go through your long list of friends, person by person, and decide who will see your posts. I'm sorry; it's hard being popular.

What's with the New Facebook — Can I Change It Back?

Inevitably, Facebook is going to change the way it looks. You're going to log in one day, and things will look different — the things you were used to seeing on the left will now be on the right, or gone completely, or someplace hidden . . . it's confusing. Facebook changes the look and feel of either the Home page or the Timeline about once per year. And trust me when I say that when you log in and this has happened to you, you're going to hate it.

Unfortunately, no matter what you do, no matter how much you hate it, Facebook rarely goes back on a redesign like that. You won't be able to change it back, and the best thing you can do is try to figure out the new site. Check out the Help Center (click the down arrow in the big blue bar on top, and then click Help in the menu that opens) or Facebook's Page (www.facebook.com/facebook) to read about the layout changes and how the site works. And then try to use Facebook a few minutes a day until you get used to it. Over time, it won't seem so bad any more. You'll look at a photo of the old Facebook, and you'll think how ugly it looks by comparison.

So, short answer: *No; you can't change it back.* But I have complete confidence in your ability to adapt to the new Facebook.

I Have a Problem with My Account — Can You Help Me?

I wish I could. Unfortunately, I am but a user like you, and that means although I can help diagnose the issue, I can't usually treat it. Sometimes the problems are Facebook's fault, and sometimes they are user errors, but either way, I don't really have the tools required to fix them. Most account problems can be resolved only by Facebook employees with special access to the specific tool required to fix an account. Here are a few of the account questions I've received recently, and the answers given:

>> **I can't remember my password. Can you reset it for me?** *Answer:* No can do. Click the Forgot Your Password link on the login page to start the reset process, which entails Facebook sending a reset link to your email account.

>> **My account was deactivated because it said I was sending too many messages. Why? Can you fix it?** *Answer:* I recently had this happen to two friends: one who was using his account to promote his music career, and one who was distributing his poetry to many, many friends through messages. This is Facebook spam detection at work. When an account starts sending a lot of messages in quick succession, especially when those messages contain links, this looks a lot like spam to the system. In most cases, the person is warned first, but if the behavior continues, his account is disabled. The only way to have this action reversed is to write in to Facebook's User Operations team and request reactivation. To write in, click Help from the Account menu — the little downward-facing arrow in the blue bar on top. Search for a FAQ entitled My Personal Facebook Account Is Disabled. Follow the instructions for contacting Facebook. The process of getting your account reactivated can sometimes take several days.

What Do I Do with Friend Requests I Don't Want to Accept?

This is a tough question. As far as I know, there isn't exactly a social convention for this yet, so the answer to this question is pretty personal. Just know that there are a number of actions you can take:

>> **Click Delete Request.** Remember, people are never notified if you have rejected their friend request. If you don't want to be their friend, you don't have to be.

>> **Many people just leave the request sitting there forever.** I admit I am guilty of this.

>> **If you don't want to accept because you don't want that person having access to your Timeline, you can accept the request and then add him to a special restricted Friend List (see the answer to "I Friended Too Many People and Now I Don't Like Sharing Stuff").** You can go into your Privacy settings and exclude that Friend List from seeing any parts of your Timeline. Then anyone you add to that list will be restricted. In this way, you can accept the Friend Request without giving up access to your Timeline.

>> **If you don't want to accept because you don't want to read about that person in your News Feed, no problem!** Simply click Confirm. The first time she shows up in News Feed, hover over the story and click the downward-pointing triangle in the upper right of the story. Choose Hide All Stories from <*Friend's Name*> in the menu that opens to prevent any future stories from that person from appearing in your News Feed.

Why Can't I Find My Friend?

I'm assuming you're asking this question after exhausting every possibility for finding friends, as described in Chapter 8. And I'm also assuming you're looking for a specific person, not friends in general.

You won't be able to find a friend for the following few reasons:

>> **She hasn't joined Facebook.** Shocking, I know. If you think she'd enjoy it, you can always invite her to join and be your friend as long as you have her email address.

>> **She goes by a different name on Facebook to protect her privacy.** For example, if her name is Jane Smith, she may list her name as Janie S. Try searching for her by her email address or phone number.

>> **She has a common name.** Facebook Search tries to get you to the right Jane Smith by looking at things like friends in common and shared hometowns, but sometimes it comes up empty.

>> **She doesn't have much information filled out on her Timeline.** If you're looking for someone you went to high school with but she never entered her high school information, you're going to have a hard time finding her.

>> **She blocked you.** Yes, this one is harsh. I put it on the list only because I've seen it happen before. Someone says to me, "I *know* she's on Facebook. And I *know* she's friends with my friend. But when I go to find her she's not there."

While it hurts to be blocked by someone, don't drive yourself crazy looking for reasons why it happened. If she doesn't want to connect with you on Facebook, that's her loss; move on to your other friends and all the things you can share with them.

Will Facebook Start Charging Me to Use the Site?

Another simple answer: *No.*

This rumor is a particularly nasty one that makes the rounds every now and again via people's statuses. There are several variations, but they always seem to involve asking you to repost the status that Facebook is shutting down/going to start charging/running out of names. Don't fall victim to this ruse. Facebook has long maintained that it will always be free to users. Unless you're advertising something, Facebook will always have space for you for free.

How Do I Convince My Friends to Join Facebook?

While the obvious answer to this question is to give them a copy of this brilliant book about how to use Facebook, there are a few other things you can try. You can tell her anecdotally the ways in which Facebook has enriched your life. Maybe you're interacting with your kids more, you're keeping in touch with friends you thought were lost, or you have a place to put your thoughts and photos where your friends might actually see them. You can let her look over your shoulder as you use the site so that she can see the experience herself — ask her questions about whether there's anyone in particular she'd like to look up. The more information she sees about the people she cares about, the more likely she is to take the next step.

One common complaint from people who haven't joined the site is that they "don't have time for yet another computer thing." To this concern, one common response is that Facebook is an efficiency tool that often saves a person time compared to using old-school methods of communication. Messaging can often replace email, and events are easier to coordinate over Facebook. Sharing phone numbers is easier. Sending and receiving links is easier. Finding rides to the airport, restaurant recommendations, and who is heading to the park on Saturday are all faster and easier than trying to use email, phone, or other methods of communication.

REMEMBER

Finally, for some people, it's just not their time. No matter what you say, they'll stick their fingers in their ears and sing *la-la-la* until you start talking about sports or the weather or the circus coming to town next week. You can't force them to Facebook; you have to let Facebook come to them. Over the years, I've watched many a nonbeliever eventually cross over and discover the value. Patience may be your only weapon for these diehards.

What If I Don't Want Everyone Knowing My Business?

To those who ask that question and don't have time to read Chapter 6 of this book, which goes into great detail about how to be a private person on Facebook, I simply try to impart the following message: You can be an extremely private person and still derive nearly all the same value out of Facebook as anyone else. All you have to do is learn how to use the Privacy controls and lock down all your information and access to your Timeline, ensuring that only those you trust can see your info. From there, you can interact in all the same ways as anyone else without feeling like your privacy is being compromised.

Note: Besides understanding the Privacy settings and taking the initial time to adjust yours until they feel just right, you will have to do a little extra work to be private on Facebook and still derive comparable value. You'll likely have to put in extra effort connecting with friends, because the more locked-down your information is, the harder you make it for not-yet-Facebook-friends to find your

Timeline, and the harder it is for your friends to find you, identify you, and connect with you. As long as you're willing to do the work of seeking out your friends and connecting with them, however, your experience should be nearly identical with everyone else's.

Does Facebook Have a Feature That Lets Me Lock Myself Out for a Few Hours?

Short answer: *Not really.*

Long answer: Many people do *deactivate* their accounts. Deactivation is a way of shutting down your account temporarily. It means that no one will see your Timeline or be able to interact with you on Facebook. Some people will deactivate their accounts, their reason being "I spend too much time using Facebook." The benefit of such an action is that you're guaranteed not to get notifications about messages, picture tags, Timeline posts, or anything else. The downside is that it will cause a lot of confusion among your friends who suddenly can't message you, tag you, or write on your Timeline. If they have your email address, they're likely to bug you anyway to ask why you disappeared from Facebook.

The reason it's not a real solution is because all you have to do to reactivate at any time is to enter your password (just like signing in), and you're completely back to normal. So if you're remotely curious how your social group has evolved without you, you may have trouble truly staying away.

Which brings me to the next suggestion: Have some self-control. Just like many good things in life, the key to keeping them good is moderation. French fries are delicious, but too many give you a tummy ache. Dancing is a blast 'til your feet are covered with blisters. Television is educational and entertaining until it's 3 a.m., you're watching your fifth infomercial, you forgot to feed the cat and put out the trash, and you find yourself wondering what life is all about. Facebook is no different. It's a brilliant utility when used to make your life easier and your social interactions richer. When you find yourself flipping through two-year-old vacation photos of a friend of a friend of a friend of a friend, it's time to blink a few times, step away from the mouse, and go out for ice cream, or dancing, or whatever else it is that gives you joy.

Chapter 18

Ten Tips for Parents of Teens on Facebook

t's hard to put the word *teenager* together with the phrase *social networking* and not get just the teensiest bit anxious. A lot of horror stories are out there about cyberbullying and online predators. Any parent is likely to be a bit worried.

However, it's unreasonable to think you can keep your teen away from Facebook, much less the Internet. That's where their friends are and that's where they want to be. So here are some tips I hope will be useful in navigating the waters of Facebook and the Internet at large.

I should acknowledge here that I'm neither a parent of a teen nor a teenager, so I don't pretend to know everything about what's going on in your family or in your teen's life. Think of these tips as a useful jumping-off place for figuring out how to keep your teen safe online.

Talk to Teens about General Internet Safety

Here are some general Internet safety tips that apply no matter what kind of website you're using:

>> Don't share any personal identifying info (address, phone number, credit card info, and so on) with anyone you don't know.

>> Create different passwords for all the sites you use. Passwords should also be difficult to guess and contain a mix of numbers, upper- and lowercase letters, and symbols.

>> Don't share your passwords with anyone, even boyfriends/girlfriends or best friends. (This is one that teenagers tend to struggle with.)

>> Click only those links you trust; be wary of scammy-sounding advertisements. They are usually scams.

Beware of Strangers

On Facebook, in general, people are who they say they are and tend to have only one account that links to their real email address and contains only real information about them. Unfortunately, like the real world, Facebook isn't completely free of malicious people who lie to take advantage of someone else.

The good news is that it's fairly easy to keep your experience free of people like this by accepting only Friend Requests from people you actually know in real life. Talk to your teen about the importance of sharing information only with people they actually know, and telling you when someone they don't know contacts them.

Teach Teens How to Report Abuse

Virtually every piece of content on Facebook has a Report link. These include photos, videos, messages, Timelines, groups, posts, and events. If you or your child comes across content that is abusive or offensive, report it by clicking any of the Report links located near these pieces of content. Facebook investigates all abuse reports and removes content that violates its Statement of Rights and Responsi-bilities. You can report Timelines for being fake or posts for being harassing.

TIP

The only caveat is that some stuff that may be offensive to you or your teen may not be considered offensive by Facebook's staff. For example, you can't report a photo for being unflattering — you can only ask that the person who posted it take it down.

Teach Teens How to Block People

Certain kinds of behaviors can eventually lead to someone being kicked off of Facebook, but you (and your teen) might not want to wait around until the offender is out for good. If someone is bothering your teen (or you) and won't leave your teen (or you) alone, don't hesitate to block the person from the Privacy Shortcuts menu. Blocking someone almost has the effect of making it seem like that person isn't on Facebook. Neither of you will be able to see each other in searches, to message each other, or to look at each other's Timeline.

Personally, I block strangers early and often. I receive my share of junk mail, and anytime a stranger sends me a weird link or comments on my looks, I both report and block the person. It just gives me peace of mind to do so. To block someone, follow these steps:

1. **Click the lock icon in the big blue bar on top to open the Privacy Shortcuts menu.**

2. **In the Privacy Shortcuts menu, click the How Do I Stop Someone from Bothering Me section.**

   This expands an interface for adding people to your blocklist.

3. **Type a name or email address in the Add Name or Email text box.**

4. **Click Block.**

   The person is then added to your blocklist. Repeat Steps 4 and 5 as needed to block more people .

Learn to Use Privacy Settings

This book contains an entire chapter on privacy. Teens in the United States on Facebook actually have very specific privacy rules that are different from most users. Their Public posts are not actually distributed to everyone via search or otherwise. Instead, the largest group of people who can see something a minor shares "publicly" is friends of his friends. When adults create a Facebook Timeline, by default most of their biographical info, like their hometown and school, is shared publicly. For teens, this information is available only to friends of friends.

That being said, you can rest easier if you go through your teen's Privacy settings with her and agree on settings that allow her to share more safely. In general, sharing only with friends or, better yet, creating a list of close friends can quickly ensure that fewer people are seeing your child's information and that, at all times, you both have a complete list of who those people are. If you have a question about anything, refer to Chapter 6 for help.

Talk about Posts and Consequences

Even with good Privacy settings, teenagers often struggle with the idea that once something is shared, it's hard to undo. This is extremely true of things like Facebook photos or posts. Encourage your teens to think about how something might be seen and interpreted by people who aren't their closest friends. Would they want a college admissions officer to see that photo? Would they want their boss to read that post? Both of these situations have happened with real consequences. The college admissions officer might decide you aren't really "Hah-vahrd" material, or the boss may fire you for complaining on Facebook about her way of speaking. The things that happen on Facebook don't always stay on Facebook; they have a way of spreading. Remind your teen to think before he posts.

Remember the Golden Rule

As much as many parents worry about their kids being the victims of cyberbullying, you have to also consider that kids can be the perpetrators of cyberbullying. Talk to your kids about the behaviors that might affect others, whether known or unknown. This includes things like creating hateful Facebook groups targeting a teacher or peer, as well as going into a forum somewhere else on the Internet and posting something inflammatory or offensive under the protection of anonymity (although, on the Internet, anonymity doesn't usually last).

The Golden Rule applies to your child just as much in adolescence as when she was in kindergarten: Do unto others as you would have them do unto you. Would you want someone saying something bad about you online? How would you feel if you posted something really personal, and people made fun of you? Part of being part of Facebook (and other online communities) is being a good citizen. That makes Facebook Nation a safe place for all.

Respect Teens' Boundaries

After you get them set up on Facebook and talk about all the general ideas for Internet and Facebook safety, you need to give them some space. As one of my teenage cousins said to me, "They should be my friend, and that's it."

Some kids are really comfortable interacting with their parents; others think it is the most embarrassing thing in the world. Hey, that's okay. When you were a teen, did you like it when your parents came along with you and your friends when you went out? Did you like it when they listened in on your phone calls or read your diary? That's what it can feel like to some teenagers when they're asked to be friends with their parents: like you're invading their space.

You can talk to them about some of the things you see on Facebook (both the good and the bad; trust me, there are both!), but commenting on their stuff and posting on their Timeline are things that are likely to get you unfriended. As long as you let them know they can come tell you whenever they're having some sort of problem (and that they always tell you when they're contacted by a stranger), it's important to let them know that you trust them to make smart choices.

Don't Send Friend Requests to Teens' Friends

If their friends friend you, it's probably okay to accept those requests (though you may want to check with your teen first; see the previous section, "Respect Their Boundaries"). However, it's generally considered weird and pushy for you to reach out to their friends.

Make Space for Your Own Social Life, and Your Family Life, on Facebook

If you joined Facebook just to understand what's going on in your teen's life, that's great. But now, having read this book, I hope you can see that there's a lot Facebook can offer you and your friends, with or without your children present. Share photos. Coordinate events with your friends. Post statuses about what's going on with you. It doesn't always have to be about them.

One way to keep your social life separate from your teen's social life, but still have a little interaction on Facebook, is to create a group for your family. You can add lots of different family members, and everyone can share the sort of stuff family members like to know: holiday newsletter–type stuff. It creates a space where it's okay for you and your son or daughter to interact on Facebook. Hopefully, it's a way to bring you both a little closer.

One parent I spoke to mentioned that he likes to send his teen messages on Facebook letting her know he loves her. It's just another way for them to connect where his daughter is comfortable, and it has strengthened their relationship.

Index

A

Aa icon, 159
About (footer), 48
About section
  about, 92–93
  Basic Information section, 95–96
  Contact Information, 95–96
  Details, 98
  Life Events, 99
  Living section, 95
  on Official Pages, 275
  Relationship and Family section, 97–98
  Work and Education section, 93–95
abuse, reporting, 346–347
accepting friend requests, 140, 176–177
account, 340
Account menu, 40–41
Acquaintances list, 185
Action buttons (Facebook Mobile), 164
Activity icon, 144
Activity Log, 40, 101, 129–130, 301
Add Files option (Facebook Chat), 200
Add Friends to Chat option (Facebook Chat), 200
Add People option (Facebook Messages), 206
adding
  colleges to Work and Education section, 94
  contact information, 95–97
  cover photos, 227

employers to Work and Education section, 93
event photos, 269–270
files to Share box, 219–220
friends, 33, 167, 175–178
friends to groups, 230–231
GIFs, 329
high schools to Work and Education section, 94–95
to Interests box, 99–101
photos
  to events, 269–270
  to Facebook, 244–252, 255, 280–281, 285–287
  with iPhone, 248–250
  to posts, 283
stickers, 248, 329
tags
  about, 328
  to photos, 255–256
text to photos, 247–248
video
  from computer, 258–259
  from Facebook app, 259–260
address books, importing, 178–181
adjusting
  cover photo, 57
  News Feed, 66–69
  notification settings for apps, 310=311
  privacy and safety, 108–109
Admin Roles section (Pages), 299

administrator (group), 231–234

Ads section, privacy for, 124–125

Advanced Settings (Chat menu), 208–209

Advertiser role, 299

advertising, 47

age limitation, 16, 32, 278

Age Restrictions check box (Manage Permissions section), 278

album view, 242–243

albums, photo

  automatic, 257

  creating, 285–286

  deleting, 253–254

  editing, 253–255

  privacy of, 253

Analysts role, 299

App Install Screen, 320

Application Activity box, 99

apps

  about, 305–306

  Basic Information section for, 95–97

  blocking

    about, 120, 320

    invites, 119, 321

  Candy Crush Saga, 308, 310

  controlling what you see from friends, 320–321

  Facebook, 137–156, 259–260

  Facebook Messenger, 156–160, 209–211

  Game Center, 312–313

  games, 308–313

  getting started, 306–308

  Goodreads, 57, 122

  Instagram, 17, 300

  Kickstarter, 121

  logging in with Facebook, 313–315

  managing, 317–321

  mobile, 160–162, 315–317

  opting out, 320

  Pinterest, 314–315

  privacy options for, 120–124

  removing, 319

  Riff, 162, 328

  sharing back to Facebook, 315

  On This Day, 325–326

  using Facebook outside of Facebook, 313–315

Apps (sidebar), 45

Apps Others Use setting, 319–320

Apps section, 300

Archive option (Facebook Messages), 204, 292

archiving conversations, 202

@ symbol, 62, 72

attachments, sending, 198

audience options, 104–106

autocomplete, 35, 41

automatic albums, 257

B

backdating posts, 284–285

Basic Information section, 95–96

Birthday option, 24

Block App Invites list, 119

Block Apps list, 120

Block Event Invites list, 119–120

Block Messages option (Facebook Chat), 200

Block Messages option (Facebook Messages), 205

Block Settings (Chat menu), 208

Block Users list, 118–119

blocking
  about, 111, 113
  app invites, 119
  apps, 120, 320
  event invites, 119–120
  friend's invites to apps, 321
  pages, 120
  users, 118–119, 347
  using Restricted List, 117–118
Blocking section (Settings page), 118–120
blue bar, 34–35, 38–41
boosting posts, 285
building
  events, 267–270
  Friend Lists, 186–187
  groups, 225–228
  pages, 277–281
  photo albums, 285–286
  photo carousel, 287
  polls, 219
  slideshows, 287
bullet list icon, 158
Buy/Sell/Trade group, 225

C

Camera icon, 159
canceling events, 270
Candy Crush Saga app, 308, 310
Careers (footer), 48
changing
  cover photo, 57
  News Feed, 66–69
  notification settings for apps, 310–311
  privacy and safety, 108–109
chat, 140, 199, 221–222. *See also* Facebook Chat

Chat Sounds (Chat menu), 208
Cheat Sheet (website), 3
check-ins/check-in tags, 56, 73, 99, 148–150
choosing friends, 177
classmates, finding, 181–183
clock icon, 158
Close All Chat Tabs setting (Chat menu), 209
Close Friends view, 185
closed groups, 215, 226
Coin icon, 160
colleges, adding to Work and Education section, 94
Comment link, 54
comments and commenting
  about, 57
  on photo albums, 243
  on posts, 61–62, 220–221, 289–290
common sense, using, 134–135
Community Pages, 275–276
computer, adding video from, 258–259
confirmation, 30
connecting, with Pages, 276–277
contact information, adding, 95–97
content
  illegal, 17
  optimizing, 325–329
controlling
  apps, 317–321
  events, 270–272
  interactions with friends, 184–191
  notifications for groups, 228–230
  Pages, 290–301
  what you see from friend's apps, 320–321
conversations. *See* Facebook Messages
Cookies (footer), 47

Country Restrictions check box (Manage Permissions section), 297

cover photo
adding, 79–84, 227
changing, 57
on Official Pages, 275

co-workers, finding, 181–183

Create Ad (footer), 42

Create Event option (Facebook Messages), 206

Create Group option (Facebook Messages), 206

Create Page (footer), 48

creating
events, 267–270
Friend Lists, 186–187
groups, 225–228
pages, 277–281
photo albums, 285–286
photo carousel, 287
polls, 219
slideshows, 287

cropping photos, 247

Custom privacy setting, 76, 105–106, 260

D

Daily Text Limit setting (Mobile Texts), 168

dating, 19

deactivated accounts, 340, 344

Delete Conversation option (Facebook Messages), 200, 204

Delete Messages option (Facebook Messages), 204–205

deleting
apps, 319
event guests, 271–272
photo albums, 253–254

photos, 256–257

Details section, 98

Developers (footer), 48

Docs feature, in groups, 223–224

E

Edit Conversation Name option (Facebook Messages), 206

Edit Conversation Picture option (Facebook Messages), 206

Edit Participants option (Facebook Messages), 206

Edit Privacy option, 101

editing
event info, 270
members of groups, 233–234
photo albums, 253–255
photos, 246–248, 252–257, 327
posts, 90–91
sections, 101

Editor role, 299

e-mail confirmation, 30

employers, adding to Work and Education section, 93

Events (sidebar), 44

Events feature
about, 14, 263
adding photos to, 269–270
blocking invites, 119–120
creating, 267–270
in groups, 222–223
inviting guests to, 263–265
managing, 270–272
posting to Pages, 287
posts, 56, 57
public events, 265–266
viewing, 155–156, 266

F

face books, defined, 21

Facebook. *See also specific topics*

   about, 7–10

   adding photos, 244–252, 285–287

   compared with other social sites, 17–18

   getting started, 25–30

   rules, 15–17

   signing up, 23–25

   uses for, 10–15, 18–20, 331–336

   website, 8, 23

Facebook app, 137–156, 259–260

Facebook Chat, 207–209

Facebook Groups

   about, 14, 75

   adding friends to, 189, 230–231

   administrator, 231–234

   Buy/Sell/Trade group, 225

   chats in, 221–222

   compared with Friend Lists, 215

   controlling notifications for, 228–230

   creating, 225–228

   Docs feature, 223–224

   editing members, 233–234

   evaluating, 214–216

   events in, 222–223

   Files feature, 223–224

   personalizing groups, 227–228

   posts, 56

   reporting offensive groups, 234–235

   searching, 230

   sharing with, 213–235

   using from mobile phone, 153–155

Facebook logo, 34–35, 38

"Facebook me!" phrase, 336

Facebook menu (Facebook Mobile), 148

Facebook Messages

   about, 140, 193–194

   Chat, 207–209

   conversations, 202–205, 207

   Facebook Messenger app, 209–211

   Inbox, 201–206, 291–293

   options for, 188–201

   sending messages, 158–160, 194–199

   setting (Mobile Texts), 168

   viewing messages, 158–160

Facebook Messenger app, 156–160,
      209–211

Facebook Mobile, 79, 162–165

Facebook Official (FBO), 335–336

Facebook Pages

   about, 15, 273–274

   Activity Log, 301

   Admin Roles section, 299

   Apps section, 300

   blocking pages, 120

   Community Pages, 275–276

   connecting with, 276–277

   creating, 277–281

   Insights section, 301–303

   interacting with, 276–277

   liking, 60–61

   managing your, 290–301

   notifications for, 293–294, 298–299

   Official Pages, 274–275

   posting events to, 287

   posting notes, 288

   settings, 295–301

   sharing on, 282–288

   using your, 289–290

Facebook Pages Terms (website), 278
Facebook Photos
  about, 239
  adding photos to Facebook, 244–252
  editing photos, 252–257
  tagging photos, 252–257
  viewing photos, 240–244
Facebook Platform, 305–306. *See also*
    apps
Facebook Suggestions, 47
Facebook Texts, 165–169
Facebook's Security Page (website), 134
FAQs, 337–344
Favorites section, 42–44
FBO (Facebook Official), 335–336
featured pages, 301
features
  Docs, 223–224
  Events
    about, 14, 263
    adding photos to, 269–270
    blocking invites, 119–120
    creating, 267–270
    in groups, 222–223
    inviting guests to, 263–265
    managing, 270–272
    posting to Pages, 287
    posts, 56, 57
    public events, 265–266
    viewing, 155–156, 266
  Files, 223–224
  Groups
    about, 14, 75
    adding friends to, 189, 230–231
    administrator, 231–234
    Buy/Sell/Trade group, 225
    chats in, 221–222

compared with Friend Lists, 215
controlling notifications for, 228–230
creating, 225–228
Docs feature, 223–224
editing members, 233–234
evaluating, 214–216
events in, 222–223
Files feature, 223–224
personalizing groups, 227–228
posts, 56
reporting offensive groups, 234–235
searching, 230
sharing with, 213–235
using from mobile phone, 153–155
Pages
  about, 15, 273–274
  Activity Log, 301
  Admin Roles section, 299
  Apps section, 300
  blocking pages, 120
  Community Pages, 275–276
  connecting with, 276–277
  creating, 277–281
  Insights section, 301–303
  interacting with, 276–277
  liking, 60
  managing your, 290–301
  notifications for, 293–294, 298–299
  Official Pages, 274–275
  posting events to, 287
  posting notes, 288
  settings, 295–301
  sharing on, 282–288
  using your, 289–290
Reactions, 60
Say Thanks, 327
Search, 10, 139–140, 230

Feedback option (Facebook Messages), 205
feeds, Social Plugins, 64
Feeling/Activity info, 53, 283–284, 328
fees, 342
files, adding to Share box, 219–220
Files feature, in groups, 223–224
filters, 247
finding
  friends, 25–27, 173–174
  friends on Facebook, 178–184
  friends with Search box, 182–184
flagging messages, 292
following friends, 190–191
footer, 47–48
Friend Finder tool
  about, 10
  classmates and co-workers, 181–183
  importing address books, 178–181
  People You May Know list, 10, 181
  using, 25–27
Friend Lists
  about, 74, 185–189
  compared with Groups, 217
  FAQs, 338–339
friend requests
  about, 27
  accepting, 140, 176–177
  icon for, 39
  ignoring, 341
  sending, 175–176, 349
friend-a-versary, 329
friending, 10
friends. *See also* friend requests
  accepting friend requests, 140, 176–177
  adding
    about, 33, 167, 175–178
    to groups, 230–231

  choosing, 177
  convincing to join, 342–343
  FAQs, 341–342
  finding
    about, 25–27, 173–174, 341–342
    on Facebook, 178–184
    in your town/city, 182–184
  following, 190–191
  Friend Finder tool, 10, 25–27, 178–183
  Friend Lists, 75, 185–189, 217, 338–339
  managing interactions with, 184–191
  prioritizing, 68
  quality compared with quantity, 177–178
  reconnecting with, 69
  Search feature, 10, 182–183
  sending
    friend requests, 175–176, 349
    messages to, 158–160, 194–199
  Timeline and, 101–102
  unfollowing, 68–69
  unfriending, 191
  viewing photos from, 240–244
Friends box, 92
Friends Except Acquaintances privacy
    setting, 93, 105
Friends of Friends privacy option, 108
Friends Only privacy setting, 74
Friends privacy setting, 74, 105, 260
Friends section, 44
friendships, stories about, 57

G

games. *See* apps
gear icon, 158
General settings, 296–297
generating
  events, 267–270

generating *(continued)*
  Friend Lists, 186–187
  groups, 225–228
  pages, 277–281
  photo albums, 285–286
  photo carousel, 287
  polls, 219
  slideshows, 287
getting started
  about, 25
  adding friends, 33
  App Install Screen, 320
  apps, 306–308
  completing your profile, 34–35
  confirmation, 30
  Facebook, 25–30
  finding friends, 25–27
  Home page, 31–32
  Inbox, 30–31
  Pages, 279–281
  profile, 28–30
  profile picture, 28–30
Gif icon, 160
GIFs, adding, 329
gifts, sending, 197
globe icon, 35
Goodreads app, 57, 122
group administrator, 225, 231–234
group chats, 207
group conversations, 207
Groups (sidebar), 40, 44
Groups app, 161
Groups feature
  about, 14, 75
  adding friends to, 189, 230–231
  administrator, 231–234

Buy/Sell/Trade group, 225
chats in, 221–222
compared with Friend Lists, 215
controlling notifications for, 228–230
creating, 225–228
Docs feature, 223–224
editing members, 233–234
evaluating, 214–216
events in, 222–223
Files feature, 223–224
personalizing groups, 227–228
posts, 56
reporting offensive groups, 234–235
searching, 230
sharing with, 213–235
using from mobile phone, 153–155
Groups icon, 158
guests (event)
  inviting to, 268–269
  messaging, 271
  removing, 271–272

H

hard drive, adding profile picture from,
    82–83
Hello app, 161
Help
  Account menu, 41
  footer, 48
Hide Section option, 101
hiding
  posts, 66–67
  sections, 101
high schools, adding to Work and
    Education section, 94–95
highlights, 228–229

Home link, 39
Home page
  about, 31–32
  for apps, 309–310
Hulu (website), 313

I

icons
 Aa, 159
 Activity, 144
 bullet list, 158
 Camera, 159
 clock, 158
 Coin, 160
 explained, 3
 for friend requests, 39
 gear, 158
 Gif, 160
 globe, 35
 Groups, 158
 Like, 160
 Links, 144
 Location, 144
 Messages, 39, 140
 Microphone, 160
 More, 141–142, 160
 Notifications, 39, 140
 padlock, 39
 People, 72, 158
 Photos, 144, 159
 Photos (Official Pages), 159
 privacy, 108
 Recent, 158
 Remember, 3
 Settings, 158

 Smiley, 160
 Tags, 144
 Tip, 3
 Warning!, 3
identity, lying about your, 16
ignoring friend requests, 341
illegal content, uploading, 17
importing address books, 178–181
Inbox, 30–31, 201–206
Info section, of groups, 298
information gathering, 18
Insights section (Pages), 301–303
Instagram, 17, 300
Instant Replies, 298
interacting
  with friends, 184–191
  with Pages, 276–277
Interested In option, 97
Interests box/section, 99
Internet resources. *See also* apps
  Cheat Sheet, 3
  Facebook, 8, 23
  Facebook Pages Terms, 278
  Hulu, 313
  Match.com, 17
  Security Page, for Facebook, 134
  Statement of Rights and
    Responsibilities, 278
Internet safety, 346
Intro box, 91
inviting
  to apps, 310–311
  guests to events, 263–265, 268–269
iPhone, adding photos with, 248–250

J

job searches, 19

K

Keyboard Shortcuts option (Facebook Messages), 205
Kickstarter app, 121

L

Languages option, 97
layout, Facebook app, 139
Learn More section, 319
Leave Conversation option (Facebook Messages), 206
Life Events, adding, 56, 88–90, 99, 152–153
Like button, on Official Pages, 275
Like icon, 160
Like link, 54
likes, 57, 59–61, 289–290
Likes box, 302
Likes icon, on Official Pages, 275
LinkedIn, 17
links, 47–48, 54, 71, 87–88, 141–142, 195–196
Links icon, 144
lists, managing, 187–188
Living section, 95
Location icon, 144
Log Out (Account menu), 40–41
Logged In With Facebook section, 121–123
logging in, with Facebook, 313–315
logo, Facebook, 34–35, 38
long-distance friends, 18

M

managing
  apps, 317–321
  events, 270–272
interactions with friends, 184–191
lists, 187–188
notifications for groups, 228–230
Pages, 290–301
Mark as Unread option (Facebook Messages), 204, 292
Match.com (website), 17
members, editing of groups, 233–234
Message button, on Official Pages, 275
Messages
  about, 140, 193–194
  Chat, 207–209
  conversations, 202–205, 207
  Facebook Messenger app, 209–211
  Inbox, 201–206, 291–293
  options for, 188–201
  sending messages, 158–160, 194–199
  setting (Mobile Texts), 168
  viewing messages, 158–160
Messages icon, 39
messaging
  about, 12
  event guests, 271
Messaging section, 298
Messenger app, 156–160
Microphone icon, 160
milestones, posting to Pages, 287–289
minors, protecting, 132–133
mobile apps, 160–162, 315–317
mobile browser, 162–165
mobile devices, viewing photos on, 243
Mobile Home Page, 163–164
Mobile Inbox, 165
Mobile PIN setting (Mobile Texts), 167
Mobile Timeline, 164–165
Moderator role, 299
Moments app, 161

More icon, 141–142, 160, 275

movements, organizing, 20–21

Mute Conversation option

  Facebook Chat, 200

  Facebook Messages, 204

N

navigation

  about, 34–35, 37–38

  blue bar, 34–35, 38–41

  Facebook app, 139

  Facebook Messenger, 157–158

  viewing News Feed, 45–46

networking, 334–335

News Feed

  about, 10–11, 52–53, 142–143

  adjusting, 66–69

  anatomy of, 53–54

  commenting, 61–62

  common story types in, 54–57

  hiding apps from, 320

  liking, 59–60

  liking and sharing, 64

  liking pages, 60

  preferences, 67

  saving, 64–65

  settings for friends, 190

  sharing, 63–64

  Ticker, 46, 58–59

  viewing

    about, 45–46

    photos in, 240–241

News Feed (sidebar), 40

notes, posting to pages, 288

notifications

  about, 140

changing settings for apps, 310–311

controlling for groups, 228–230

Mobile Texts, 168–169

for pages, 293–294, 298–299

Notifications icon, 39, 140

O

offensive apps, reporting, 321

offensive groups, reporting, 234–235

Official Pages, 274–275

On This Day app, 325–326

Only Me privacy setting, 105, 260

open groups, 215, 226

Open in Chat option (Facebook Chat), 204

opting out, 320

Options icon, on Official Pages, 275

organizing movements, 20–21

outreach emails, 31

P

padlock icon, 39

Page Info section, 298

Page Roles, 299

Page Support, 301

Page Visibility check box (Manage Permissions section), 296

Pages (sidebar), 44

Pages feature

  about, 15, 273–274

  Activity Log, 301

  Admin Roles section, 299

  Apps section, 300

  blocking pages, 120

  Community Pages, 275–276

  connecting with, 276–277

  creating, 277–281

Pages feature *(continued)*
  Insights section, 301–303
  interacting with, 276–277
  liking, 60–61
  managing your, 290–301
  notifications for, 293–294, 298–299
  Official Pages, 274–275
  posting
    events to, 287
    notes, 288
  settings, 295–301
  sharing on, 282–288
  using your, 289–290
Paper app, 161
parenting tips, 345–350
password, 340
payments, sending, 197–198
People icon, 72, 158
People You May Know list, 10, 181
permissions, 308
phishing, preventing, 133–134
photo albums
  automatic, 257
  creating, 285–286
  deleting, 253–254
  editing, 253–255
  privacy of, 253
photo carousel, 287
photo viewer, 241–242
photos. *See also* Facebook Photos
  adding
    to events, 269–270
    with iPhone, 248–250
    to posts, 283
    stickers, 248
    tags, 255–256
    text to, 247–248
  albums, 253–255, 257, 285–286
  cover photo, 57, 227
  deleting, 256–257
  editing, 246–248, 252–257, 327
  as posts, 54, 88, 144–148
  privacy for, 260–262
  profile picture, 29–30, 53, 57
  reordering photos in albums, 254
  rotating, 256
  sending, 196
  sharing, 13
  tagged, 244
  uploading, 245–250, 285
  viewing
    from friends, 240–244
    on mobile devices, 243
    in News Feed, 240–241
Photos box, 92
Photos icon, 144, 159, 275
pictures. *See* photos
pinning posts, 234
Pinterest app, 314–315
Places box, 99
Political Views option, 97
polls, creating, 219
Post Attribution settings, 298
posts and posting
  about, 13, 51–52, 85
  adding photos, 283
  for apps, 311–321
  backdating posts, 284–285
  boosting posts, 285
  commenting on, 220–221
  consequences from, 348
  editing, 90–91

events, 265

events to Pages, 287

from Facebook app, 143–144

hiding, 66–67, 91

with links, 87–88

milestones to Pages, 287–288

notes, 288

photos, 144–148

pinning posts, 234

privacy of, 73–76

reading, 220–221

scheduling posts, 284–285

status updates, 53–54, 85–88

unfollowing, 66–67

writing in Share box, 218

Preferred Page Audience, 300

privacy and safety

about, 29, 103–104

Ads section, 124–125

apps, 120–124

audience options, 104–106

changing privacy, 108–109

FAQs, 343–344

minors, 132–133

phishing, 133–134

photo albums, 253

of photos, 13, 260–262

of posts, 73–76

Privacy section, 111–113

privacy settings, 111–125, 348

privacy shortcuts, 109–111

reporting options, 131–132

Share box, 63

spam, 133

tagging, 113–116

of Timeline, 126–128, 338

tools, 128–131

using common sense, 134–135

videos, 260–262

viruses, 133

Privacy Checkup tool, 130–131

Privacy section (Settings page), 111–113

Privacy Shortcuts (lock icon) (sidebar), 109

Private privacy setting, 264

profile, completing your, 28–30, 34–35

profile picture

about, 29–30, 39

adding, 79–84

changing, 57

on Official Pages, 275

profile videos, 151–152

protecting minors, 132–133

public events, 265–266

public groups, 215, 226

Public or Everyone privacy setting, 74, 105

Public privacy setting, 260, 264

Publisher box, 46, 69, 106, 217–220, 282–285

Publishing Tools tab, 294–295

R

Reactions feature, 60

reading posts in Groups, 220–221

Read/Watch/Listen stories, 57

Recent icon, 158

reconnecting with friends, 69

Relationship and Family section, 97–98

Relationship Status option, 97–98

Religion option, 97

relocations, 19

Remember icon, 3

Reminders, 46
removing
  apps, 319
  event guests, 271–272
  photo albums, 253–254
  photos, 256–257
reordering photos in albums, 254
Report as Spam or Abuse option
  Facebook Chat, 201
  Facebook Messages, 205, 292
reporting
  abuse, 346–347
  offensive apps, 321
  offensive groups, 234–235
  options for, 131–132
requests, for apps. *See* friend requests
resources, Internet. *See also* apps
  Cheat Sheet, 3
  Facebook, 8, 23
  Facebook Pages Terms, 278
  Hulu, 313
  Match.com, 17
  Security Page, for Facebook, 134
  Statement of Rights and Responsibilities, 278
respecting boundaries, 349
Response Time Display, 298
Restricted List, 117–118, 185
reunions, 20
Riff app, 162, 328
Rooms app, 162
rotating photos, 256
RSVP, for Events, 264–265

S

safety and privacy
  about, 29, 103–104
  Ads section, 124–125
  apps, 120–124
  audience options, 104–106
  changing privacy, 108–109
  FAQs, 343–344
  minors, 132–133
  phishing, 133–134
  photo albums, 253
  of photos, 13, 260–262
  of posts, 73–76
  Privacy section, 111–113
  privacy settings, 111–125, 348
  privacy shortcuts, 109–111
  reporting options, 131–132
  Share box, 63
  spam, 133
  tagging, 113–116
  of Timeline, 126–128, 338
  tools, 128–131
  using common sense, 134–135
  videos, 260–262
  viruses, 133
saving, 65, 285
Say Thanks feature, 327
scheduling posts, 284–285
Scrapbook, 326
scrolling Timeline, 78–79
Search box
  about, 38–39, 41
  finding friends with, 182–184
Search feature, 10, 139–140, 230
secret groups, 215, 226
sections
  about, 99–101
  About
    about, 92–93
    Basic Information section, 95–96

Contact Information, 95–96
Details, 98
Life Events, 99
Living section, 95
on Official Pages, 275
Relationship and Family section, 97–98
Work and Education section, 93–95
Admin Roles (Pages), 299
Ads, 124–125
Apps, 300
Basic Information, 95–96
Blocking (Settings page), 118–120
Details, 98
Favorites, 42–44
Friends, 44
Info, 298
Insights (Pages), 301–303
Interests, 99
Learn More, 319
Living, 95
Logged In With Facebook, 121–123
Messaging, 298
Page Info, 298
Privacy (Settings page), 111–113
Relationship and Family, 97–98
This App Can, 318
Work and Education, 93–95
Security Page, for Facebook (website), 134
See Full Conversation option (Facebook Chat), 200
Send button (Social Plugins), 315
sending
  attachments, 198
  friend requests, 175–176
  gifts, 197
  links, 195–196

messages
  on Facebook Messages, 194–199
  in Facebook Messenger, 158–160
payments, 197–198
photos, 196
stickers, 196–197
setting(s)
Account menu, 40–41
Advanced (Chat menu), 208–209
Apps Others Use, 319–320
changing for app notifications, 310–311
Custom Privacy, 76
Daily Text Limit (Mobile Texts), 168
Facebook Messages, 168
Friends Except Acquaintances privacy, 93, 105
Friends privacy, 73–74
News Feed, 190
Only Me privacy, 105, 260
Page, 295–301
privacy, 111–125
Public or Everyone privacy, 74, 105
Public privacy, 260, 264
Similar Page Suggestions (Pages), 297
Text Messaging (Mobile Texts), 167
Settings icon, 158
Sex (I Am) option, 25
share box, 46
Share box
  about, 46
  adding files, 219–220
  privacy in, 62
  writing posts in, 218
Share link, 54, 64–65
sharing. *See also* Groups feature
  about, 69

sharing. *(continued)*
  apps back to Facebook, 315
  back to Facebook, 315
  on friend's Timeline, 64
  in groups, 64
  with Groups, 213–235
  as messages, 64
  on Pages, 282–290
  on pages you manage, 64
  in private messages, 64
  status updates, 70
  on your own Timeline, 64
Short Message Service (SMS), 166
shortcuts, privacy, 109–111
sidebar
  about, 42
  Apps section, 45
  Events section, 44
  Favorites section, 42–44
  Friends section, 44
  Groups section, 44
  links to apps, 310
  Pages section, 44
signing up, 23–25
Similar Page Suggestions setting (Pages), 297
slideshows, 287
Slingshot app, 162
Smart Lists, 185–186
Smiley icon, 160
SMS (Short message Service), 166
social graph, 7
Social Plugins, 64–65
spam, 16–17, 30, 133
Specific People of Lists privacy option, 105–106

Sponsored Ads, 47
sponsored stories, 58
Start Video/Voice Call option (Facebook Chat), 200
Statement of Rights and Responsibilities (website), 278
status updates
  about, 53–54, 85–88
  sharing, 70
  subscribing to, 167
  unsubscribing from, 167
stickers
  adding, 248, 329
  sending, 196–197
suggested stories, 58

T

tagging
  about, 13, 53, 57
  adding tags, 71–72, 255–256, 328
  in comments, 62
  photos, 247, 252–257
  privacy settings for, 113–116
  videos, 244
Tagging Ability check box (Manage Permissions section), 297
Tags icon, 144
Terms (footer), 47
text, adding to photos, 247–248
Text Messaging setting (Mobile Texts), 167
This App Can section, 318
thread. *See* Facebook Messages
Ticker, 46, 58–59
Time of Day setting (Mobile Texts), 168
Timeline
  about, 11–12, 77–78, 84, 150–153

About section, 92–101
cover photo, 79–84
editing posts, 90–91
friends and, 101–102
Life Events, 88–90
on Official Pages, 275
posts, 55–56, 85
privacy settings for, 113–116, 126–128
profile picture, 79–84
scrolling, 78–79
timestamp, 53
Tip icon, 3
tools, privacy, 128–131
Trending, 46
trolling, 16–17
Turn Off Chat option (Facebook Chat), 200
Turn Off Chat setting (Chat menu), 209
Turn Off Video/Voice Calls setting (Chat menu), 209
tweets, 17
Twitter, 17

U

unfollowing
  friends, 68–69
  posts, 66
unfriending, 191
unsubscribing from outreach emails, 31
updating
  Friend Lists, 188–189
  status. *See* status updates
uploading
  illegal content, 17
  photos, 245–250, 285
users, blocking, 118–119

V

video chats, 199
videos
  about, 257
  adding
    from computer, 258–259
    from Facebook app, 259–260
  as posts, 54, 88
  privacy settings for, 260–262
  profile, 151–152
  tagging, 244
  viewing, 258
  writing in Share box, 218
View As tool, 128–129
View Photos in Thread option (Facebook Messages), 204
viewing
  events, 266
  messages in Facebook Messenger, 158–160
  News Feed, 45–46
  photos
    from friends, 240–244
    on mobile devices, 243
    in News Feed, 240–241
  videos, 244, 258
viruses, preventing, 133
visibility, of apps, 317–318

W

Warning! icon, 3
web interactions, 14–15
webcam, taking profile pictures using, 83–84
websites. *See also* apps
  Cheat Sheet, 3
  Facebook, 8, 23

websites. *(continued)*
  Facebook Pages Terms, 278
  Hulu, 313
  Match.com, 17
  Security Page, for Facebook, 134
  Statement of Rights and
    Responsibilities, 278
Work and Education section, 93–95
writing posts in Share box, 218

Y

Year in Review videos, 327–328
Your Pages (Account menu), 40

Z

Zuckerberg, Mark (CEO), 21

About the Author

Carolyn Abram is a writer. She was the first user of Facebook at Stanford in 2004 and worked for Facebook from 2006-2009. She has used Facebook every day for most of her adult life, acquiring 767 Facebook friends. Despite that, she managed to receive a BA from Stanford ('06) and an MFA from California College of the Arts ('12). Her short fiction has appeared in *New California Writing 2013* and *Switchback*. She currently lives in Seattle with her husband and children.

Author's Acknowledgments

A huge thank you to a very flexible and supportive editorial staff, including Steve Hayes and Colleen Diamond. The rest of the Wiley crew also has my gratitude.

On the home front, I have to thank my husband, Eric, and our children, Connor and Lina, who are the best like-bait a Facebook-er could ask for. I also want to acknowledge the enormous web of people who actually make it possible for me to get work done by helping care for my children: the phenomenal staff at Stroum Early Childhood School, our friends, and our families.

In closing, I'd like to thank the millions of Facebook users around the world who are busy connecting, sharing, and generally having fun on Facebook. Keep on signin' on.

Publisher's Acknowledgments

Executive Editor: Steve Hayes

Project Manager: Colleen Diamond

Development Editor: Colleen Diamond

Copy Editor: Colleen Diamond

Technical Editor: Michelle Krasniak

Editorial Assistant: Matthew Lowe

Sr. Editorial Assistant: Cherie Case

Production Editor: Antony Sami

Cover credit: ©Juli Hansen/Shutterstock

Apple & Mac

iPad For Dummies,
6th Edition
978-1-118-72306-7

iPhone For Dummies,
7th Edition
978-1-118-69083-3

Macs All-in-One
For Dummies, 4th Edition
978-1-118-82210-4

OS X Mavericks
For Dummies
978-1-118-69188-5

Blogging & Social Media

Facebook For Dummies,
5th Edition
978-1-118-63312-0

Social Media Engagement
For Dummies
978-1-118-53019-1

WordPress For Dummies,
6th Edition
978-1-118-79161-5

Business

Stock Investing
For Dummies, 4th Edition
978-1-118-37678-2

Investing For Dummies,
6th Edition
978-0-470-90545-6

Personal Finance
For Dummies, 7th Edition
978-1-118-11785-9

QuickBooks 2014
For Dummies
978-1-118-72005-9

Small Business Marketing
Kit For Dummies,
3rd Edition
978-1-118-31183-7

Careers

Job Interviews
For Dummies, 4th Edition
978-1-118-11290-8

Job Searching with Social
Media For Dummies,
2nd Edition
978-1-118-67856-5

Personal Branding
For Dummies
978-1-118-11792-7

Resumes For Dummies,
6th Edition
978-0-470-87361-8

Starting an Etsy Business
For Dummies, 2nd Edition
978-1-118-59024-9

Diet & Nutrition

Belly Fat Diet For Dummies
978-1-118-34585-6

Mediterranean Diet
For Dummies
978-1-118-71525-3

Nutrition For Dummies,
5th Edition
978-0-470-93231-5

Digital Photography

Digital SLR Photography
All-in-One For Dummies,
2nd Edition
978-1-118-59082-9

Digital SLR Video &
Filmmaking For Dummies
978-1-118-36598-4

Photoshop Elements 12
For Dummies
978-1-118-72714-0

Gardening

Herb Gardening
For Dummies, 2nd Edition
978-0-470-61778-6

Gardening with Free-Range
Chickens For Dummies
978-1-118-54754-0

Health

Boosting Your Immunity
For Dummies
978-1-118-40200-9

Diabetes For Dummies,
4th Edition
978-1-118-29447-5

Living Paleo For Dummies
978-1-118-29405-5

Big Data

Big Data For Dummies
978-1-118-50422-2

Data Visualization
For Dummies
978-1-118-50289-1

Hadoop For Dummies
978-1-118-60755-8

Language & Foreign Language

500 Spanish Verbs
For Dummies
978-1-118-02382-2

English Grammar
For Dummies, 2nd Edition
978-0-470-54664-2

French All-in-One
For Dummies
978-1-118-22815-9

German Essentials
For Dummies
978-1-118-18422-6

Italian For Dummies,
2nd Edition
978-1-118-00465-4

 Available in print and e-book formats.

Available wherever books are sold. **For more information or to order direct visit www.dummies.com**

Math & Science

Algebra I For Dummies,
2nd Edition
978-0-470-55964-2

Anatomy and Physiology
For Dummies, 2nd Edition
978-0-470-92326-9

Astronomy For Dummies,
3rd Edition
978-1-118-37697-3

Biology For Dummies,
2nd Edition
978-0-470-59875-7

Chemistry For Dummies,
2nd Edition
978-1-118-00730-3

1001 Algebra II Practice
Problems For Dummies
978-1-118-44662-1

Microsoft Office

Excel 2013 For Dummies
978-1-118-51012-4

Office 2013 All-in-One
For Dummies
978-1-118-51636-2

PowerPoint 2013
For Dummies
978-1-118-50253-2

Word 2013 For Dummies
978-1-118-49123-2

Music

Blues Harmonica
For Dummies
978-1-118-25269-7

Guitar For Dummies,
3rd Edition
978-1-118-11554-1

iPod & iTunes
For Dummies, 10th Edition
978-1-118-50864-0

Programming

Beginning Programming
with C For Dummies
978-1-118-73763-7

Excel VBA Programming
For Dummies, 3rd Edition
978-1-118-49037-2

Java For Dummies,
6th Edition
978-1-118-40780-6

Religion & Inspiration

The Bible For Dummies
978-0-7645-5296-0

Buddhism For Dummies,
2nd Edition
978-1-118-02379-2

Catholicism For Dummies,
2nd Edition
978-1-118-07778-8

Self-Help & Relationships

Beating Sugar Addiction
For Dummies
978-1-118-54645-1

Meditation For Dummies,
3rd Edition
978-1-118-29144-3

Seniors

Laptops For Seniors
For Dummies, 3rd Edition
978-1-118-71105-7

Computers For Seniors
For Dummies, 3rd Edition
978-1-118-11553-4

iPad For Seniors
For Dummies, 6th Edition
978-1-118-72826-0

Social Security
For Dummies
978-1-118-20573-0

Smartphones & Tablets

Android Phones
For Dummies, 2nd Edition
978-1-118-72030-1

Nexus Tablets
For Dummies
978-1-118-77243-0

Samsung Galaxy S 4
For Dummies
978-1-118-64222-1

Samsung Galaxy Tabs
For Dummies
978-1-118-77294-2

Test Prep

ACT For Dummies,
5th Edition
978-1-118-01259-8

ASVAB For Dummies,
3rd Edition
978-0-470-63760-9

GRE For Dummies,
7th Edition
978-0-470-88921-3

Officer Candidate Tests
For Dummies
978-0-470-59876-4

Physician's Assistant Exam
For Dummies
978-1-118-11556-5

Series 7 Exam For Dummies
978-0-470-09932-2

Windows 8

Windows 8.1 All-in-One
For Dummies
978-1-118-82087-2

Windows 8.1 For Dummies
978-1-118-82121-3

Windows 8.1 For Dummies,
Book + DVD Bundle
978-1-118-82107-7

Available in print and e-book formats.

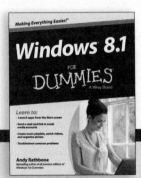

Available wherever books are sold. **For more information or to order direct visit www.dummies.com**